ABOUT THIS PUBLICATION

FOR SERVICE ASSISTANCE

Customer Service
1.704.898.0770

North Carolina General Statues is published by The Muliti-Media Group of Greater Charlotte in Charlotte, North Carolina. Copyright 2015 by the Multi-Media Group of Greater Charlotte. This book or parts thereof may not be reproduced in any form, stored in a retrieval system, or transmitted in any form by any means—electronic, mechanical, photocopy, recording or otherwise—without prior written permission of the publisher, except as provided by United States of America copyright law.

The records required by U.S. Code 2257(a) through (c) and the pertinent regulations 28 C.F.R. Cli. 1, Part 75 with respect to this publication and all materials associated with such records are maintained by The Multi-Media Group of Greater Charlotte, Publisher and available for review by Attorney General.

www.visionbooks.org

Copyright © 2015 by MMGGC
All rights reserved!

TID: 5061505
ISBN (10) digit: 1502913593
ISBN (13) digit: 978-1502913593

123-4-56789-01239-Paperback
123-4-56789-01239-Hardback

First Edition

090520140547

Printed in the United States of America

2015 EDITION

North Carolina Criminal Law And Procedure-Pamphlet # 38

Printed In conjunction with the Administration of the Courts

North Carolina Criminal Law and Procedure
Pamphlet Reference Guide

Chapters	Pamphlet
Chapter 1 Civil Procedure	1
Chapter 1 Civil Procedure (Continue)	2
Chapter 1A Rules of Civil Procedure	2
Chapter 1B Contribution.	2
Chapter 1C Enforcement of Judgments.	2
Chapter 1D Punitive Damages.	2
Chapter 1E Eastern Band of Cherokee Indians.	2
Chapter 1F North Carolina Uniform Interstate Depositions and Discovery Act.	2
Chapter 2 - Clerk of Superior Court [Repealed and Transferred.]	3
Chapter 3 - Commissioners of Affidavits and Deeds [Repealed.]	3
Chapter 4 - Common Law	3
Chapter 5 - Contempt [Repealed.]	3
Chapter 5A - Contempt	3
Chapter 6 - Liability for Court Costs	3
Chapter 7 - Courts [Repealed and Transferred.]	3
Chapter 7A – Judicial Department	3
Chapter 7A – Continuation (Judicial Department)	4
Chapter 7A – Continuation (Judicial Department)	5
Chapter 7B - Juvenile Code	5
Chapter 8 - Evidence	6
Chapter 8A - Interpreters for Deaf Persons [Recodified.]	6
Chapter 8B - Interpreters for Deaf Persons	6
Chapter 8C - Evidence Code	6
Chapter 9 - Jurors	6
Chapter 10 - Notaries [Repealed.]	6
Chapter 10A - Notaries [Recodified.]	6
Chapter 10B - Notaries	6
Chapter 11 - Oaths	6
Chapter 12 - Statutory Construction	6
Chapter 13 - Citizenship Restored	6
Chapter 14 - Criminal Law	7
Chapter 14 –Criminal Law (Continuation)	8
Chapter 15 - Criminal Procedure	9
Chapter 15A - Criminal Procedure Act (Continuation)	10
Chapter 15A - Criminal Procedure Act (Continuation)	11
Chapter 15B - Victims Compensation	11
Chapter 15C - Address Confidentiality Program	11
Chapter 16 - Gaming Contracts and Futures	11
Chapter 17 - Habeas Corpus	11

Chapter 17A - Law-Enforcement Officers [Recodified.]	11
Chapter 17B - North Carolina Criminal Justice Education and Training System [Recodified.] Chapter 17C - North Carolina Criminal Justice Education and Training Standards Commission	11
Chapter 17D - North Carolina Justice Academy	11
Chapter 17E - North Carolina Sheriffs' Education and Training Standards Commission	11
Chapter 18 - Regulation of Intoxicating Liquors [Repealed.]	12
Chapter 18A - Regulation of Intoxicating Liquors [Repealed.]	12
Chapter 18B - Regulation of Alcoholic Beverages	12
Chapter 18C - North Carolina State Lottery	12
Chapter 19 - Offenses against Public Morals	12
Chapter 19A - Protection of Animals	12
Chapter 20 - Motor Vehicles	13
Chapter 20 - Motor Vehicles (Continuation)	14
Chapter 20 - Motor Vehicles (Continuation)	15
Chapter 20 - Motor Vehicles (Continuation)	16
Chapter 21 - Bills of Lading	17
Chapter 22 - Contracts Requiring Writing	17
Chapter 22A - Signatures	17
Chapter 22B - Contracts Against Public Policy	17
Chapter 22C - Payments to Subcontractors	17
Chapter 23 - Debtor and Creditor. r 24 - Interest	17
Chapter 24 – Interest	17
Chapter 25 – Uniform Commercial Code	18
Chapter 25 – Uniform Commercial Code (Continuation)	19
Chapter 25A – Retail Installment Sales Act	20
Chapter 25B - Credit	20
Chapter 25C - Sales of Artwork	20
Chapter 26 - Suretyship	20
Chapter 27 - Warehouse Receipts [Repealed.]	20
Chapter 28 - Administration [Repealed.]	20
Chapter 28A - Administration of Decedents' Estates	20
Chapter 28B - Estates of Absentees in Military Service	20
Chapter 28C - Estates of Missing Persons	20
Chapter 29 - Intestate Succession	21
Chapter 30 - Surviving Spouses	21
Chapter 31 - Wills	21
Chapter 31A - Acts Barring Property Rights	21
Chapter 31B - Renunciation of Property and Renunciation of Fiduciary Powers Act	21
Chapter 31C - Uniform Disposition of Community Property Rights at Death Act	21
Chapter 32 - Fiduciaries	21
Chapter 32A - Powers of Attorney	21
Chapter 33 - Guardian and Ward [Repealed and Recodified.]	21

Chapter 33A - North Carolina Uniform Transfers to Minors Act	21
Chapter 33B - North Carolina Uniform Custodial Trust Act	21
Chapter 34 - Veterans' Guardianship Act	22
Chapter 35 - Sterilization Procedures	22
Chapter 35A - Incompetency and Guardianship	22
Chapter 36 - Trusts and Trustees [Repealed.]	22
Chapter 36A - Trusts and Trustees	22
Chapter 36B - Uniform Management of Institutional Funds Act [Repealed.]	22
Chapter 36C - North Carolina Uniform Trust Code	22
Chapter 36D - North Carolina Community Third Party Trusts, Pooled Trusts	23
Chapter 36E - Uniform Prudent Management of Institutional Funds Act	23
Chapter 37 - Allocation of Principal and Income [Repealed.]	23
Chapter 37A - Uniform Principal and Income Act	23
Chapter 38 - Boundaries	23
Chapter 38A - Landowner Liability	23
Chapter 39 - Conveyances	23
Chapter 39A - Transfer Fee Covenants Prohibited	23
Chapter 40 - Eminent Domain [Repealed.]	23
Chapter 40A - Eminent Domain	23
Chapter 41 - Estates	23
Chapter 41A - State Fair Housing Act	23
Chapter 42 - Landlord and Tenant	23
Chapter 42A - Vacation Rental Act	23
Chapter 43 - Land Registration	23
Chapter 44 - Liens	24
Chapter 44A - Statutory Liens and Charges	24
Chapter 45 - Mortgages and Deeds of Trust	24
Chapter 45A - Good Funds Settlement Act	24
Chapter 46 - Partition	24
Chapter 47 - Probate and Registration	25
Chapter 47A - Unit Ownership	25
Chapter 47B - Real Property Marketable Title Act	25
Chapter 47C - North Carolina Condominium Act	25
Chapter 47D - Notice of Settlement Act [Expired.]	25
Chapter 47E - Residential Property Disclosure Act	25
Chapter 47F - North Carolina Planned Community Act	25
Chapter 47G - Option to Purchase Contracts	25
Chapter 47H - Contracts for Deed	25
Chapter 48 - Adoptions +	26
Chapter 48A - Minors	26
Chapter 49 - Bastardy	26
Chapter 49A - Rights of Children	26
Chapter 50 - Divorce and Alimony	26
Chapter 50A - Uniform Child-Custody Jurisdiction and	

Enforcement Act	26
Chapter 50B - Domestic Violence	26
Chapter 50C - Civil No-Contact Orders	26
Chapter 51 - Marriage	26
Chapter 52 - Powers and Liabilities of Married Persons	27
Chapter 52A - Uniform Reciprocal Enforcement of Support Act [Repealed.]	27
Chapter 52B - Uniform Premarital Agreement Act	27
Chapter 52C - Uniform Interstate Family Support Act	27
Chapter 53 - Banks	27
Chapter 53A - Business Development Corporations and North Carolina Capital Resource Corporations	28
Chapter 53B - Financial Privacy Act	28
Chapter 54 - Cooperative Organizations	28
Chapter 54A - Capital Stock Savings and Loan Associations [Repealed.]	28
Chapter 54B - Savings and Loan Associations	29
Chapter 54C - Savings Banks	29
Chapter 55 - North Carolina Business Corporation Act	30
Chapter 55A - North Carolina Nonprofit Corporation Act	31
Chapter 55B - Professional Corporation Act	31
Chapter 55C - Foreign Trade Zones	31
Chapter 55D - Filings, Names, and Registered Agents for Corporations, Nonprofit Corporations, and Partnerships	31
Chapter 56 - Electric, Telegraph and Power Companies [Repealed.]	31
Chapter 57 - Hospital, Medical and Dental Service Corporations [Recodified.]	31
Chapter 57A - Health Maintenance Organization Act [Recodified.]	31
Chapter 57B - Health Maintenance Organization Act [Recodified.]	31
Chapter 57C - North Carolina Limited Liability Company Act.	31
Chapter 58 - Insurance.	32
Chapter 58 - Insurance (Continuation)	33
Chapter 58 - Insurance (Continuation)	34
Chapter 58 - Insurance (Continuation)	35
Chapter 58 - Insurance (Continuation)	36
Chapter 58 - Insurance (Continuation)	37
Chapter 58 - Insurance (Continuation)	38
Chapter 58A - North Carolina Health Insurance Trust Commission [Recodified.]	38
Chapter 59 - Partnership.	39
Chapter 59B - Uniform Unincorporated Nonprofit Association Act.	39
Chapter 60 - Railroads and Other Carriers [Repealed and Transferred.]	39
Chapter 61 - Religious Societies	39
Chapter 62 - Public Utilities	39

Chapter 62 - Public Utilities (Continuation)	40
Chapter 62A - Public Safety Telephone Service And Wireless Telephone Service	40
Chapter 63 - Aeronautics	40
Chapter 63A - North Carolina Global TransPark Authority	40
Chapter 64 - Aliens	40
Chapter 65 – Cemeteries	40
Chapter 66 - Commerce and Business	41
Chapter 67 - Dogs	41
Chapter 68 - Fences and Stock Law	41
Chapter 69 - Fire Protection	41
Chapter 70 - Indian Antiquities, Archaeological Resources and Unmarked Human Skeletal Remains Protection	42
Chapter 71 - Indians [Repealed.]	42
Chapter 71A - Indians	42
Chapter 72 - Inns, Hotels and Restaurants	42
Chapter 73 - Mills	42
Chapter 74 - Mines and Quarries	42
Chapter 74A - Company Police [Repealed.]	42
Chapter 74B - Private Protective Services Act [Repealed.]	42
Chapter 74C - Private Protective Services	42
Chapter 74D - Alarm Systems	42
Chapter 74E - Company Police Act	42
Chapter 74F - Locksmith Licensing Act	42
Chapter 74G - Campus Police Act	42
Chapter 75 - Monopolies, Trusts and Consumer Protection	42
Chapter 75A - Boating and Water Safety	43
Chapter 75B - Discrimination in Business	43
Chapter 75C - Motion Picture Fair Competition Act	43
Chapter 75D - Racketeer Influenced and Corrupt Organizations	43
Chapter 75E - Unlawful Activities in Connection With Certain Corporate Transactions	43
Chapter 76 - Navigation	43
Chapter 76A - Navigation and Pilotage Commissions	43
Chapter 77 - Rivers, Creeks, and Coastal Waters	43
Chapter 78 - Securities Law [Repealed.]	43
Chapter 78A - North Carolina Securities Act	43
Chapter 78B - Tender Offer Disclosure Act [Repealed.]	43
Chapter 78C - Investment Advisers	43
Chapter 78D - Commodities Act	43
Chapter 79 - Strays [Repealed.]	43
Chapter 80 - Trademarks, Brands, etc.	44
Chapter 81 - Weights and Measures [Recodified.]	44
Chapter 81A - Weights and Measures Act of 1975.	44
Chapter 82 - Wrecks [Repealed.]	44
Chapter 83 - Architects [Recodified.]	44

Chapter 83A - Architects	44
Chapter 84 - Attorneys-at-Law	44
Chapter 84A - Foreign Legal Consultants	44
Chapter 85 - Auctions and Auctioneers [Repealed.]	44
Chapter 85A - Bail Bondsmen and Runners [Recodified.]	44
Chapter 85B - Auctions and Auctioneers	44
Chapter 85C - Bail Bondsmen and Runners [Recodified.]	44
Chapter 86 - Barbers [Recodified.]	44
Chapter 86A - Barbers	44
Chapter 87 - Contractors	44
Chapter 88 - Cosmetic Art [Repealed.]	44
Chapter 88A - Electrolysis Practice Act	44
Chapter 88B - Cosmetic Art	45
Chapter 89 - Engineering and Land Surveying [Recodified.]	45
Chapter 89A - Landscape Architects	45
Chapter 89B - Foresters	45
Chapter 89C - Engineering and Land Surveying	45
Chapter 89D - Landscape Contractors	45
Chapter 89E - Geologists Licensing Act	45
Chapter 89F - North Carolina Soil Scientist Licensing Act	45
Chapter 89G - Irrigation Contractors	45
Chapter 90 - Medicine and Allied Occupations	45
Chapter 90 - Medicine and Allied Occupations (Continuation)	46
Chapter 90 - Medicine and Allied Occupations (Continuation)	47
Chapter 90 - Medicine and Allied Occupations (Continuation)	48
Chapter 90A - Sanitarians and Water and Wastewater Treatment Facility Operators	48
Chapter 90B - Social Worker Certification and Licensure Act	48
Chapter 90C - North Carolina Recreational Therapy Licensure Act	48
Chapter 90D - Interpreters and Transliterators	48
Chapter 91 - Pawnbrokers [Repealed.]	48
Chapter 91A - Pawnbrokers Modernization Act of 1989	48
Chapter 92 - Photographers [Deleted.]	48
Chapter 93 - Certified Public Accountants	48
Chapter 93A - Real Estate License Law	49
Chapter 93B - Occupational Licensing Boards	49
Chapter 93C - Watchmakers [Repealed.]	49
Chapter 93D - North Carolina State Hearing Aid Dealers and Fitters Board.	49
Chapter 93E - North Carolina Appraisers Act	49
Chapter 94 - Apprenticeship	49
Chapter 95 - Department of Labor and Labor Regulations	49
Chapter 95 - Department of Labor and Labor Regulations (Continuation)	50
Chapter 96 - Employment Security	50
Chapter 97 - Workers' Compensation Act	50
Chapter 97 - Workers' Compensation Act (Continuation)	51

Chapter 98 - Burnt and Lost Records	51
Chapter 99 - Libel and Slander	51
Chapter 99A - Civil Remedies for Criminal Actions	51
Chapter 99B - Products Liability	51
Chapter 99C - Actions Relating to Winter Sports Safety and Accidents	51
Chapter 99D - Civil Rights	51
Chapter 99E - Special Liability Provisions	51
Chapter 100 - Monuments, Memorials and Parks	51
Chapter 101 - Names of Persons	51
Chapter 102 - Official Survey Base	51
Chapter 103 - Sundays, Holidays and Special Days	51
Chapter 104 - United States Lands	51
Chapter 104A - Degrees of Kinship	51
Chapter 104B - Hurricanes or Other Acts of Nature	51
Chapter 104C - Atomic Energy, Radioactivity and Ionizing Radiation [Repealed and Recodified.]	51
Chapter 104D - Southern States Energy Compact	51
Chapter 104E - North Carolina Radiation Protection Act	51
Chapter 104F - Southeast Interstate Low-Level Radioactive Waste Management Compact [Repealed]	51
Chapter 104G - North Carolina Low-Level Radioactive Waste Management Authority Act of 1987 [Repealed]	51
Chapter 105 - Taxation	51
Chapter 105 - Taxation (Continuation)	52
Chapter 105 - Taxation (Continuation)	53
Chapter 105 - Taxation (Continuation)	54
Chapter 105A - Setoff Debt Collection Act	55
Chapter 105B - Defaulted Student Loan Recovery Act	55
Chapter 106 - Agriculture	55
Chapter 106 - Agriculture (Continue)	56
Chapter 106 - Agriculture (Continue)	57
Chapter 107 - Agricultural Development Districts [Repealed.]	57
Chapter 108 - Social Services [Repealed and Recodified.]	57
Chapter 108A - Social Services	57
Chapter 108B - Community Action Programs	58
Chapter 108C Medicaid and Health Choice Provider Requirements.	58
Chapter 108D Medicaid Managed Care for Behavioral Health Services.	58
Chapter 109 - Bonds [Recodified.]	58
Chapter 110 - Child Welfare	58
Chapter 111 - Aid to the Blind	58
Chapter 112 - Confederate Homes and Pensions [Repealed.]	58
Chapter 113 - Conservation and Development	58
Chapter 113 - Conservation and Development (Continuation)	59

Chapter 113A - Pollution Control and Environment	59
Chapter 113A - Pollution Control and Environment (Continuation)	60
Chapter 113B - North Carolina Energy Policy Act of 1975	60
Chapter 114 - Department of Justice	60
Chapter 115 - Elementary and Secondary Education [Repealed.]	60
Chapter 115A - Community Colleges, Technical Institutes, and Industrial Education Centers [Repealed.]	60
Chapter 115B - Tuition and Fee Waivers	60
Chapter 115C - Elementary and Secondary Education	60
Chapter 115C - Elementary and Secondary Education (Continuation)	61
Chapter 115C - Elementary and Secondary Education (Continuation)	62
Chapter 115C - Elementary and Secondary Education (Continuation)	63
Chapter 115D - Community Colleges	63
Chapter 115E - Private Educational Facilities Finance Act [Recodified]	63
Chapter 116 - Higher Education	63
Chapter 116 - Higher Education (Continuation)	63
Chapter 116A - Escheats and Abandoned Property [Repealed.]	64
Chapter 116B - Escheats and Abandoned Property	64
Chapter 116C - Continuum of Education Programs	64
Chapter 116D - Higher Education Bonds	64
Chapter 117 - Electrification	64
Chapter 118 - Firemen's and Rescue Squad Workers' Relief and Pension Funds [Recodified.]	64
Chapter 118A - Firemen's Death Benefit Act [Repealed.]	64
Chapter 118B - Members of a Rescue Squad Death Benefit Act [Repealed.]	64
Chapter 119 - Gasoline and Oil Inspection and Regulation	64
Chapter 120 - General Assembly	65
Chapter 120 - General Assembly (Continuation)	66
Chapter 120 - General Assembly (Continuation)	67
Chapter 120C - Lobbying	67
Chapter 121 - Archives and History	67
Chapter 122 - Hospitals for the Mentally Disordered [Repealed.]	67
Chapter 122A - North Carolina Housing Finance Agency	67
Chapter 122B - North Carolina Agricultural Facilities Finance Act [Repealed.]	67
Chapter 122C - Mental Health, Developmental Disabilities, and Substance Abuse Act of 1985	67
Chapter 122C - Mental Health, Developmental Disabilities, and Substance Abuse Act of 1985 (Continuation)	68
Chapter 122D - North Carolina Agricultural Finance Act	68

Chapter 122E - North Carolina Housing Trust and Oil Overcharge Act	68
Chapter 123 - Impeachment	69
Chapter 123A - Industrial Development [Repealed.]	69
Chapter 124 - Internal Improvements	69
Chapter 125 - Libraries	69
Chapter 126 - State Personnel System	69
Chapter 127 - Militia [Repealed.]	69
Chapter 127A - Militia	69
Chapter 127B - Military Affairs	69
Chapter 127C - Advisory Commission on Military Affairs	69
Chapter 128 - Offices and Public Officers	69
Chapter 128 - Offices and Public Officers (Continuation)	70
Chapter 129 - Public Buildings and Grounds	70
Chapter 130 - Public Health [Repealed.]	70
Chapter 130A - Public Health	70
Chapter 130A - Public Health (Continuation)	71
Chapter 130A - Public Health (Continuation)	72
Chapter 130B - Hazardous Waste Management Commission [Repealed.]	72
Chapter 131 - Public Hospitals [Repealed.]	72
Chapter 131A - Health Care Facilities Finance Act	72
Chapter 131B - Licensing of Ambulatory Surgical Facilities [Repealed.]	72
Chapter 131C - Charitable Solicitation Licensure Act [Repealed.]	72
Chapter 131D - Inspection and Licensing of Facilities	72
Chapter 131E - Health Care Facilities and Services	72
Chapter 131E - Health Care Facilities and Services (Continuation)	73
Chapter 131F - Solicitation of Contributions	73
Chapter 132 - Public Records	73
Chapter 133 - Public Works	74
Chapter 134 - Youth Development [Recodified.]	74
Chapter 134A - Youth Services [Repealed.]	74
Chapter 135 - Retirement System for Teachers and State Employees; Social Security; Health Insurance Program for Children	74
Chapter 135 - Retirement System for Teachers and State Employees; Social Security; Health Insurance Program for Children	75
Chapter 136 - Transportation	75
Chapter 136 - Transportation (Continuation)	76
Chapter 137 - Rural Rehabilitation [Repealed.]	76
Chapter 138 - Salaries, Fees and Allowances	76
Chapter 138A - State Government Ethics Act	76
Chapter 139 - Soil and Water Conservation Districts	76

Chapter 140 - State Art Museum; Symphony and Art Societies	76
Chapter 140A - State Awards System	76
Chapter 141 - State Boundaries	76
Chapter 142 - State Debt	76
Chapter 143 - State Departments, Institutions, and Commissions	77
Chapter 143 - State Departments, Institutions, and Commissions (Continuation)	78
Chapter 143 - State Departments, Institutions, and Commissions (Continuation)	79
Chapter 143 - State Departments, Institutions, and Commissions (Continuation)	80
Chapter 143A - State Government Reorganization	80
Chapter 143B - Executive Organization Act of 1973	80
Chapter 143B - Executive Organization Act of 1973 (Continuation)	81
Chapter 143B - Executive Organization Act of 1973 (Continuation)	82
Chapter 143C - State Budget Act	83
Chapter 143D - The State Governmental Accountability and Internal Control Act	83
Chapter 144 - State Flag, Official Governmental Flags, Motto, and Colors	83
Chapter 145 - State Symbols and Other Official Adoptions.	83
Chapter 146 - State Lands	83
Chapter 147 - State Officers	83
Chapter 148 - State Prison System	84
Chapter 149 - State Song and Toast	84
Chapter 150 - Uniform Revocation of Licenses [Repealed.]	84
Chapter 150A - Administrative Procedure Act [Recodified.]	84
Chapter 150B - Administrative Procedure Act	84
Chapter 151 - Constables [Repealed.]	84
Chapter 152 - Coroners	84
Chapter 152A - County Medical Examiner [Repealed.]	84
Chapter 152A - County Medical Examiner [Repealed.] (Continuation)	85
Chapter 153 - Counties and County Commissioners [Repealed.]	85
Chapter 153A - Counties	85
Chapter 153B - Mountain Resources Planning Act	85
Chapter 153C - Uwharrie Regional Resources Act	85
Chapter 154 - County Surveyor [Repealed.]	85
Chapter 155 - County Treasurer [Repealed.]	85
Chapter 156 - Drainage	85
Chapter 156 – Drainage (Continuation)	86

Chapter 157 - Housing Authorities and Projects	86
Chapter 157A - Historic Properties Commissions [Transferred.]	86
Chapter 158 - Local Development	86
Chapter 159 - Local Government Finance	86
Chapter 159 - Local Government Finance (Continuation)	87
Chapter 159A - Pollution Abatement and Industrial Facilities Financing Act [Unconstitutional.]	87
Chapter 159B - Joint Municipal Electric Power and Energy Act	87
Chapter 159C - Industrial and Pollution Control Facilities Financing Act	87
Chapter 159D - The North Carolina Capital Facilities Financing Act	87
Chapter 159E - Registered Public Obligations Act	87
Chapter 159F - North Carolina Energy Development Authority [Repealed.]	87
Chapter 159G - Water Infrastructure	87
Chapter 159H - [Reserved.]	87
Chapter 159I - Solid Waste Management Loan Program and Local Government Special Obligation Bonds	87
Chapter 160 - Municipal Corporations [Repealed And Transferred.]	87
Chapter 160A - Cities and Towns	88
Chapter 160A - Cities and Towns (Continuation)	89
Chapter 160B - Consolidated City-County Act	89
Chapter 160C - Baseball Park Districts [Repealed.]	90
Chapter 161 - Register of Deeds	90
Chapter 162 - Sheriff	90
Chapter 162A - Water and Sewer Systems	90
Chapter 162B Continuity of Local Government in Emergency.	90
Chapter 163 Elections and Election Laws.	90
Chapter 163 Elections and Election Laws. (Continuation)	91
Chapter 164 Concerning the General Statutes of North Carolina.	92
Chapter 165 Veterans.	92
Chapter 166 Civil Preparedness Agencies [Repealed.]	92
Chapter 166A North Carolina Emergency Management Act.	92
Chapter 167 State Civil Air Patrol [Repealed.]	92
Chapter 168 Persons with Disabilities.	92
Chapter 168A Persons With Disabilities Protection Act.	92

§ 58-68-55. Exclusion of certain plans.

(a) Exception for Certain Benefits. - The requirements of Subparts 1 and 2 of this Part do not apply to any group health insurance coverage in relation to its provision of excepted benefits described in G.S. 58-68-25(b)(1).

(b) Exception for Certain Benefits if Certain Conditions Met. -

(1) Limited, excepted benefits. - The requirements of Subparts 1 and 2 of this Part do not apply to any group health insurance plan in relation to its provision of excepted benefits described in G.S. 58-68-25(b)(2) if the benefits:

a. Are provided under a separate policy, certificate, or contract of insurance; or

b. Are otherwise not an integral part of the plan.

(2) Noncoordinated, excepted benefits. - The requirements of Subparts 1 and 2 of this Part do not apply to any group health insurance plan in relation to its provision of excepted benefits described in G.S. 58-68-25(b)(3) if all of the following conditions are met:

a. The benefits are provided under a separate policy, certificate, or contract of insurance.

b. There is no coordination between the provision of the benefits and any exclusion of benefits under any group health insurance plan maintained by the same policyholder.

c. The benefits are paid with respect to an event without regard to whether benefits are provided with respect to that event under any group health insurance plan maintained by the same policyholder.

(3) Supplemental, excepted benefits. - The requirements of this Part do not apply to any group health insurance plan in relation to its provision of excepted benefits described in G.S. 58-68-25(b)(4) if the benefits are provided under a separate policy, certificate, or contract of insurance. (1997-259, s. 1(c).)

Part B. Individual Market Reforms.

§ 58-68-60. Guaranteed availability of individual health insurance coverage to certain individuals with prior group coverage.

(a) Guaranteed Availability. -

(1) In general. - Subject to the succeeding subsections of this section, each health insurer that offers health insurance coverage in the individual market in this State shall not, with respect to an eligible individual desiring to enroll in individual health insurance coverage:

a. Decline to offer the coverage to, or deny enrollment of, the individual; or

b. Impose any preexisting condition exclusion with respect to the coverage.

(2) Reserved.

(b) Eligible Individual Defined. - In this Part, "eligible individual" means an individual:

(1) (i) For whom, as of the date on which the individual seeks coverage under this section, the aggregate of the periods of creditable coverage is 18 or more months and (ii) whose most recent prior creditable coverage was under a group health plan, governmental plan, or church plan (or health insurance coverage offered in connection with any such plan);

(2) Who is not eligible for coverage under (i) a group health plan, (ii) part A or part B of title XVIII of the Social Security Act, or (iii) a State plan under title XIX of the Act (or any successor program), and does not have other health insurance coverage;

(3) With respect to whom the most recent coverage within the coverage period described in subdivision (1)(i) was not terminated based on a factor described in G.S. 58-68-45(b)(1) or (b)(2);

(4) If the individual had been offered the option of continuation coverage under a COBRA continuation provision or under Article 53 of this Chapter, who elected the coverage; and

(5) Who, if the individual elected the continuation coverage, has exhausted the continuation coverage under the provision or program.

(c) Alternative Coverage Permitted. -

(1) In general. - In the case of health insurance coverage offered in this State, a health insurer may elect to limit the coverage offered under subsection (a) of this section as long as it offers at least two different policy forms of health insurance coverage both of which:

a. Are designed for, made generally available to, and actively marketed to, and enroll both eligible and other individuals by the health insurer; and

b. Meet the requirement of subdivision (2) or (3) of this subsection, as elected by the health insurer.

For the purposes of this subsection, policy forms that have different cost-sharing arrangements or different riders shall be considered to be different policy forms.

(2) Choice of most popular policy forms. - The requirement of this subdivision is met, for health insurance coverage policy forms offered by a health insurer in the individual market, if the health insurer offers the policy forms for individual health insurance coverage with the largest, and next to largest, premium volume of all the policy forms offered by the health insurer in this State or applicable marketing or service area (as may be prescribed by rules or regulations) by the health insurer in the individual market in the period involved.

(3) Choice of two policy forms with representative coverage. -

a. In general. - The requirement of this subdivision is met, for health insurance coverage policy forms offered by a health insurer in the individual market, if the health insurer offers a lower-level coverage policy form (as described in sub-subdivision b. of this subdivision) and a higher-level coverage policy form (as described in sub-subdivision c. of this subdivision) each of which includes benefits substantially similar to other individual health insurance coverage offered by the health insurer in this State.

b. Lower-level of coverage described. - A policy form is described in this sub-subdivision if the actuarial value of the benefits under the coverage is at least eighty-five percent (85%) but not greater than one hundred percent (100%) of a weighted average (described in sub-subdivision d. of this subdivision).

c. Higher-level of coverage described. - A policy form is described in this sub-subdivision if: (i) the actuarial value of the benefits under the coverage is at least fifteen percent (15%) greater than the actuarial value of the coverage described in sub-subdivision b. of this subdivision offered by the health insurer in the area involved; and (ii) the actuarial value of the benefits under the coverage is at least one hundred percent (100%) but not greater than one hundred twenty percent (120%) of a weighted average (described in sub-subdivision d. of this subdivision).

d. Weighted average. - For the purposes of this subdivision, the weighted average described in this sub-subdivision is the average actuarial value of the benefits provided by all the health insurance coverage issued, as elected by the health insurer, either by that health insurer or by all health insurers in this State in the individual market during the previous year, not including coverage issued under this section, weighted by enrollment for the different coverage.

(4) Election. - The health insurer elections under this subsection shall apply uniformly to all eligible individuals in this State for that health insurer. The election shall be effective for policies offered during a period of not less than two years.

(5) Assumptions. - For the purposes of subdivision (3) of this subsection, the actuarial value of benefits provided under individual health insurance coverage shall be calculated based on a standardized population and a set of standardized utilization and cost factors.

(d) Special Rules for Network Plans. -

(1) In general. - In the case of a health insurer that offers health insurance coverage in the individual market through a network plan, the health insurer may:

a. Limit the individuals who may be enrolled under the coverage to those who live, reside, or work within the service area for the network plan; and

b. Within the service area of the plan, deny the coverage to the individuals if the health insurer has demonstrated to the Commissioner that: (i) it will not have the capacity to deliver services adequately to additional individual enrollees because of its obligations to existing group contract holders and enrollees and individual enrollees, and (ii) it is applying this subdivision uniformly to individuals without regard to any health status-related factor of the individuals and without regard to whether the individuals are eligible individuals.

(2)   180-day suspension upon denial of coverage. - A health insurer, upon denying health insurance coverage in any service area in accordance with sub-subdivision (1)b. of this subdivision, shall not offer coverage in the individual market within the service area for a period of 180 days after the coverage is denied.

(e)   Application of Financial Capacity Limits. -

(1)   In general. - A health insurer may deny health insurance coverage in the individual market to an eligible individual if the health insurer has demonstrated to the Commissioner that:

a.   It does not have the financial reserves necessary to underwrite additional coverage; and

b.   It is applying this subdivision uniformly to all individuals in the individual market in this State consistent with this Chapter and without regard to any health status-related factor of the individuals and without regard to whether the individuals are eligible individuals.

(2)   180-day suspension upon denial of coverage. - A health insurer, upon denying individual health insurance coverage in any service area in accordance with subdivision (1) of this subsection, shall not offer the coverage in the individual market within the service area for a period of 180 days after the date the coverage is denied or until the health insurer has demonstrated to the Commissioner that the health insurer has sufficient financial reserves to underwrite additional coverage, whichever is later.

(f)   Market Requirements. -

(1)   In general. - Subsection (a) of this section does not require that a health insurer offering health insurance coverage only in connection with ERISA group health plans or through one or more bona fide associations, or both, offer the health insurance coverage in the individual market.

(2)   Conversion policies. - A health insurer offering health insurance coverage in connection with group health plans under title XXVII of the federal Public Health Service Act shall not be deemed to be a health insurer offering

individual health insurance coverage solely because the health insurer offers a conversion policy.

(g) Construction. - Nothing in this section shall be construed:

(1) To restrict the amount of the premium rates that a health insurer may charge an individual for health insurance coverage provided in the individual market under this Chapter; or

(2) To prevent a health insurer offering health insurance coverage in the individual market from establishing premium discounts or rebates or modifying otherwise applicable copayments or deductibles in return for adherence to programs of health promotion and disease prevention.

(h) Other Definitions. - As used in this section:

(1) "Church plan". - The meaning given the term under section 3(33) of the Employee Retirement Income Security Act of 1974.

(2) "Governmental plan". -

a. The meaning given the term under section 3(32) of the Employee Retirement Income Security Act of 1974 and any federal governmental plan.

b. Federal governmental plan. - A governmental plan established or maintained for its employees by the government of the United States or by any agency or instrumentality of the government.

c. Nonfederal governmental plan. - A governmental plan that is not a federal governmental plan.

(i) Rights of Replacement Coverage Upon Termination. - Subsection (a) of this section shall apply to an eligible individual whose coverage issued under this section is terminated by a health insurer under G.S. 58-68-65(c)(2) the application for the replacement coverage is dated not more than 63 days following the termination date.

(j) Waiting Period. - In determining the length of any break in coverage for an individual as prescribed in G.S. 58-68-60(b)(1)(i), a significant break in coverage does not occur during the waiting period. The "waiting period" is defined as the period that begins on the date the individual submits a substantially complete application for coverage and ends on:

(1) The date coverage begins, if the application results in coverage, or

(2) The date on which the application is denied by the issuer or the date on which the offer for coverage lapses, if the application does not result in coverage. (1997-259, s. 1(c); 1999-132, s. 4.7; 2005-224, s. 3; 2009-382, s. 5.)

§ 58-68-65. Guaranteed renewability of individual health insurance coverage.

(a) In General. - Except as provided in this section, a health insurer that provides individual health insurance coverage to an individual shall renew or continue in force the coverage at the option of the individual.

(b) General Exceptions. - A health insurer may nonrenew or discontinue health insurance coverage of an individual in the individual market based only on one or more of the following:

(1) Nonpayment of premiums. - The individual has failed to pay premiums or contributions in accordance with the terms of the health insurance coverage or the health insurer has not received timely premium payments.

(2) Fraud. - The individual has performed an act or practice that constitutes fraud or made an intentional misrepresentation of material fact under the terms of the coverage.

(3) Termination of plan. - The health insurer is ceasing to offer coverage in the individual market in accordance with subsection (c) of this section and this Chapter.

(4) Movement outside service area. - In the case of a health insurer that offers health insurance coverage in the market through a network plan, the individual no longer resides, lives, or works in the service area (or in an area for which the health insurer is authorized to do business) but only if the coverage is terminated under this subdivision uniformly without regard to any health status-related factor of covered individuals.

(5) Association membership ceases. - In the case of health insurance coverage that is made available in the individual market only through one or more bona fide associations, the membership of the individual in the association (on the basis of which the coverage is provided) ceases but only if the coverage is terminated under this subdivision uniformly without regard to any health status-related factor of covered individuals.

(c) Requirements for Uniform Termination of Coverage. -

(1) Particular type of coverage not offered. - In any case in which a health insurer decides to discontinue offering a particular type of health insurance coverage offered in the individual market, coverage of the type may be discontinued by the health insurer only if:

a. The health insurer provides notice, notwithstanding G.S. 58-51-20 or G.S. 58-65-60(c)(3)b., to each covered individual provided coverage of this type in the market of the discontinuation at least 90 days before the date of the discontinuation of the coverage;

b. The health insurer offers to each individual in the individual market provided coverage of this type, the option to purchase any other individual health insurance coverage currently being offered by the health insurer for individuals in the market; and

c. In exercising the option to discontinue coverage of this type and in offering the option of coverage under sub-subdivision b. of this subdivision, the health insurer acts uniformly without regard to any health status-related factor of enrolled individuals or individuals who may become eligible for the coverage.

(2) Discontinuance of all coverage. -

a. In general. - Subject to sub-subdivision c. of this subdivision, in any case in which a health insurer elects to discontinue offering all health insurance coverage in the individual market in this State, health insurance coverage may be discontinued by the health insurer only if: (i) the health insurer provides notice to the Commissioner and to each individual of the discontinuation at least 180 days before the date of the expiration of the coverage, and (ii) all health insurance coverage issued or delivered for issuance in this State in the market is discontinued and the health insurance coverage in the market is not renewed.

b. Prohibition on market reentry. - In the case of a discontinuation under sub-subdivision a. of this subdivision in the individual market, the health insurer shall not provide for the issuance of any health insurance coverage in the market and this State during the five-year period beginning on the date of the discontinuation of the last health insurance coverage not so renewed.

(d) Exception for Uniform Modification of Coverage. - At the time of coverage renewal, a health insurer may modify the health insurance coverage for a policy form offered to individuals in the individual market as long as the modification is consistent with State law and effective on a uniform basis among all individuals with that policy form.

(e) Application to Coverage Offered Only Through Associations. - In applying this section in the case of health insurance coverage that is made available by a health insurer in the individual market to individuals only through one or more associations, a reference to an "individual" is deemed to include a reference to the association of which the individual is a member. (1997-259, s. 1(c).)

§ 58-68-70. Certification of coverage.

G.S. 58-68-30(e) applies to health insurance coverage offered by a health insurer in the individual market in the same manner that it applies to health insurance coverage offered by a health insurer in the small or large group market. (1997-259, s. 1(c).)

§ 58-68-75. General exceptions.

(a) Exception for Certain Benefits. - This Part does not apply to any health insurance coverage in relation to its provision of excepted benefits described in G.S. 58-68-25(b)(1).

(b) Exception for Certain Benefits if Certain Conditions Met. - This Part does not apply to any health insurance coverage in relation to its provision of excepted benefits described in G.S. 58-68-25(b)(2), (3), or (4) if the benefits are provided under a separate policy, certificate, or contract of insurance. (1997-259, s. 1(c).)

Article 68A.

Health Care Reform Planning.

§§ 58-68A-1 through 58-68A-10: Repealed by Session Laws 1995 (Regular Session, 1996), c. 17, s. 16.

Article 69.

Motor Clubs and Associations.

§ 58-69-1. Repealed by Session Laws 1999-132, s. 12.1.

§ 58-69-2. Definitions.

As used in this Article:

(1) "Branch or district office" means any physical location, other than a motor club's home office, that is used by the motor club or its representatives as a principal place of business for conducting any type of business authorized under this Article and as a place of business that is used by clients or prospective clients in meeting or dealing with the motor club or its representatives in the normal course of business authorized under this Article.

(2) "Licensee" means a motor club to which a license has been issued under this Article.

(3) "Motor club" means any person, whether or not residing, domiciled, or chartered in this State, that, in consideration of dues, assessments, or periodic payments of money, promises its members to assist them in matters relating to

the ownership, operation, use, or maintenance of motor vehicles by rendering three or more of the following services:

a. Automobile theft reward service. - A reward payable to any person, law enforcement agency, or officer for information leading to the recovery of a member's stolen vehicle and to the apprehension and conviction of the person or persons unlawfully taking the vehicle.

b. Bail or cash appearance bond service. - The furnishing of cash or a surety bond for a member accused of a violation of the motor vehicle law, or of any law of this State by reason of an automobile accident to secure the member's release and subsequent appearance in court.

c. Emergency road service. - Roadside adjustment of a motor vehicle so that the vehicle may be operated under its own power.

d. Legal service. - Providing for reimbursement to a member for attorneys' fees if criminal proceedings are instituted against the member as a result of the operation of a motor vehicle.

e. Map service. - The furnishing of road maps to members without cost.

f. Personal travel and accident insurance service. - Making available to members a personal travel and accident insurance policy issued by a duly licensed insurance company in this State.

g. Touring service. - The furnishing of touring information to members without cost.

h. Towing service. - Furnishing means to move a motor vehicle from one place to another under power other than its own. (1963, c. 698; 1983, c. 542; 1985, c. 666, s. 81; 1991, c. 401, s. 1; 1999-132, s. 12.2; 2000-122, s. 7.)

§ 58-69-5. License required.

No motor club, district or branch office of a motor club, or franchise motor club shall engage in business in this State unless it holds a valid license issued to it by the Commissioner as provided in this Article. The license shall at all times be prominently displayed in each office of the entity to which the license is issued. (1963, c. 698; 1991, c. 644, s. 15.)

§ 58-69-10. Applications for licenses; fees; bonds or deposits.

Licenses hereunder shall be obtained by filing a written application with the Commissioner in such form and manner as the Commissioner shall require. As a prerequisite to issuance of a license:

(1)   The applicant shall furnish to the Commissioner such data and information as the Commissioner may deem reasonably necessary to enable him to determine, in accordance with the provisions of G.S. 58-69-15, whether or not a license should be issued to the applicant.

(1a)   If the applicant has never been issued a motor club license it shall be required to submit an audited financial statement. If the applicant has previously been licensed the Commissioner may require that the financial statement be audited if it is reasonably necessary to determine whether or not a license should be issued to the applicant.

(2)   If the applicant is a motor club it shall be required to pay to the Commissioner a nonrefundable annual license fee of six hundred dollars ($600.00) and to deposit or file with the Commissioner a bond, in favor of the State of North Carolina and executed by a surety company duly authorized to transact business in this State, in the amount of fifty thousand dollars ($50,000), or securities of the type hereinafter specified in the amount of fifty thousand dollars ($50,000), pledged to or made payable to the State of North Carolina and conditioned upon the full compliance by the applicant with the provisions of this Article and the regulations and orders issued by the Commissioner pursuant thereto, and upon the good faith performance by the applicant of its contracts for motor club services.

(3)   If the applicant is a branch or district office of a motor club licensed under this Article it shall pay to the Commissioner a nonrefundable license fee of one hundred dollars ($100.00).

(4)   If the applicant is a franchise motor club it shall pay to the Commissioner a nonrefundable annual license fee of two hundred dollars ($200.00) and shall deposit or file with the Commissioner a bond, in favor of the State of North

Carolina and executed by a surety company duly authorized to transact business in this State, in the amount of fifty thousand dollars ($50,000), or securities of the type hereinafter specified in the amount of fifty thousand dollars ($50,000), pledged to or made payable to the State of North Carolina and conditioned upon the full compliance by the applicant with the provisions of this Article and the regulations and orders issued by the Commissioner pursuant thereto and upon the good faith performance by the applicant of its contracts for motor club services.

(5) Any applicant depositing securities under this section shall do so in the form and manner as prescribed in Article 5 of this Chapter, and the provisions of Article 5 of this Chapter, shall be applicable to securities pledged under this Article. (1963, c. 698; 1983, c. 790, ss. 7-9; 1991, c. 425, s. 1; c. 721, s. 2; 2009-451, s. 21.6(a).)

§ 58-69-15. Issuance or refusal of license; notice of hearing on refusal; renewal.

Within 60 days after an application for license is filed, the Commissioner shall issue a license to the applicant unless he shall find:

(1) That the applicant has not met all of the requirements of this Article, or

(2) That the applicant does not have sufficient financial responsibility to engage in business as a motor club in this State, or

(3) That the applicant has failed to make a reasonable showing that its managers, officers, directors and agents are persons of reliability and integrity. If any such finding is made, the Commissioner shall notify the applicant as soon as practicable of the reason for his refusal to issue the license, and inform the applicant of its right to a hearing on the matters as provided in G.S. 58-69-25. All licenses issued hereunder, and all renewals thereof, shall expire on June 30 following such issuance or renewal. Renewal of all licenses not previously revoked or suspended shall be automatic upon timely payment by the licensee of the annual fee. (1963, c. 698.)

§ 58-69-20. Powers of Commissioner.

The Commissioner shall have the same powers and authority for the purpose of conducting investigations and hearings under this Article as that vested in him by G.S. 58-2-50 and 58-2-70.

(1) To investigate possible violation of this Article and to report evidence thereof to the Attorney General who may recommend prosecution to the appropriate solicitor;

(2) To suspend or revoke any license issued under this Article upon a finding, after notice and opportunity for hearing, that the holder of said license has violated any of the provisions of this Article, or has failed to maintain the standards requisite to original licensing as indicated in G.S. 58-69-15 hereof;

(3) To require any licensee to cease doing business through any particular agent or representative upon a finding after notice and opportunity for hearing, that such agent or representative has intentionally made false or misleading statements concerning the motor club services offered by the motor club represented by him;

(4) To approve or disapprove the name, trademarks, emblems, and all forms which an applicant for license or licensee employs or proposes to employ in connection with its business. If such name, trademarks or emblems is distinctive and not likely to confuse or mislead the public as to the nature or identity of the motor club using or proposing to use it, then it shall be approved, otherwise, the Commissioner may disapprove its use and effectuate such disapproval by the issuance of an appropriate order; and

(5) To make any rules or regulations necessary to enforce the provisions of this Article. (1963, c. 698; 1987, c. 864, s. 3(c).)

§ 58-69-25. Hearing on denial of license.

Whenever the Commissioner denies an initial application for a license, he shall notify the applicant and advise, in writing, the applicant of the reasons for the denial or nonrenewal of the license. Within 30 days of receipt of notification the applicant may make written demand upon the Commissioner for a hearing to determine the reasonableness of the Commissioner's action. Such hearing shall be scheduled within 30 days from the date of receipt of the written demand. (1963, c. 698; 1989, c. 485, s. 32.)

§ 58-69-30. Agent for service of process.

Every motor club licensed hereunder shall appoint and maintain at all times an agent for service of process who shall be a resident of North Carolina. (1963, c. 698.)

§ 58-69-35. Violations; penalty.

Any person, firm, association or corporation who shall violate any of the provisions of this Article shall be guilty of a Class 1 misdemeanor. (1963, c. 698; 1993, c. 539, s. 471; 1994, Ex. Sess., c. 24, s. 14(c).)

§ 58-69-40. Disposition of fees.

All fees collected by the Commissioner under this Article shall be credited to the Insurance Regulatory Fund created under G.S. 58-6-25. (1963, c. 698; 1991, c. 689, s. 292; 1993 (Reg. Sess., 1994), c. 678, s. 30; 2003-221, s. 7.)

§ 58-69-45. Insurance licensing provisions not affected.

Nothing in this Article shall be construed as amending, repealing, or in any way affecting any laws now in force relating to the licensing of Motor Club Membership Sales Agents or to the licensing or regulation of insurance agents and insurance companies, as provided in Articles 1 through 64 of this Chapter. (1963, c. 698; 1983, c. 802, s. 3.)

§ 58-69-50. Authority for qualified surety companies to guarantee certain arrest bond certificates.

(a) Any domestic or foreign surety company that is authorized to do business in this State may become a surety, by filing with the Department an undertaking to become a surety, in an amount not to exceed one thousand five hundred dollars ($1,500) with respect to each guaranteed arrest bond certificate issued by a motor club.

(b) The undertaking shall be in a form to be prescribed by the Department and shall state:

(1) The name and address of the motor club or clubs with respect to which the surety company undertakes to guarantee the arrest bond certificates.

(2) The unqualified obligation of the surety company to pay the fine or forfeiture, in an amount not to exceed one thousand five hundred dollars ($1,500) of any person who, after posting a guaranteed arrest bond certificate which the surety has undertaken to guarantee, fails to make the appearance for which the guaranteed arrest bond certificate was posted. (1985, c. 623, s. 1; 1989, c. 663, s. 1; 1999-132, s. 12.3.)

§ 58-69-55. Guaranteed arrest bond certificates accepted.

(a) Any guaranteed arrest bond certificate guaranteed by a surety company under G.S. 58-69-50 shall be accepted in lieu of cash bail or other bond in an amount not to exceed one thousand five hundred dollars ($1,500) as a bail bond, when signed by the person whose signature appears on the certificate, to guarantee the appearance of that person in any court in this State at the time set by the court when the person is arrested for the violation of any motor vehicle law of this State or any motor vehicle ordinance of any municipality of this State. The guaranteed arrest bond certificate shall not apply to, and shall not be accepted in lieu of, cash bail or bond when the person has been arrested for any impaired driving offense or for any felony.

(b) A guaranteed arrest bond certificate that is posted as a bail bond in any court shall be subject to the forfeiture and enforcement provisions with respect to bail bonds in criminal cases as provided by law. (1985, c. 623, s. 1; 1989, c. 663, s. 2; 1999-132, s. 12.4.)

§ 58-69-60. Notification of criminal or administrative actions.

(a) If an individual proprietor, officer, or partner of a motor club has been convicted in any court of competent jurisdiction for any crime involving dishonesty or breach of trust, the motor club shall notify the Commissioner in writing of the conviction within 10 days after the date of the conviction. As used in this subsection, "conviction" includes an adjudication of guilt, a plea of guilty, or a plea of nolo contendere.

(b) A motor club shall report to the Commissioner any administrative action taken against the motor club by another state or by another governmental agency in this State within 30 days after the final disposition of the matter. This report shall include a copy of the order or consent order and other information or documents filed in the proceeding necessary to describe the action. (2009-566, s. 18.)

Article 70.

Collection Agencies.

Part 1. Permit Procedures.

§ 58-70-1. Permit from Commissioner of Insurance; penalty for violation; exception.

No person, firm, corporation, or association shall conduct or operate a collection agency or do a collection agency business, as the same is hereinafter defined in this Article, until he or it shall have secured a permit therefor as provided in this Article. Any person, firm, corporation or association conducting or operating a collection agency or doing a collection agency business without the permit shall be guilty of a Class I felony. Any officer or agent of any person, firm, corporation or association, who shall personally and knowingly participate in any violation of the remaining provisions of this Part shall be guilty of a Class 1 misdemeanor. Provided, however, that nothing in this section shall be construed to require a regular employee of a duly licensed collection agency licensed pursuant to this Article to procure a collection agency permit. (1931, c. 217, s. 1; 1943, c. 170;

1959, c. 1194, s. 1; 1969, c. 906, s. 1; 1979, c. 835; 1989, c. 441, s. 1; 1993, c. 539, ss. 472, 1275; 1994, Ex. Sess., c. 24, s. 14(c); 2011-320, s. 1.)

§ 58-70-5. Application to Commissioner for permit.

Any person, firm, corporation or association desiring to secure a permit as provided by G.S. 58-70-1, shall make application to the Commissioner of Insurance for each location at which such person, firm, corporation or association desires to carry on the collection agency business as hereinafter defined. Such applicant shall be entitled to a permit upon submission to the Commissioner of Insurance of the following:

(a) The name, trade name if any, street address, and telephone number of the applicant, including any home office address and telephone number, if different;

(b) If the applicant is a corporation,

(1) A certified copy of the board of director's resolution authorizing the submission of the application;

(2) An authenticated copy of the Articles of Incorporation and all amendments thereto;

(3) An authenticated copy of the bylaws or other governing instruments;

(4) If the applicant is a foreign corporation, a copy of the certificate of authority to transact business in this State issued by the North Carolina Secretary of State;

(b1) In addition to the information required by subsection (b) of this section, if the applicant is an alien corporation, the corporation must be owned or majority controlled ultimately by a parent entity incorporated or organized under the laws of the United States or any jurisdiction within the United States, and the alien corporation may only service accounts held by an affiliate or subsidiary of the same parent entity. For purposes of this subsection, "control" is defined by G.S. 58-19-5(2). Should the alien corporation be sold to an entity unrelated to the parent entity, notice shall be provided to the Department of the pending sale 30 days in advance of the sale. Provision of Form 8-K, properly filed with the

Securities and Exchange Commission, shall be deemed compliance with the notice requirement of this subsection. In the event of a sale, the new parent entity shall provide evidence to the Department within 30 days of the sale of its and the alien corporation's compliance with the requirements of this section. In the event that the new parent entity does not provide the evidence within 30 days after the sale, the alien corporation's permit shall be automatically suspended until the Department is provided the evidence of compliance which is satisfactory to the Commissioner;

(c)   If the applicant is a partnership, an authenticated copy of the then current partnership agreement;

(d)   If the trade name is used, certificates showing that the trade name has been filed as required by G.S. 66-68;

(e)   A surety bond as required by G.S. 58-70-20. In the case of an alien corporation, the surety bond requirements shall be double the amount set by G.S. 58-70-20;

(f)   A completed statement by each stockholder owning ten percent (10%) or more of the applicant's outstanding voting stock and each partner, director, and officer actively engaged in the collection agency business, containing: the name of the collection agency, the name and address of the individual completing the form, the positions held by the individual, each conviction of any criminal offense and any criminal charges pending other than minor traffic violations of the individual, and the name and address of three people not related to the individual who can attest to the individual's reputation for honesty and fair dealings;

(g)   A statement sworn to by an appropriate corporate officer, partner, or individual proprietor giving a description of the collection method to be employed in North Carolina;

(h)   A statement certifying that there are no unsatisfied judgments against the applicant;

(i)   A list of all telephone numbers assigned to, or to be used by the applicant in the operation of the collection agency;

(j)   The appropriate permit fee as required by G.S. 58-70-35;

(k)   A balance sheet as of the last day of the month prior to the date of submission of the application, certified true and correct by a corporate officer, partner, or proprietor, setting forth the current assets, fixed assets, current liabilities and positive net worth of the applicant;

(l)   The address of the location at which the applicant will make those records of its collection agency business described in G.S. 58-70-25 available for inspection by the Commissioner of Insurance.

(m)   A statement certifying that no officer, individual proprietor or partner of the applicant has been convicted of a felony involving moral turpitude, or any violation of any State or federal debt collection law.

(n)   If the collection agency's office or records, as described in G.S. 58-70-25, are located outside of North Carolina, a statement sworn to by an appropriate corporate officer, partner, or individual proprietor consenting to and authorizing the reimbursement, to the Commissioner by the collection agency, of expenses incurred by the Commissioner in conducting routine examinations, audits, and in investigating written complaints against the collection agency or its employees. All reimbursements shall be paid to the Commissioner no more than 30 days after the date of billing. In the case of an alien corporation, the sworn statement must provide that the corporation will make available to the Commissioner for his inspection, in North Carolina, those records described in G.S. 58-70-25, at the expense of the corporation;

(o)   If the applicant is a foreign corporation, a statement authorizing the Commissioner to be its agent for service of process, which shall be administered pursuant to the provisions of G.S. 58-16-30.

(p)   In the case of an alien corporation, when the corporation is in violation of this Article, the parent entity must agree to cure the violation by the alien corporation.

(q)   For purposes of this Article, the following definitions apply:

(1)   "Alien corporation" means a company incorporated or organized under the laws of any jurisdiction outside of the United States.

(2)   "Foreign corporation" means a company incorporated or organized under the laws of the United States or of any jurisdiction within the United States other than this State.

(r) If the applicant is a subsidiary in a holding company system and if the applicant's ultimate parent regularly files financial information with the U.S. Securities and Exchange Commission, in lieu of complying with subsection (k) of this section, the applicant may file the ultimate parent company's balance sheet as of the most recent fiscal year-end, as certified by the ultimate parent's independent auditors, and accompanied by a guarantee of the applicant's performance from the ultimate parent company for the benefit of the Department, limited to those portions of this Article that are applicable to the applicant.

(s) After a permit is issued by the Commissioner, the permittee's ultimate parent, as specified in subsection (r) of this section, shall remain responsible for the guarantee of performance as provided in subsection (r) of this section notwithstanding any change in the corporate structure of the ultimate parent company. If the permittee is acquired by any other person that has control over the permittee, the controlling person shall provide its own guarantee of performance as provided in subsection (r) of this section for the permittee to retain its permit. If the permittee does not have an ultimate parent company, it shall file its own balance sheet as specified in subsection (k) of this section. (1931, c. 217, s. 2; 1943, c. 170; 1959, c. 1194, s. 2; 1969, c. 906, s. 2; 1979, c. 835; 1989, c. 441, ss. 2, 3; 2001-269, s. 1.1; 2006-134, s. 1; 2009-566, s. 21.)

§ 58-70-6. Definitions.

For purposes of G.S. 58-70-5 and this section, the following definitions apply:

(1) An "affiliate" of or a person "affiliated" with a specific person. - A person that indirectly through one or more intermediaries or directly controls, is controlled by, or is under common control with the person specified.

(2) Control, including the terms "controlling," "controlled by," and "under common control with." - The direct or indirect possession of the power to direct or cause the direction of the management and policies of a person, whether through the ownership of voting securities, by contract other than a commercial contract for goods or nonmanagement services, or otherwise. Control is presumed to exist if any person directly or indirectly owns, controls, holds with the power to vote, or holds proxies representing ten percent (10%) or more of the voting securities of any other person.

(3) Holding company system. - An entity comprising two or more affiliated persons.

(4) Person. - An individual, corporation, partnership, limited liability company, association, joint stock company, trust, unincorporated organization, or any similar entity or any combination of the foregoing acting in concert.

(5) Subsidiary of a specified person. - An affiliate controlled by that person indirectly through one or more intermediaries or directly.

(6) Voting security. - Includes any security convertible into or evidencing a right to acquire a voting security. (2009-566, s. 22.)

§ 58-70-10. Application to Commissioner for permit renewal.

Any person, firm, corporation or association desiring to renew a permit issued pursuant to G.S. 58-70-5 shall make application to the Commissioner of Insurance not less than 30 days prior to the expiration date of the then current permit. Such renewal applicant shall be entitled to a renewal permit upon submission to the Commissioner of Insurance of all the information as required by G.S. 58-70-5; provided, however, it shall be sufficient, wherever applicable, to reference the prior year's application if there has been no change as to any of the required information and it shall not be necessary to submit with a renewal application a new director's resolution. In addition, the applicant shall submit to the Commissioner a copy of a "continuation certificate" or paid receipt for renewal premiums for the collection agency bond for the year for which the renewal permit is applied. The application shall include a calculation in accordance with G.S. 58-70-20, and if the bond is increased, an endorsement by the surety. With a renewal application, the applicant shall submit a balance sheet for the last fiscal year ending prior to the application, certified true and correct by a corporate officer, partner, or proprietor, setting forth the current assets, fixed assets, current liabilities and positive net worth of the applicant. (1979, c. 835.)

§ 58-70-15. Definition of collection agency and collection agency business.

(a) "Collection agency" means a person directly or indirectly engaged in soliciting, from more than one person delinquent claims of any kind owed or due or asserted to be owed or due the solicited person and all persons directly or indirectly engaged in the asserting, enforcing or prosecuting of those claims.

(b) "Collection agency" includes any of the following:

(1) Any person that procures a listing of delinquent debtors from any creditor and that sells the listing or otherwise receives any fee or benefit from collections made on the listing.

(2) Any person that attempts to or does transfer or sell to any person not holding the permit prescribed by this Article any system or series of letters or forms for use in the collection of delinquent accounts or claims which by direct assertion or by implication indicate that the claim or account is being asserted or collected by any person, firm, corporation, or association other than the creditor or owner of the claim or demand.

(3) An in-house collection agency, whereby a person, firm, corporation, or association sets up a collection service for his or its own business and the agency has a name other than that of the business.

(4) A "debt buyer." As used in this subdivision, the term "debt buyer" means a person or entity that is engaged in the business of purchasing delinquent or charged-off consumer loans or consumer credit accounts, or other delinquent consumer debt for collection purposes, whether it collects the debt itself or hires a third party for collection or an attorney-at-law for litigation in order to collect such debt.

(c) "Collection agency" does not mean:

(1) Regular employees of a single creditor;

(2) Banks, trust companies, or bank-owned, controlled or related firms, corporations or associations engaged in accounting, bookkeeping or data processing services where a primary component of such services is the rendering of statements of accounts and bookkeeping services for creditors;

(3) Mortgage banking companies;

(4) Savings and loan associations;

(5) Building and loan associations;

(6) Duly licensed real estate brokers and agents when the claims or accounts being handled by the broker or agent are related to or are in connection with the broker's or agent's regular real estate business;

(7) Express, telephone and telegraph companies subject to public regulation and supervision;

(8) Attorneys-at-law handling claims and collections in their own name and not operating a collection agency under the management of a layman;

(9) Any person, firm, corporation or association handling claims, accounts or collections under an order or orders of any court;

(10) A person, firm, corporation or association which, for valuable consideration purchases accounts, claims, or demands of another, which such accounts, claims, or demands of another are not delinquent at the time of such purchase, and then, in its own name, proceeds to assert or collect the accounts, claims or demands;

(11) Any person attempting to collect or collecting claims, in that person's name, of a business or businesses owned wholly or substantially by that person;

(12) Any nonprofit tax exempt corporation organized for the purpose of providing mediation or other dispute resolution services; and

(13) The designated representatives of programs as defined by G.S. 110-129(5). (1969, c. 906, s. 3; 1973, c. 785; 1979, c. 835; 1989, c. 441, ss. 4, 5, 12; 1991, c. 387, s. 1; 1993, c. 553, s. 22; 1999-419, s. 1; 2001-269, s. 1.2; 2009-573, s. 4(a).)

§ 58-70-20. Bond requirement.

(a) As a condition precedent to the issuance of any permit under this Article, every applicant for a permit shall file with the Commissioner a bond in favor of the State of North Carolina that is executed by a surety company licensed to transact surety business in this State. The bond shall be maintained in force during the permit period, continuous in form, and remain in effect until all moneys collected have been accounted for. The bond shall expressly provide that the bond is for the benefit of any person, firm or corporation for whom the collection agency engages in the collection of accounts. The bond shall be in the amount of ten thousand dollars ($10,000) for the initial permit. The amount of the bond for any renewal permit shall be no less than ten thousand dollars ($10,000), nor more than seventy-five thousand dollars ($75,000), and shall be computed as follows: The total collections paid directly to the collection agency less commissions earned by the collection agency on those collections for the calendar year ending immediately prior to the date of application, multiplied by one-sixth.

(b) A person required by this section to maintain a bond may, in lieu of that bond, deposit with the Commissioner the equivalent amount in cash, in certificates of deposit issued by banks organized under the laws of the State of North Carolina, or any national bank having its principal office in North Carolina, or securities, which shall be held in accordance with Article 5 of this Chapter. Securities may only be obligations of the United States or of federal agencies listed in G.S. 147-69.1(c) (2) guaranteed by the United States, obligations of the State of North Carolina, or obligations of a city or county of this State. Any proposed deposit of an obligation of a city or county of this State is subject to the prior approval of the Commissioner.

(c) In addition to the requirements of subsections (a) and (b) of this section, as a condition precedent to the issuance of any permit under this Article, every nonresident applicant for a permit shall file with the Commissioner a bond in the amount of ten thousand dollars ($10,000) in favor of the Department that is executed by a surety company licensed to transact surety business in this State. The bond shall be maintained in force during the permit period, be continuous in form, and remain in effect until terminated by the Commissioner. The bond shall expressly provide that the bond is for the purpose of reimbursing the Department for expenses incurred in visiting and examining a nonresident collection agency in connection with a federal bankruptcy or State receivership proceeding in which the collection agency is the subject of the proceeding. (1943, c. 170; 1959, c. 1194, s. 3; 1979, c. 835; 1991, c. 212, s. 4; 2001-269, s. 1.3.)

§ 58-70-25. Record of business in State.

(a) Each person, firm, or corporation licensed as a collection agency in North Carolina shall keep a full and correct record of all business done in this State as set forth below. All such records pertaining to collection activity, concerning debtor records and client accounting records, but not general operating records, shall be open to inspection by the Commissioner of Insurance or his duly authorized deputy upon demand.

(b) Every permit holder shall maintain adequate records which shall contain the items listed below. These records must be kept separate from records of any other business and must be maintained for not less than three years after the final entry has been made:

(1) A daily collection record or cash receipt journal in which all collections are recorded and allocated as to total collections, setting forth:

a. The amount credited to principal and to interest, if any;

b. The amount due creditors or forwarders.

(2) The amount retained as commission or commission paid to forwardees.

(3) Payments made directly to creditors as reported to the collection agency by those creditors and commissions due the collection agency on those payments.

(4) A record of each debtor's account shall be maintained consisting of the following:

a. The name and address of the debtor;

b. The name of the creditor or forwarder or forwardee if the account has been forwarded;

c. The principal amount owing and, if available, the date of the last credit or debit;

d. The amount and date of each payment made by the debtor; and

e. The date and time of each telephone or personal contact with the debtor.

(5) A master alphabetical record by name and address of every creditor or forwarder with whom the permit holder engages in the business of collecting accounts.

(6) A check register or carbon copies of each check issued or numerically numbered check stubs corresponding with all checks issued on the trust account for funds collected on behalf of creditors. Cancelled checks, together with voided or unused checks (adequately explained) drawn on the trust account shall be maintained in numerical order with the monthly bank statements.

(7) A record by client or client number showing the number of accounts received from the client, the date received and the principal amount of the accounts.

(8) A duplicate copy of each remittance statement furnished a creditor or forwarder, or other listing of the information contained on the statement. (1959, c. 1194, s. 3; 1979, c. 835; 1989, c. 441, s. 6.)

§ 58-70-30. Hearing granted applicant if application denied; appeal.

If, upon application, the Commissioner finds that the permit should not be issued or renewed and denies an application, he shall notify the applicant or permittee and advise, in writing, the applicant or permittee of the reasons for the denial or nonrenewal of the permit. Within 30 days of receipt of notification the applicant or permittee may make written demand upon the Commissioner for a hearing to determine the reasonableness of the Commissioner's action. Such hearing shall be scheduled within 30 days and held within 90 days from the date of receipt of the written demand. An applicant or permittee has the right to appeal any order or any unreasonable delay pursuant to Article 4 of Chapter 150B of the General Statutes. If the Commissioner shall decline an application for renewal, that applicant may continue to do business pending any appeal taken pursuant hereto. (1931, c. 217, s. 3; 1979, c. 835; 1989, c. 441, s. 7, c. 770, s. 51.)

§ 58-70-35. Application fee; issuance of permit; contents and duration.

(a) Upon the filing of the application and information required by this Article, the applicant shall pay a nonrefundable fee of one thousand dollars ($1,000), and no permit may be issued until this fee is paid. Fees collected under this subsection shall be credited to the Insurance Regulatory Fund created under G.S. 58-6-25.

(b) Each permit shall state the name of the applicant, his place of business, and the nature and kind of business in which he is engaged. The Commissioner shall assign to the permit a serial number for each year, and each permit shall be for a period of one year, beginning with July 1 and ending with June 30 of the following year.

(c) A permit is assignable or transferable only if the assignee or transferee qualifies under the provisions of this Article. Upon any change in ownership of a permittee, if a sole proprietorship or partnership, or upon a change in ownership of more than fifty percent (50%) of the shares or voting rights of a corporate permittee, a permit issued to a permittee is void unless within 30 days of the change of ownership the new owner or owners have satisfied the Commissioner that he or they qualify for a permit under this Article, and he or they maintain a bond in accordance with and in the amount required for a renewal bond under G.S. 58-70-20. (1931, c. 217, s. 4; 1979, c. 835; 1983, c. 790, s. 10; 1989, c. 441, s. 8; 1991, c. 721, s. 3; 2009-451, s. 21.5(a); 2011-330, s. 47(a).)

§ 58-70-40. Restraining orders; criminal convictions; permit revocations; other permit requirements.

(a) When it appears to the Commissioner that any person has violated, is violating, or threatens to violate any provision of this Article, he may apply to the superior court of any county in which the violation has occurred, is occurring, or may occur for a restraining order and injunction to restrain such violation, or threatened violation. If upon application the court finds that any provision of this Article has been violated, is being violated, or a violation thereof is threatened, the court shall issue an order restraining and enjoining such violations; and such relief may be granted regardless of whether criminal prosecution is instituted under any provision of this Article.

(b) If an individual proprietor, officer, or partner of the collection agency has been convicted in any court of competent jurisdiction for any crime involving dishonesty or breach of trust, the collection agency shall notify the

Commissioner in writing of the conviction within 10 days after the date of the conviction. As used in this subsection, "conviction" includes an adjudication of guilt, a plea of guilty, or a plea of nolo contendere. The conviction by a court of competent jurisdiction of any permittee for a violation of this Article shall automatically have the effect of suspending the permit of that permittee until such time that the permit is reinstated by the Commissioner. As used in this subsection, "conviction" includes an adjudication of guilt, a plea of guilty, and a plea of nolo contendere.

(c) In addition to the other qualifications for a permit under this Article, no collection agency shall be issued or be entitled to hold a permit if the Commissioner finds as to the applicant or permittee any one or more of the following conditions:

(1) An individual proprietor, officer, or partner of the collection agency has been convicted of a felony involving moral turpitude, or any State or federal debt collection law.

(2) There is an unsatisfied judgment which is not currently the subject of litigation against any partner, individual proprietor, or officer of the collection agency or against the collection agency.

(3) There is any materially false or misleading information in the permit application.

(4) The applicant has obtained or attempted to obtain the permit through misrepresentation or fraud.

(5) There has been an adjudication that a partner, individual proprietor, or officer of the collection agency has violated any State or federal unfair trade practice law.

(6) A partner, individual proprietor, or officer of the collection agency has violated or refused to comply with any provision of this Article or any order of the Commissioner.

(7) Another jurisdiction has suspended or revoked a collection agency or similar license or permit of the collection agency.

(d) In the case of an alien corporation that has been issued a permit under this Article, in an action brought by the Commissioner, service of process upon the parent entity is sufficient service of process on the alien corporation.

(e) A collection agency shall report to the Commissioner any administrative action taken against the collection agency by another state or by another governmental agency in this State within 30 days after the final disposition of the matter. This report shall include a copy of the order or consent order and other information or documents filed in the proceeding necessary to describe the action. (1931, c. 217, s. 5; 1979, c. 835; 1989, c. 441, s. 9; 2006-134, s. 2; 2009-566, ss. 16, 17.)

§ 58-70-45. Disposition of permit fees.

All permit fees collected under this Article shall be credited to the Insurance Regulatory Fund created under G.S. 58-6-25. (1931, c. 217, s. 8; 1943, c. 170; 1979, c. 835; 1991, c. 689, s. 293; 2003-221, s. 8.)

§ 58-70-50. All collection agencies to identify themselves in correspondence.

All collection agencies licensed under this Part to do the business of a collection agency in this State, shall in all correspondence with debtors use stationery or forms which contain the permit number and the true name and address of such collection agency.

The permit to engage in the business of a collection agency shall at all times be prominently displayed in each office of the person, firm, corporation or association to whom or to which the permit is issued. (1931, c. 217, s. 9; 1969, c. 906, s. 5; 1979, c. 835.)

Part 2. Operating Procedures.

§ 58-70-55. Office hours.

If an office of a duly licensed collection agency does not maintain normally accepted business hours, the hours the office is open shall be posted so as to be prominently displayed to the public at all times. If at any time it is anticipated that the permit holder's office will be closed to the public for a period exceeding seven days, the Department of Insurance shall be notified thereof in writing. (1979, c. 835.)

§ 58-70-60. Statements to be furnished each collection creditor.

(a) Acknowledgment of Accounts. - When any account is received for collection, the permit holder shall upon request furnish the collection creditor or forwarder with a written listing or acknowledgment of the accounts received.

(b) Remittance Statements. - Each permit holder shall remit all moneys due to any collection creditor or forwarder within 30 days after the end of the collection month during which the collection was effected. The remittance shall be accompanied by a statement setting forth:

(1) The date of remittance;

(2) The debtor's name;

(3) The date or month of collection and amount collected from each debtor; and

(4) A breakdown showing money collected from each debtor and the amount due the creditor or forwarder. (1979, c. 835.)

§ 58-70-65. Remittance trust account.

(a) Each permit holder shall deposit, no later than two banking days after receipt, in a separate trust account in any bank located in North Carolina or in any other bank approved by the Commissioner, sufficient funds to pay all moneys due or owed to all collection creditors or forwarders. The funds shall remain in the trust account until remitted to the creditor or forwarder, and shall not be commingled with any other operating funds. The trust account shall be used only for the purpose of:

(1) Remitting to collection creditors or forwarders the proceeds to which they are entitled.

(2) Remitting to the collection agency the commission that is due the collection agency.

(3) Reimbursing consumers for overpayments.

(4) Making adjustments to the trust account balance for bank service charges.

(b) No refund for overpayment by a debtor in an amount of less than one dollar ($1.00) is required.

(c) Each permit holder located outside this State shall deposit in a separate trust account, designated for its North Carolina creditors, funds to pay all monies due or owing all collection creditors or forwarders located within this State. In the case of alien corporations that are permit holders, the trust account must be established with a bank located in the United States or in any bank approved by the Commissioner. (1979, c. 835; 1989, c. 441, s. 10; c. 770, s. 52; 1991, c. 644, s. 23; 1993 (Reg. Sess., 1994), c. 678, s. 31; 2006-134, s. 3.)

§ 58-70-70. Receipt requirement.

(a) Whenever a payment is received in cash from a debtor, forwardee, or other person, an original receipt or an exact copy thereof shall be furnished the individual from whom payment is received. Evidence of all receipts issued shall be kept in the permit holder's office for three years. All receipts issued must:

(1) Be prenumbered by the printer and used and filed in consecutive numerical order;

(2) Show the name, street address and permit number of the permit holder;

(3) Show the name of the creditor or creditors for whom collected;

(4) Show the amount and date paid; and

(5) Show the last name of the person accepting payment.

(b) Whenever payment in any form is received by or on behalf of a debt buyer, in addition to meeting the requirements set forth in subsection (a) of this section, the receipt shall also:

(1) Show the name of the creditor or creditors for whom collected, the account number assigned by the creditor or creditors for whom collected, and if the current creditor is not the original creditor, the account number assigned by the original creditor.

(2) State clearly whether the payment is accepted as either payment in full or as a full and final compromise of the debt, and if not, the receipt shall state clearly the balance due after payment is credited. (1979, c. 835; 2009-573, s. 4(b).)

§ 58-70-75. Creditor may request return of accounts.

The written request of a creditor or forwarder for the return of any account which is not in the actual process of collection shall be complied with by the permit holder in writing within a reasonable length of time, but in any event not to exceed 60 days. All valuable papers furnished by the creditor or forwarder in connection with the account shall be returned. (1979, c. 835.)

§ 58-70-80. Return of accounts and all valuable papers upon termination of permit.

Whenever the permit of a collection agency is revoked, cancelled, or terminated for any reason, all accounts and valuable papers placed with the agency for collection shall be returned to the person placing the account for collection within five days of the termination of said permit unless, upon written application, an extension of time is granted by the Department of Insurance. All agreements between the collection agency and creditor or forwarder are automatically cancelled as of the date on which said permit is revoked, cancelled or terminated. If any of the accounts placed for collection are in the hands of others at the time of the permit termination, they shall immediately be notified by the collection agency to thereafter correspond, remit and be solely responsible to the creditor placing the accounts with the agency for collection unless the creditor has authorized a successor or other permit holder to continue to collect the accounts. In the case of dissolution of the collection agency, all accounts shall be returned within a reasonable period of time, but in any event not to exceed 60 days. Valuable papers shall include, but not be limited to, notes payable, creditor account cards and any other items placed within the collection agency by the creditor. (1979, c. 835.)

§ 58-70-85. Application of funds where there is a debtor-creditor relationship.

If a creditor has listed accounts with a permit holder for collection and also has had accounts on which he is debtor listed with the permit holder by any other creditors, collections effected in his behalf as a creditor may not be applied on accounts that he owes unless the permit holder has a written authorization on file as to how the moneys collected are to be applied. (1979, c. 835.)

Part 3. Prohibited Practices by Collecton Agencies Engaged in the Collection of Debts from Consumers.

§ 58-70-90. Definitions.

As used in this Part, the following terms have the meanings specified:

(1) "Collection agency" means a collection agency as defined in G.S. 58-70-15 which engages, directly or indirectly, in debt collection from a consumer.

(2) "Consumer" means an individual, aggregation of individuals, corporation, company, association, or partnership that has incurred a debt or alleged debt.

(3) "Debt" means any obligation owed or due or alleged to be owed or due from a consumer. (1961, c. 782; 1971, c. 814, ss. 1-3; 1979, c. 835.)

§ 58-70-95. Threats and coercion.

No collection agency shall collect or attempt to collect any debt alleged to be due and owing from a consumer by means of any unfair threat, coercion, or attempt to coerce. Such unfair acts include, but are not limited to, the following:

(1) Using or threatening to use violence or any illegal means to cause harm to the person, reputation or property of any person;

(2) Falsely accusing or threatening to accuse any person of fraud or any crime, or of any conduct that would tend to cause disgrace, contempt or ridicule;

(3) Making or threatening to make false accusations to another person, including any credit reporting agency, that a consumer has not paid, or has willfully refused to pay a just debt;

(4) Threatening to sell or assign, or to refer to another for collection, the debt of the consumer with an attending representation that the result of such sale, assignment or reference would be that the consumer would lose any defense to the debt or would be subject to harsh, vindictive, or abusive collection attempts;

(5) Representing that nonpayment of an alleged debt may result in the arrest of any person;

(6) Representing that nonpayment of an alleged debt may result in the seizure, garnishment, attachment, or sale of any property or wages unless such action is in fact contemplated by the debt collector and permitted by law;

(7) Threatening to take any action not in fact taken in the usual course of business, unless it can be shown that such threatened action was actually intended to be taken in the particular case in which the threat was made;

(8) Threatening to take any action not permitted by law. (1979, c. 835.)

§ 58-70-100. Harassment.

No collection agency shall use any conduct, the natural consequence of which is to oppress, harass, or abuse any person in connection with the attempt to collect any debt. Such conduct includes, but is not limited to, the following:

(1) Using profane or obscene language, or language that would ordinarily abuse the typical hearer or reader;

(2) Placing collect telephone calls or sending collect telegrams unless the caller fully identifies himself and the company he represents;

(3) Causing a telephone to ring or engaging any person in telephone conversation with such frequency as to be unreasonable or to constitute a harassment to the person under the circumstances or at times known to be times other than normal waking hours of the person;

(4) Placing telephone calls or attempting to communicate with any person, contrary to his instructions, at his place of employment, unless the collection agency does not have a telephone number where the consumer can be reached during the consumer's nonworking hours. (1979, c. 835.)

§ 58-70-105. Unreasonable publication.

No collection agency shall unreasonably publicize information regarding a consumer's debt. Such unreasonable publication includes, but is not limited to, the following:

(1) Any communication with any person other than the debtor or his attorney, except:

a. With the permission of the debtor or his attorney;

b. To persons employed by the collection agency, to a credit reporting agency, to a person or business employed to collect the debt on behalf of the creditor, or to a person who makes a legitimate request for the information;

c. To the spouse (or one who stands in place of the spouse) of the debtor, or to the parent or guardian of the debtor if the debtor is a minor;

d. For the sole purpose of locating the debtor, if no indication of indebtedness is made;

e. Through legal process.

(2) Using any form of communication which ordinarily would be seen or heard by any person other than the consumer that displays or conveys any information about the alleged debt other than the name, address and phone number of the collection agency except as otherwise provided in this Part.

(3) Disclosing any information relating to a consumer's debt by publishing or posting any list of consumers, except for credit reporting purposes. (1979, c. 835.)

§ 58-70-110. Deceptive representation.

No collection agency shall collect or attempt to collect a debt or obtain information concerning a consumer by any fraudulent, deceptive or misleading representation. Such representations include, but are not limited to, the following:

(1) Communicating with the consumer other than in the name of the person making the communication, the collection agency and the person or business on whose behalf the collection agency is acting or to whom the debt is owed;

(2) Failing to disclose in the initial written communication with the consumer and, in addition, if the initial communication with the consumer is oral, in that initial oral communication, that the debt collector is attempting to collect a debt and that any information obtained will be used for that purpose, and the failure to disclose in subsequent communications that the communication is from a debt collector; provided, however, that this subdivision does not apply to a formal pleading made in connection with legal action;

(3) Falsely representing that the collection agency has in its possession information or something of value for the consumer;

(4) Falsely representing the character, extent, or amount of a debt against a consumer or of its status in any legal proceeding; falsely representing that the collection agency is in any way connected with any agency of the federal, State or local government; or falsely representing the creditor's rights or intentions;

(5) Using or distributing or selling any written communication which simulates or is falsely represented to be a document authorized, issued, or

approved by a court, an official, or any other legally constituted or authorized authority, or which creates a false impression about its source;

(6)   Falsely representing that an existing obligation of the consumer may be increased by the addition of attorney's fees, investigation fees, service fees, or any other fees or charges;

(7)   Falsely representing the status or true nature of the services rendered by the collection agency or its business.

(8)   Communicating with the consumer in violation of the provisions of G.S. 62-159.1(a), 153A-277(b1), or 160A-314(b1). (1979, c. 835; 2001-269, s. 1.4; 2009-302, s. 4.)

§ 58-70-115. Unfair practices.

No collection agency shall collect or attempt to collect any debt by use of any unfair practices. Such practices include, but are not limited to, the following:

(1)   Seeking or obtaining any written statement or acknowledgment in any form containing an affirmation of any debt by a consumer who has been declared bankrupt, an acknowledgment of any debt barred by the statute of limitations, or a waiver of any legal rights of the debtor without disclosing the nature and consequences of such affirmation or waiver and the fact that the consumer is not legally obligated to make such affirmation or waiver.

(2)   Collecting or attempting to collect from the consumer all or any part of the collection agency's fee or charge for services rendered, collecting or attempting to collect any interest or other charge, fee or expense incidental to the principal debt unless legally entitled to such fee or charge.

(3)   Communicating with a consumer whenever the collection agency has been notified by the consumer's attorney that he represents said consumer.

(4)   When the collection agency is a debt buyer or is acting on behalf of a debt buyer, bringing suit or initiating an arbitration proceeding against the debtor or otherwise attempting to collect on a debt when the collection agency knows, or reasonably should know, that such collection is barred by the applicable statute of limitations.

(5) When the collection agency is a debt buyer or acting on behalf of a debt buyer, bringing suit or initiating an arbitration proceeding against the debtor, or otherwise attempting to collect on the debt without (i) valid documentation that the debt buyer is the owner of the specific debt instrument or account at issue and (ii) reasonable verification of the amount of the debt allegedly owed by the debtor. For purposes of this subdivision, reasonable verification shall include documentation of the name of the original creditor, the name and address of the debtor as appearing on the original creditor's records, the original consumer account number, a copy of the contract or other document evidencing the consumer debt, and an itemized accounting of the amount claimed to be owed, including all fees and charges.

(6) When the collection agency is a debt buyer or acting on behalf of a debt buyer, bringing suit or initiating an arbitration proceeding against the debtor to collect on a debt without first giving the debtor written notice of the intent to file a legal action at least 30 days in advance of filing. The written notice shall include the name, address, and telephone number of the debt buyer, the name of the original creditor and the debtor's original account number, a copy of the contract or other document evidencing the consumer debt, and an itemized accounting of all amounts claimed to be owed.

(7) Failing to comply with Part 5 of this Article. (1979, c. 835; 2009-573, s. 5.)

§ 58-70-120. Unauthorized practice of law; court appearances.

Neither a collection agency nor any representative thereof who is not a duly licensed attorney shall engage in the practice of law. As used in this section, "practice of law" includes the preparation of warrants or subpoenas. A collection agency's representative is prohibited from appearing in court on behalf of a creditor except as required by court order or subpoena, and except to submit and explain claims in bankruptcy court. (1979, c. 835; 1989, c. 441, s. 11.)

§ 58-70-125. Shared office space.

The office of a collection agency shall not be shared or have a common waiting room with a practicing attorney or any type of lending institution. The office may be located in a private residence only if it is solely for business purposes, has an outside entrance and can be isolated from the remainder of the residence. (1979, c. 835.)

Part 4. Enforcement.

§ 58-70-130. Civil liability.

(a)   Any collection agency which violates Part 3 of this Article with respect to any debtor shall be liable to that debtor in an amount equal to the sum of any actual damages sustained by the debtor as a result of the violation.

(b)   Any collection agency which violates Part 3 of this Article with respect to any debtor shall, in addition to actual damages sustained by the debtor as a result of the violation, also be liable to the debtor for a penalty in such amount as the court may allow, which shall not be less than five hundred dollars ($500.00) for each violation nor greater than four thousand dollars ($4,000) for each violation.

(c)   The specific and general provisions of Part 3 of this Article shall constitute unfair or deceptive acts or practices proscribed herein or by G.S. 75-1.1 in the area of commerce regulated thereby; provided, however, that, notwithstanding the provisions of G.S. 75-16, the civil penalties provided in this section shall not be trebled. Civil penalties in excess of four thousand dollars ($4,000) for each violation shall not be imposed.

(d)   The remedies provided by this section shall be cumulative, and in addition to remedies otherwise available. Any punitive damages assessed against a collection agency shall not be reduced by the amount of the civil penalty assessed against such agency pursuant to subsection (b) of this section.

(e)   The clear proceeds of civil penalties imposed under this section in suits instituted by the Attorney General shall be remitted to the Civil Penalty and Forfeiture Fund in accordance with G.S. 115C-457.2. (1979, c. 835; 1991, c. 68, s. 2; 1998-215, s. 89(a); 2009-573, s. 6.)

Part 5. Special Requirements in Actions Filed by Collection Agency Plaintiffs.

§ 58-70-145. Complaint of a collection agency plaintiff must contain certain allegations.

In any cause of action that arises out of the conduct of a business for which a plaintiff must secure a permit pursuant to this Article, the complaint shall allege as part of the cause of action that the plaintiff is duly licensed under this Article and shall contain the name and number, if any, of the license and the governmental agency that issued it. (2009-573, s. 8.)

§ 58-70-150. Complaint of a debt buyer plaintiff must be accompanied by certain materials.

In addition to the requirements of G.S. 58-70-145, in any cause of action initiated by a debt buyer, as that term is defined in G.S. 58-70-15, all of the following materials shall be attached to the complaint or claim:

(1)   A copy of the contract or other writing evidencing the original debt, which must contain a signature of the defendant. If a claim is based on credit card debt and no such signed writing evidencing the original debt ever existed, then copies of documents generated when the credit card was actually used must be attached.

(2)   A copy of the assignment or other writing establishing that the plaintiff is the owner of the debt. If the debt has been assigned more than once, then each assignment or other writing evidencing transfer of ownership must be attached to establish an unbroken chain of ownership. Each assignment or other writing evidencing transfer of ownership must contain the original account number of the debt purchased and must clearly show the debtor's name associated with that account number. (2009-573, s. 8.)

§ 58-70-155. Prerequisites to entering a default or summary judgment against a debtor under this Part.

(a) Prior to entry of a default judgment or summary judgment against a debtor in a complaint initiated by a debt buyer, the plaintiff shall file evidence with the court to establish the amount and nature of the debt.

(b) The only evidence sufficient to establish the amount and nature of the debt shall be properly authenticated business records that satisfy the requirements of Rule 803(6) of the North Carolina Rules of Evidence. The authenticated business records shall include at least all of the following items:

(1) The original account number.

(2) The original creditor.

(3) The amount of the original debt.

(4) An itemization of charges and fees claimed to be owed.

(5) The original charge-off balance, or, if the balance has not been charged off, an explanation of how the balance was calculated.

(6) An itemization of post charge-off additions, where applicable.

(7) The date of last payment.

(8) The amount of interest claimed and the basis for the interest charged. (2009-573, s. 8; 2011-326, s. 7.)

Article 71.

Bail Bondsmen and Runners.

§ 58-71-1. Definitions.

The following definitions apply in this Article:

(1) Accommodation bondsman. - A person who shall not charge a fee or receive any consideration for action as surety and who endorses the bail bond

after providing satisfactory evidences of ownership, value, and marketability of real or personal property to the extent necessary to reasonably satisfy the official taking bond that the real or personal property will in all respects be sufficient to assure that the full principal sum of the bond will be realized if there is a breach of the conditions of the bond. "Consideration" as used in this subdivision does not include the legal rights of a surety against a principal by reason of breach of the conditions of a bail bond nor does it include collateral furnished to and securing the surety as long as the value of the surety's rights in the collateral do not exceed the principal's liability to the surety by reason of a breach in the conditions of the bail bond.

(2) Bail bond. - An undertaking by the principal to appear in court as required upon penalty of forfeiting bail to the State in a stated amount; and may include an unsecured appearance bond, a premium-secured appearance bond, an appearance bond secured by a cash deposit of the full amount of the bond, an appearance bond secured by a mortgage pursuant to G.S. 58-74-5, and an appearance bond secured by at least one surety. A bail bond may also include a bond securing the return of a motor vehicle subject to forfeiture in accordance with G.S. 20-28.3(e).

(3) Bail bondsman. - A surety bondsman, professional bondsman or an accommodation bondsman as defined in this section.

(4) Commissioner. - The North Carolina Commissioner of Insurance.

(4a) First-year licensee. - Any person who has been licensed as a bail bondsman or runner under this Article and who has held the license for a period of less than 12 months.

(5) Insurer. - Any domestic, foreign, or alien surety company which has qualified generally to transact surety business and specifically to transact bail bond business in this State.

(6) Obligor. - A principal or a surety on a bail bond.

(7) Principal. - A defendant or witness obligated to appear in court as required upon penalty of forfeiting bail under a bail bond or a person obligated to return a motor vehicle subject to forfeiture in accordance with G.S. 20-28.3(e).

(8) Professional bondsman. - Any person who is approved and licensed by the Commissioner and who pledges cash or approved securities with the

Commissioner as security for bail bonds written in connection with a judicial proceeding and who receives or is promised money or other things of value in exchange for writing the bail bonds.

(8a)   Resident. - A person who lives in this State for at least six consecutive months immediately before applying for a license under this Article.

(9)   Runner. - A person employed by a bail bondsman for the purpose of assisting the bail bondsman in presenting the defendant in court when required, assisting in the apprehension and surrender of defendant to the court, keeping the defendant under necessary surveillance, or executing bonds on behalf of the licensed bondsman when the power of attorney has been duly recorded. "Runner" does not include a duly licensed attorney-at-law or a law-enforcement officer assisting a bondsman.

(9a)   Supervising bail bondsman. - Any person licensed by the Commissioner as a professional bondsman or surety bondsman who employs or contracts with any new licensee under this Article.

(10)   Surety. - One who, with the principal, is liable for the amount of the bail bond upon forfeiture of bail.

(11)   Surety bondsman. - Any person who is licensed by the Commissioner as a surety bondsman under this Article, is appointed by an insurer by power of attorney to execute or countersign bail bonds for the insurer in connection with judicial proceedings, and who receives or is promised consideration for doing so. (1963, c. 1225, s. 1; 1975, c. 619, s. 1; 1995 (Reg. Sess., 1996), c. 726, s. 1; 1998-182, s. 16; 2000-180, ss. 1, 2; 2001-269, s. 2.1; 2007-228, s. 1.)

§ 58-71-5. Commissioner of Insurance to administer Article; rules and regulations; employees; evidence of Commissioner's actions.

(a)   The Commissioner shall have full power and authority to administer the provisions of this Article, which regulates bail bondsmen and runners and to that end to adopt and promulgate rules and regulations to enforce the purposes and provisions of this Article. Subject to the provisions of the North Carolina Human Resources Act, the Commissioner may employ and discharge such employees, examiners, investigators and such other assistants as shall be deemed necessary, and he shall prescribe their duties.

(b) Any written instrument purporting to be a copy of any action, proceeding, or finding of fact by the Commissioner, or any record of the Commissioner authenticated under the head of the Commissioner by the seal of his office shall be accepted by all the courts of this State as prima facie evidence of the contents thereof. (1963, c. 1225, s. 2; 1975, c. 619, s. 1; 2013-382, s. 9.1(c).)

§ 58-71-10. Defects not to invalidate undertakings; liability not affected by agreement or lack of qualifications.

(a) No undertaking shall be invalid because of any defect of form, omission or recital or of condition, failure to note or record the default of any principal or surety, or because of any other irregularity, if it appears from the tenor of the undertaking before what magistrate or at what court the principal was bound to appear, and that the official before whom it was entered into was legally authorized to take it and the amount of bail is stated.

(b) The liability of a person on an undertaking shall not be affected by reason of the lack of any qualifications, sufficiency or competency provided in the criminal procedure law, or by reason of any other agreement whether or not the agreement is expressed in the undertaking, or because the defendant has not joined in the undertaking. (1963, c. 1225, s. 3; 1975, c. 619, s. 1; 2001-269, s. 2.2.)

§ 58-71-15. Qualifications of sureties on bail.

Each and every surety for the release of a person on bail shall be qualified as:

(1) An insurer and represented by a surety bondsman or bondsmen; or

(2) A professional bondsman; or

(3) An accommodation bondsman. (1963, c. 1225, s. 4; 1971, c. 1231, s. 1; 1975, c. 619, s. 1.)

§ 58-71-16. No return of premium; bond reduction.

Notwithstanding any other provision of law or rules adopted by the Commissioner under this Article, if, after an agreement has been entered into between a defendant and a surety, the defendant's bond is reduced, the surety shall not be required to return any portion of the premium to the defendant. (2011-377, s. 1.)

§ 58-71-20. Surrender of defendant by surety; when premium need not be returned.

At any time before there has been a breach of the undertaking in any type of bail or fine and cash bond the surety may surrender the defendant to the sheriff of the county in which the defendant is bonded to appear or to the sheriff where the defendant was bonded; in such case the full premium shall be returned within 72 hours after the surrender. The defendant may be surrendered without the return of premium for the bond if the defendant does any of the following:

(1)   Willfully fails to pay the premium to the surety or willfully fails to make a premium payment under the agreement specified in G.S. 58-71-167.

(2)   Changes his or her address without notifying the surety before the address change.

(3)   Physically hides from the surety.

(4)   Leaves the State without the permission of the surety.

(5)   Violates any order of the court.

(6)   Fails to disclose information or provides false information regarding any failure to appear in court, any previous felony convictions within the past 10 years, or any charges pending in any State or federal court.

(7)   Knowingly provides the surety with incorrect personal identification, or uses a false name or alias. (1963, c. 1225, s. 5; 1975, c. 619, s. 1; 1998-211, s. 30; 2001-269, s. 2.3; 2007-399, s. 1.)

§ 58-71-25. Procedure for surrender.

After there has been a breach of the undertaking in a bail bond, the surety may surrender the defendant as provided in G.S. 15A-540. (1963, c. 1225, s. 6; 1975, c. 619, s. 1; 2000-133, s. 7.)

§ 58-71-30. Arrest of defendant for purpose of surrender.

For the purpose of surrendering the defendant, the surety may arrest him before the forfeiture of the undertaking, or by his written authority endorsed on a certified copy of the undertaking, may request any judicial officer to order arrest of the defendant. (1963, c. 1225, s. 7; 1975, c. 619, s. 1.)

§ 58-71-35. Forfeiture of bail.

(a)   Except for bonds issued to secure the return of a motor vehicle subject to forfeiture in accordance with G.S. 20-28.3(e), the procedure for forfeiture of bail shall be that provided in Article 26 of Chapter 15A of the General Statutes and all provisions of that Article shall continue in full force and effect.

(b)   At any time before execution is issued on a judgment of forfeiture against a principal or his surety, the court may direct that the judgment be remitted in whole or in part, upon such conditions as the court may impose, if it appears that justice requires the remission of part or all of the judgment. (1963, c. 1225, s. 8; 1975, c. 619, s. 1; 1998-182, s. 17.)

§ 58-71-40. Bail bondsmen and runners to be qualified and licensed; license applications generally.

(a)   No person shall act in the capacity of a professional bondsman, surety bondsman, or runner or perform any of the functions, duties, or powers prescribed for professional bondsmen, surety bondsmen, or runners under this

Article unless that person is qualified and licensed under this Article. No license shall be issued under this Article except to an individual natural person.

(b)   The applicant shall apply for a license on forms prepared and supplied by the Commissioner. The Commissioner may propound any reasonable interrogatories to an applicant for a license under this Article about the applicant's qualifications, residence, prospective place of business, and any other matters that the Commissioner considers necessary to protect the public and ascertain the qualifications of the applicant. The Commissioner may also conduct any reasonable inquiry or investigation relative to the determination of the applicant's fitness to be licensed or to continue to be licensed.

(c)   A person whose application is denied may reapply, but the Commissioner shall not consider more than one application submitted by the same person within any one-year period.

(d)   When a license is issued under this section, the Commissioner shall issue a picture identification card, of design, size, and content approved by the Commissioner, to the licensee. Each licensee must carry this card at all times when working in the scope of the licensee's employment. A licensee whose license terminates or is terminated shall surrender the identification card to the Commissioner within 10 working days after the termination. The Commissioner may contract directly with persons for the processing and issuance of picture identification cards required by this section and may charge a reasonable fee in addition to the license fee charged under G.S. 58-71-55 in an amount that offsets the cost of the service, including the costs associated with the contract authorized by this subsection. Contracts entered into pursuant to this subsection shall not be subject to Article 3 of Chapter 143 of the General Statutes. However, the Commissioner shall: (i) submit all proposed contracts for supplies, materials, printing, equipment, and contractual services that exceed one million dollars ($1,000,000) authorized by this subsection to the Attorney General or the Attorney General's designee for review as provided in G.S. 114-8.3; and (ii) include in all contracts to be awarded by the Commissioner under this subsection a standard clause which provides that the State Auditor and internal auditors of the Commissioner may audit the records of the contractor during and after the term of the contract to verify accounts and data affecting fees and performance. The Commissioner shall not award a cost plus percentage of cost agreement or contract for any purpose.

(d1)   While engaged in official duties, a licensee is authorized to carry, possess, and display a shield as described in this subsection. The shield shall fulfill all of the following requirements:

(1)   Be an exact duplicate in size, shape, color, and design of the shield approved under G.S. 74C-5(12) and pictured in 12 NCAC 07D. 0405 on May 1, 2013.

(2)   Include the licensee's last name and corresponding license number in the same locations as the shield referenced in subdivision (1) of this subsection.

(3)   With reference to the shield described in subdivision (1) of this subsection, in lieu of the word "Private," the shield shall have the words "North Carolina," and in lieu of the word "Investigator," the shield shall have the words "Bail Agent."

Any shield that deviates from the design requirements as specified in this section shall be an unauthorized shield and its possession by a licensee shall constitute a violation of the statute by the licensee.

(e)   This section does not prohibit the hiring of personnel by a bail bondsman to perform only normal office duties. As used in this subsection, "normal office duties" do not include acting as a bail bondsman or runner. (1963, c. 1225, s. 9; 1975, c. 619, s. 1; 1995 (Reg. Sess., 1996), c. 726, s. 2; 2001-269, s. 2.4; 2007-507, s. 11; 2010-194, s. 10; 2011-326, s. 15(j); 2013-209, s. 1.)

§ 58-71-41. First-year licensees; limitations.

(a)   Except as provided in this section, a first-year licensee shall have the same authority as other persons licensed as bail bondsmen or runners under this Article. Except as provided in subsection (d) of this section, a first-year licensee shall operate only under the supervision of and from the official business address of a licensed supervising bail bondsman for the first 12 months of licensure. A first-year licensee may only be employed by or contract with one supervising bail bondsman.

(b)   When a first-year licensee has completed 12 months of supervision, six of which shall be uninterrupted, the supervising bail bondsman shall give notice of that fact to the Commissioner in writing. If the licensee will continue to be employed by or contract with the supervising bail bondsman beyond the initial 12-month period, the supervising bail bondsman shall continue to supervise and be responsible for the licensee's acts.

(c)   If the employment of or contract with a first-year licensee is terminated, the supervising bail bondsman shall notify the Commissioner in writing and shall specify the reason for the termination.

(d)   If, after exercising due diligence, a first-year licensed bail bondsman is unable to become employed by or to contract with a supervising bail bondsman, the first-year licensed bail bondsman must submit to the Department a sworn affidavit stating the relevant facts and circumstances regarding the first-year licensed bail bondman's inability to become employed by or contract with a supervising bail bondsman. The Department shall review the affidavit and determine whether the first-year licensed bail bondsman will be allowed to operate as an unsupervised bail bondsman. A first-year licensed bail bondsman is prohibited from becoming a supervising bail bondsman during the first two years of licensure.

(e)   Provided all other licensing requirements are met, an applicant for a bail bondsman or runner's license who has previously been licensed with the Commissioner for a period of at least 18 consecutive months and who has been inactive or unlicensed for a period of not more than three consecutive years shall not be deemed a new licensee for purposes of this section. (2000-180, s. 3.)

§ 58-71-45. Terms of licenses.

A license issued to a bail bondsman or to a runner authorizes the licensee to act in that capacity until the license is suspended or revoked. Upon the suspension or revocation of a license, the licensee shall return the license to the Commissioner. A license of a bail bondsman and a license of a runner shall be renewed in accordance with G.S. 58-71-75. After notifying the Commissioner in writing, a professional bondsman who employs a runner may cancel the runner's authority to act for the professional bondsman. (1963, c. 1225, s. 10; 1975, c. 619, s. 1; 1995 (Reg. Sess., 1996), c. 726, s. 3; 2009-536, ss. 1, 6; 2009-566, s. 14.)

§ 58-71-50. Qualification for bail bondsmen and runners.

(a) Criminal History Record Check. - Upon receipt of an application for a license as a bail bondsman or runner, the Commissioner shall conduct a criminal history record check in accordance with G.S. 58-71-51 to determine whether the applicant meets the requirements for a license as provided in this section.

(b) Qualifications. - Every applicant for a license under this Article as a bail bondsman or runner must meet all of the following qualifications:

(1) Be 18 years of age or over.

(1a) Have obtained a high school diploma or its equivalent.

(2) Be a resident of this State.

(3) Repealed by Session Laws 1998-211, s. 23, effective November 1, 1998.

(4) Have knowledge, training, or experience of sufficient duration and extent to provide the competence necessary to fulfill the responsibilities of a licensee.

(5) Have no outstanding bail bond obligations.

(6) Have no current or prior violations of any provision of this Article or of Article 26 of Chapter 15A of the General Statutes or of any similar provision of law of any other state.

(7) Not have been in any manner disqualified under the laws of this State or any other state to engage in the bail bond business.

(8) Hold a valid and current North Carolina drivers license or valid North Carolina identification card issued by the Division of Motor Vehicles.

(c) Proof of Residency. - An applicant for a license as a bail bondsman or runner shall provide to the Commissioner at least two of the documents listed in this subsection as proof of residency in this State. Subject to rules adopted by the Commissioner, an applicant may be required to provide additional documentation. The permissible documents are:

(1) A pay stub showing the applicant's residential address in this State.

(2) A utility bill showing the applicant's residential address in this State.

(3) A written lease agreement or contract for purchase and sale signed by the applicant and for a residence located in this State.

(4) A receipt for personal property taxes paid by the applicant to a North Carolina unit of local government.

(5) A receipt for real property taxes paid by the applicant to a North Carolina unit of local government.

(6) A monthly or quarterly statement showing the applicant's residential address in this State and issued by a financial institution for an account held by the applicant. (1963, c. 1225, s. 11; 1971, c. 1231, s. 1; 1975, c. 619, s. 1; 1987, c. 728, s. 1; 1989, c. 485, s. 39; 1991, c. 720, s. 41; 1995 (Reg. Sess., 1996), c. 726, s. 4; 1998-211, s. 23; 2007-228, ss. 2, 3; 2009-536, ss. 2, 6; 2009-566, s. 12.)

§ 58-71-51. Criminal history record checks.

(a) Authorization. - The Department of Justice may provide a criminal history record check to the Commissioner for a person who has applied to the Commissioner for a new or renewal license as a bail bondsman or runner. The Commissioner shall provide to the Department of Justice, along with the request, the fingerprints of the new or renewal applicant. The applicant shall furnish the Commissioner with a complete set of the applicant's fingerprints in a manner prescribed by the Commissioner. The Department of Justice shall provide a criminal history record check based upon the new or renewal applicant's fingerprints. The Commissioner shall provide any additional information required by the Department of Justice and a form signed by the applicant consenting to the check of the criminal record and to the use of the fingerprints and other identifying information required by the State or national repositories. The new or renewal applicant's fingerprints shall be forwarded to the State Bureau of Investigation for a search of the State's criminal history record file, and the State Bureau of Investigation shall forward a set of the fingerprints to the Federal Bureau of Investigation for a national criminal history check. The Department of Justice may charge each new or renewal applicant a fee for conducting the checks of criminal history records authorized by this subsection.

(b) Confidentiality. - The Commissioner shall keep all information obtained pursuant to this section confidential in accordance with applicable State law and federal guidelines, and the information shall not be a public record under Chapter 132 of the General Statutes. (2009-536, s. 3.)

§ 58-71-55. License fees.

A nonrefundable license fee of two hundred dollars ($200.00) shall be paid to the Commissioner with each application for license as a bail bondsman and a license fee of one hundred twenty dollars ($120.00) shall be paid to the Commissioner with each application for license as a runner. (1963, c. 1225, s. 12; 1975, c. 619, s. 1; 1983, c. 790, s. 11; 1991, c. 721, s. 4; 1995 (Reg. Sess., 1996), c. 726, s. 5; 2009-451, s. 21.7(a).)

§ 58-71-60: Repealed by Session Laws 1995 (Regular Session, 1996), c. 726, s. 6.

§ 58-71-65. Contents of application for runner's license; endorsement by professional bondsman.

In addition to the other requirements of this Article, an applicant for a license to be a runner must affirmatively show:

(1) That the applicant will be employed by only one professional bondsman, who will supervise the work of the applicant and be responsible for the runner's conduct in the bail bond business.

(2) That the application is endorsed by the appointing professional bondsman, who must agree in the application to supervise the runner's activities.

(3) Whether or not the applicant has ever been licensed as a bail bondsman or runner. An applicant who has been licensed as a bail bondsman must list all outstanding bail bond obligations. An applicant who has been licensed as a runner must list all prior employment as such, indicating the name of each supervising professional bondsman and the reasons for the termination of the employment. (1963, c. 1225, s. 14; 1975, c. 619, s. 1; 1987, c. 728, s. 2; 1995 (Reg. Sess., 1996), c. 726, s. 7.)

§ 58-71-70. Examination; fees.

Each applicant for a license as a professional bondsman, surety bondsman, or runner shall appear in person and take an examination prepared by the Commissioner testing the applicant's ability and qualifications. Each applicant is eligible for examination 30 days after the date the application is received by the Commissioner. If an applicant is unable to complete the examination requirement within 30 days after notification from the Commissioner of the applicant's eligibility to take the examination, the applicant shall again be subject to the criminal history record check prescribed by G.S. 58-71-50(a) so that current information is available for review with the application. Each examination shall be held at a time and place as designated by the Commissioner. Each applicant shall be given notice of the designated time and place no sooner than 15 days before the examination. The Commissioner may contract with a person to process applications for the examination and administer and grade the examination in the same manner as for agent examinations under Article 33 of this Chapter.

The fee for each examination is twenty-five dollars ($25.00) plus an amount that offsets the cost of any contract for examination services. This examination fee is nonrefundable.

An applicant who fails an examination may take a subsequent examination, but at least one year must intervene between examinations. (1963, c. 1225, s. 15; 1975, c. 619, s. 1; 1991, c. 721, s. 5; 1995 (Reg. Sess., 1996), c. 726, s. 8; 2009-566, s. 13.)

§ 58-71-71. Examination; educational requirements; penalties.

(a) In order to be eligible to take the examination required to be licensed as a runner or bail bondsman under G.S. 58-71-70, each person shall complete at least 12 hours of education as provided by the North Carolina Bail Agents Association in subjects pertinent to the duties and responsibilities of a runner or bail bondsman, including all laws and regulations related to being a runner or bail bondsman.

(b) Each year every licensee shall complete at least three hours of continuing education as provided by the North Carolina Bail Agents Association in subjects related to the duties and responsibilities of a runner or bail bondsman before renewal of the license. This continuing education shall not include a written or oral examination. A person who receives his first license on or after January 1 of any year does not have to comply with this subsection until the period between his first and second license renewals.

(c) Any person licensed as a runner or bail bondsman before January 1, 1994, is not subject to the prelicensing education requirement of this section, but is subject to the continuing education requirement of this section. A licensed runner or bail bondsman who is 65 years of age or older and who has been licensed as a runner or bail bondsman for 15 years or more is exempt from both the prelicensing education and continuing education requirements of this section.

(d) Educational courses offered by the North Carolina Bail Agents Association under this section must be approved by the Commissioner before they may be offered. Before approving a course, the Commissioner must be satisfied that the course will enhance the professional competence and professional responsibility of bail bondsmen and runners. The North Carolina Bail Agents Association shall not offer, sponsor, or conduct any course under this section unless the Commissioner has given authorization to do so.

(e) The license of any person who fails to comply with the continuing education requirements under this section shall lapse. The Commissioner may, for good cause shown, grant extensions of time to licensees to comply with these requirements. Any licensee who, after obtaining an extension under this subsection, offers evidence satisfactory to the Commissioner that the licensee has satisfactorily completed the required continuing professional education courses is in compliance with this section.

(f)   The Commissioner may adopt rules for the effective administration of this section. (1993, c. 409, s. 22; 1993 (Reg. Sess., 1994), c. 678, s. 32; 1995 (Reg. Sess., 1996), c. 726, s. 9; 1998-211, ss. 25, 26, 28; 2004-124, s. 21.3; 2012-183, s. 1.)

§ 58-71-72. Qualifications of instructors.

(a)   A person who provides, presents, or instructs a prelicensing course or continuing education course under G.S. 58-71-71 must have a certificate of authority issued by the Commissioner. The Commissioner may establish requirements for the issuance or renewal of a certificate of authority and grounds for the summary suspension or termination of a certificate of authority.

(b)   The Commissioner may summarily suspend or terminate a certificate of authority to provide, present, or instruct a course if the Commissioner finds that the course is inaccurate or it received a poor evaluation from both a Department monitor and a majority of those who attended the course and responded to a Department questionnaire about the course. (1995 (Reg. Sess., 1996), c. 726, s. 10.)

§ 58-71-75. License renewal; criminal history record checks; renewal fees.

(a)   Annual Renewal. - A license of a bail bondsman and a license of a runner shall be renewed on July 1 of each year upon payment of the applicable annual renewal fee. In even-numbered years, in addition to paying the annual renewal fee, an applicant seeking renewal must submit an application for renewal in accordance with this section. The Commissioner is not required to print renewal licenses.

(b)   Renewal Application. - In even-numbered years, a bail bondsman or runner seeking to renew a license shall provide the Commissioner, not less than 30 days prior to the expiration date of the bail bondsman's or runner's current license, all of the following:

(1) A renewal application containing all of the following:

a. Proof that the applicant is a resident of this State as required by G.S. 58-71-50(c).

b. Proof that the applicant meets the qualifications set out in G.S. 58-71-50(b)(5) through G.S. 58-71-50(b)(7).

c. The information required by G.S. 58-2-69.

(2) The annual renewal fee as provided in subsection (d) of this section.

(3) A complete set of fingerprints of the bail bondsman or runner and a fee to cover the cost of conducting the criminal history record check. The fingerprints shall be submitted in the manner prescribed by the Commissioner and shall be certified by an authorized law enforcement officer.

(c) Criminal History Record Check. - Upon receipt of a license renewal application in an even-numbered year, the Commissioner shall conduct a criminal history record check of the applicant seeking renewal in accordance with G.S. 58-71-51.

(d) Fee. - The renewal fee for a runner's license is sixty dollars ($60.00). The renewal fee for a bail bondsman's license is one hundred dollars ($100.00). A renewed license continues in effect until suspended or revoked for cause. (1963, c. 1225, s. 16; 1975, c. 619, s. 1; 1991, c. 721, s. 6; 1995 (Reg. Sess., 1996), c. 726, s. 11; 2009-536, s. 4; 2010-96, s. 10.)

§ 58-71-80. Grounds for denial, suspension, probation, revocation, or nonrenewal of licenses.

(a) The Commissioner may deny, place on probation, suspend, revoke, or refuse to renew any license issued under this Article, in accordance with the provisions of Article 3A of Chapter 150B of the General Statutes, for any one or more of the following causes:

(1) For any cause sufficient to deny, suspend, or revoke the license under any other provision of this Article.

(2) A conviction of any misdemeanor committed in the course of dealings under the license issued by the Commissioner.

(3) Material misstatement, misrepresentation or fraud in obtaining the license.

(4) Misappropriation, conversion or unlawful withholding of moneys belonging to insurers or others and received in the conduct of business under the license.

(5) Fraudulent, coercive, or dishonest practices in the conduct of business or demonstrating incompetence, untrustworthiness, or financial irresponsibility in the conduct of business in this State or any other jurisdiction.

(6) Conviction of a crime involving dishonesty, breach of trust, or moral turpitude.

(7) Failure to comply with or violation of the provisions of this Article or of any order, subpoena, rule or regulation of the Commissioner or person with similar regulatory authority in another jurisdiction.

(8) When in the judgment of the Commissioner, the licensee has in the conduct of the licensee's affairs under the license, demonstrated incompetency, financial irresponsibility, or untrustworthiness; or that the licensee is no longer in good faith carrying on the bail bond business; or that the licensee is guilty of rebating, or offering to rebate, or offering to divide the premiums received for the bond.

(9) For failing to pay any judgment or decree rendered on any forfeited undertaking in any court of competent jurisdiction.

(10) For charging or receiving, as premium or compensation for the making of any deposit or bail bond, any sum in excess of that permitted by this Article.

(11) For requiring, as a condition of executing a bail bond, that the principal agree to engage the services of a specified attorney.

(12) For cheating on an examination for a license under this Article.

(13) For entering into any business association or agreement with any person who is at that time found by the Commissioner to be in violation of any of

the bail bond laws of this State, or who has been in any manner disqualified under the bail bond laws of this State or any other state, whereby the person has any direct or indirect financial interest in the bail bond business of the licensee or applicant.

(14) For knowingly aiding or abetting others to evade or violate the provisions of this Article.

(14a) Having any professional license denied, suspended, or revoked in this State or any other jurisdiction for causes substantially similar to those listed in this subsection.

(14b) Violation of (i) any law governing bail bonding or insurance in this State or any other jurisdiction or (ii) any rule of the Financial Industry Regulatory Authority (FINRA).

(14c) Failure to comply with an administrative order or court order imposing a child support obligation after entry of a final judgment or order finding the violation to have been willful.

(14d) Failure to pay State income tax or comply with any administrative or court order directing payment of State income tax after entry of a final judgment or order finding the violation to have been willful.

(14e) Forging another's name to any document related to a bail bond transaction.

(15) Any cause for which issuance of the license could have been refused had it then existed and been known to the Commissioner at the time of issuance.

(b) The Commissioner shall deny, revoke, or refuse to renew any license under this Article if the applicant or licensee is or has ever been convicted of a felony.

(b1) The Commissioner shall revoke or refuse to renew any license under this Article if the licensee has been convicted on or after October 1, 2009, of a misdemeanor drug violation under Article 5 of Chapter 90 of the General Statutes.

(b2) The Commissioner shall deny any license under this Article if the applicant has been convicted of a misdemeanor drug violation under Article 5 of Chapter 90 of the General Statutes within the previous 24 months of the date of the application for the license.

(c) In the case of a first-year licensee whose employment or contract is terminated prior to the end of the 12-month supervisory period, the Commissioner may consider all information provided in writing by the supervising bail bondsman in determining whether sufficient cause exists to suspend, revoke, or refuse to renew the license or to warrant criminal prosecution of the first-year licensee. If the Commissioner determines there is not sufficient cause for adverse administrative action or criminal prosecution, the termination shall not be deemed an interruption and the period of time the licensee was employed by or contracted with the terminating supervising bail bondsman will be credited toward the licensee's completion of the required 12 months of supervision with a subsequent supervising bail bondsman. (1963, c. 1225, s. 17; 1975, c. 619, s. 1; 1989, c. 485, s. 40; 1991, c. 644, s. 17; 1993, c. 409, s. 16; 1998-211, s. 24; 2000-180, s. 4; 2009-536, s. 5; 2011-377, s. 2.)

§ 58-71-81. Notice of receivership.

Upon the filing for protection under the United States Bankruptcy Code or any state receivership law by any bail bondsman licensed under this Article or by any bail bond business in which the bondsman holds a position of management or ownership, the bondsman shall notify the Commissioner of the filing for protection within three business days after the filing. Upon the appointment of a receiver by a State or federal court for any professional bondsman licensed under this Article, or for any bail bond business in which the bondsman holds a position of management or ownership, the bondsman shall notify the Commissioner of the filing for protection within three business days after the filing. The failure to notify the Commissioner within three business days after the filing for bankruptcy protection shall, after hearing, cause the license of any person failing to make the required notification to be suspended for a period of not less than 60 days nor more than three years, in the discretion of the Commissioner. (1993, c. 409, s. 17; 1995 (Reg. Sess., 1996), c. 726, s. 12.)

§ 58-71-82. Dual license holding.

If an individual holds a professional bondsman's license or a runner's license and a surety bondsman's license simultaneously, they are considered one license for the purpose of disciplinary actions involving suspension, revocation, or nonrenewal under this Article. Separate renewal fees must be paid for each license, however. Nothing in this Article shall be construed to prohibit a person from simultaneously holding a professional bondsman's license and a runner's license. (1995 (Reg. Sess., 1996), c. 726, ss. 13, 15; 1999-132, s. 5; 2011-377, s. 3.)

§ 58-71-85. License sanction and denial procedures.

(a) The suspension or revocation of, or refusal to renew, any license under G.S. 58-71-80 shall be in accordance with the provisions of Chapter 150B of the General Statutes.

(b) Whenever the Commissioner denies an initial application for a license or an application for a reissuance of a license, the Commissioner shall notify the applicant and advise, in writing, the applicant of the reasons for the denial of the license. The application may also be denied for any reason for which a license may be suspended or revoked or not renewed under G.S. 58-71-80(a). In order for an applicant to be entitled to a review of the Commissioner's action to determine the reasonableness of the action, the applicant must make a written demand upon the Commissioner for a review no later than 30 days after service of the notification upon the applicant. The review shall be completed without undue delay, and the applicant shall be notified promptly in writing of the outcome of the review. In order for an applicant who disagrees with the outcome of the review to be entitled to a hearing under Article 3A of Chapter 150B of the General Statutes, the applicant must make a written demand upon the Commissioner for a hearing no later than 30 days after service upon the applicant of the notification of the outcome. (1963, c. 1225, s. 18; 1975, c. 619, s. 1; 1989, c. 485, s. 33; 1993, c. 504, s. 33; 1998-211, s. 29; 2005-240, s. 2.)

§ 58-71-90. Repealed by Session Laws 1999-132, s. 1.1.

§ 58-71-95. Prohibited practices.

No bail bondsman or runner shall:

(1) Pay a fee or rebate or give or promise anything of value, directly or indirectly, to a jailer, law-enforcement officer, committing magistrate, or any other person who has power to arrest or hold in custody, or to any public official or public employee in order to secure a settlement, compromise, remission or reduction of the amount of any bail bond or the forfeiture thereof, including the payment to law-enforcement officers, directly or indirectly, for the arrest or apprehension of a principal or principals who have caused or will cause a forfeiture.

(2) Pay a fee or rebate or give anything of value to an attorney in bail bond matters, except in defense of any action on a bond.

(3) Pay a fee or rebate or give or promise anything of value to the principal or anyone in his behalf.

(4) Participate in the capacity of an attorney at a trial or hearing of one on whose bond he is surety, nor suggest or advise the employment of, or name for employment any particular attorney to represent his principal.

(5) Accept anything of value from a principal or from anyone on behalf of a principal except the premium, which shall not exceed fifteen percent (15%) of the face amount of the bond; provided that the bondsman shall be permitted to accept collateral security or other indemnity from a principal or from anyone on behalf of a principal. Such collateral security or other indemnity required by the bondsman must be reasonable in relation to the amount of the bond and shall be returned within 72 hours after final termination of liability on the bond. Any bail bondsman who knowingly and willfully fails to return any collateral security, the value of which exceeds one thousand five hundred dollars ($1,500), is guilty of a Class I felony. All collateral security, such as personal and real property, subject to be returned must be done so under the same conditions as requested and received by the bail bondsman.

(6) Solicit business in any of the courts or on the premises of any of the courts of this State, in the office of any magistrate and in or about any place where prisoners are confined. Loitering in or about a magistrate's office or any place where prisoners are confined shall be prima facie evidence of soliciting.

(7) Advise or assist the principal for the purpose of forfeiting bond.

(8) Impersonate a law-enforcement officer.

(9) Falsely represent that the bail bondsman or runner is in any way connected with an agency of the federal government or of a state or local government. (1963, c. 1225, s. 20; 1975, c. 619, s. 1; 1993, c. 409, s. 18; 1995 (Reg. Sess., 1996), c. 726, s. 16; 1998-211, s. 31; 2000-180, s. 5.)

§ 58-71-100. Receipts for collateral; trust accounts.

(a) When a bail bondsman accepts collateral he shall give a written receipt for the collateral. The receipt shall give in detail a full description of the collateral received. Collateral security shall be held and maintained in trust. When collateral security is received in the form of cash or check or other negotiable instrument, the licensee shall deposit the cash or instrument within two banking days after receipt, in an established, separate noninterest-bearing trust account in any bank located in North Carolina. The trust account funds under this section shall not be commingled with other operating funds.

(b) With the approval of the Commissioner, bail bondsmen operating out of the same business office or location may establish a shared trust account for collateral security received by them. The Commissioner may require the bondsmen desiring to establish the shared trust account to furnish the Commissioner information about their business that the Commissioner considers necessary to administer this Article effectively. (1963, c. 1225, s. 21; 1975, c. 619, s. 1; 2000-180, s. 6; 2001-269, s. 2.5.)

§ 58-71-105. Persons prohibited from becoming surety or runners.

No sheriff, deputy sheriff, other law-enforcement officer, judicial official, attorney, parole officer, probation officer, jailer, assistant jailer, employee of the General Court of Justice, nor other public employee assigned to duties relating to the administration of criminal justice, nor the spouse of any such person, may in any case become surety on a bail bond for any person. In addition, no person covered by this section may act as an agent for any bonding company or bail bondsman. No such person may have an interest, directly or indirectly, in the financial affairs of any firm or corporation whose principal business is acting as a bail bondsman. However, nothing in this section prohibits any such person from being surety upon the bond of his or her spouse, parent, brother, sister, child, or descendant. (1963, c. 1225, s. 22; 1973, c. 108, s. 39; 1975, c. 619, s. 1; 1991, c. 644, s. 18; 1995 (Reg. Sess., 1996), c. 726, s. 17.)

§ 58-71-110. Bonds not to be signed in blank; authority to countersign only given to licensed employee.

A bail bondsman shall not sign nor countersign in blank bail bonds, nor shall he give a power of attorney to, or otherwise authorize, anyone to countersign his name to bonds unless the person so authorized is a licensed bondsman or runner directly employed by the bondsman giving such power of attorney. Copies of all such powers of attorney and revocations of such powers of attorney must be filed immediately with the Commissioner and the clerk of superior court of any county in the State where said bondsman giving the power of attorney is currently writing or is obligated on bail bonds. (1963, c. 1225, s. 23; 1975, c. 619, s. 1.)

§ 58-71-115. Insurers to annually report surety bondsmen; notices of appointments and terminations; information confidential.

(a) Before July 1 of each year, every insurer shall furnish the Commissioner a list of all surety bondsmen appointed by the insurer to write bail bonds on the insurer's behalf. An insurer who appoints a surety bondsman in the State on or after July 1 of each year shall notify the Commissioner of the appointment. All appointments are subject to the issuance of the proper license to the appointee under this Article.

(b) An insurer terminating the appointment of a surety bondsman shall file a written notice of the termination with the Commissioner, together with a statement that the insurer has given or mailed notice of the termination to the surety bondsman. The notice to the Commissioner shall state the reasons, if any, for the termination. Information furnished in the notice to the Commissioner shall be privileged and shall not be used as evidence in or basis for any action against the insurer or any of its representatives.

(c) Notwithstanding any other provision of this Article, any documents, materials, or other information in the control or possession of the Commissioner or any organization of which the Commissioner is a member and (i) furnished by an insurer or an employee or agent thereof acting on behalf of the insurer under this section or (ii) obtained by the Commissioner in an investigation under this section shall be confidential by law and privileged, shall not be considered public records under G.S. 58-2-100 or Chapter 132 of the General Statutes, shall not be subject to subpoena, and shall not be subject to discovery in any civil action other than a proceeding brought by the Commissioner against a person to whom the documents, materials, or other information relate. However, the Commissioner may use the documents, materials, or other information in the furtherance of any regulatory or legal action brought as a part of the Commissioner's duties. Neither the Commissioner nor any person who receives documents, materials, or other information while acting under the authority of the Commissioner shall be permitted or required to testify in any civil action other than a proceeding brought by the Commissioner against a person to whom the documents, materials, or other information relate. (1963, c. 1225, s. 24; 1975, c. 619, s. 1; 1995 (Reg. Sess., 1996), c. 726, s. 18; 2007-507, s. 12; 2011-377, s. 4.)

§ 58-71-120. Bail bondsman to give notice of discontinuance of business; cancellation of license.

Any bail bondsman who discontinues writing bail bonds during the period for which the bail bondsman is licensed shall return the license to the Commissioner for cancellation within 30 days after the discontinuance. (1963, c. 1225, s. 25; 1975, c. 619, s. 1; 2009-566, s. 15.)

§ 58-71-121. Death, incapacitation, or incompetence of a bail bondsman.

In the case of death, incapacitation, or incompetence of a licensed bail bondsman, the spouse or surviving spouse, next of kin, person or persons holding a power of attorney, guardian, executor, or administrator of the licensed bail bondsman may contract with another licensed bail bondsman to perform those duties to have the licensee's outstanding bail bond obligations resolved to the satisfaction of the courts. The contract must be filed with the Commissioner and every clerk of superior court where it can be determined the licensee has pending outstanding bail bond obligations. The licensed bail bondsman who has agreed to perform these duties shall not, at the time of the execution of the contract, have any administrative or criminal actions pending against him or her. (2000-180, s. 7.)

§ 58-71-122. Transfer of business by bail bondsman.

A licensed professional bondsman may contract to transfer, convey, or assign the professional bondsman's business to another professional bondsman licensed under this Article. The contract shall include a list of the transferring professional bondsman's pending outstanding bail bond obligations and shall be filed with the Commissioner. The contract shall allow for the transferring professional bondsman to transfer, convey, or assign assets to the purchasing professional bondsman that include, but are not limited to, any pledged cash or any pledged approved securities with the Commissioner as security for bail bonds. Notwithstanding the filing of the contract with the Commissioner, the transferor remains responsible for all outstanding bond obligations until relieved from an individual obligation pursuant to G.S. 15A-534(h), by a substitution of surety pursuant to G.S. 15A-538, or satisfaction of any final judgment of forfeiture entered thereon. (2011-377, s. 5.)

§ 58-71-125. Persons eligible as runners; bail bondsmen to annually report runners; notices of appointments and terminations; information confidential.

Every person duly licensed as a bail bondsman may appoint as runner any person who has been issued runner's license. Each bail bondsman must, on or before July 1 of each year, furnish to the Commissioner a list of all runners appointed by him. Each such bail bondsman who shall, subsequent to the filing of this list, appoint additional persons as runners shall file written notice with the Commissioner of such appointment.

A bail bondsman terminating the appointment of a runner shall file written notice thereof with the Commissioner, together with a statement that he has given or mailed notice to the runner. Such notice filed with the Commissioner shall state the reasons, if any, for such termination. Information so furnished the Commissioner shall be privileged and shall not be used as evidence in any action against the bail bondsman. (1963, c. 1225, s. 26; 1975, c. 619, s. 1.)

§ 58-71-130. Substituting bail by sureties for deposit.

If money or bonds have been deposited, bail by sureties may be substituted therefor at any time before a breach of the undertaking, and the official taking the new bail shall make an order that the money or bonds be refunded to the person depositing the same and they shall be refunded accordingly, and the original undertakings shall be canceled. (1963, c. 1225, s. 27; 1975, c. 619, s. 1.)

§ 58-71-135. Deposit for defendant admitted to bail authorizes release and cancellation of undertaking.

When the defendant has been admitted to bail, he, or another in his behalf, may deposit with an official authorized to take bail, a sum of money, or nonregistered bonds of the United States, or of the State, or of any county, city or town within the State, equal in market value to the amount of such bail, together with his personal undertaking, and an undertaking of such other person, if the money or bonds are deposited by another. Upon delivery to the official in whose custody the defendant is of a certificate of such deposit, he shall be discharged from custody in the cause.

When bail other than a deposit of money or bonds has been given, the defendant or the surety may, at any time before a breach of the undertaking, deposit the sum mentioned in the undertaking, and upon such deposit being made, accompanied by a new undertaking, the original undertaking shall be canceled. (1963, c. 1225, s. 28; 1975, c. 619, s. 1.)

§ 58-71-140. Registration of licenses and power of appointments by insurers.

(a)   Before the date of the notice provided for in subsection (e) of this section, no professional bail bondsman shall become a surety on an undertaking unless he or she has registered his or her current license in the office of the clerk of superior court in the county in which he or she resides and a certified copy of the same with the clerk of superior court in any other county in which he or she shall write bail bonds.

(b)   Before the date of the notice provided for in subsection (e) of this section, a surety bondsman shall register his or her current surety bondsman's license and a certified copy of his or her power of appointment with the clerk of superior court in the county in which the surety bondsman resides and with the clerk of superior court in any other county in which the surety bondsman writes bail bonds on behalf of an insurer.

(c)   Before the date of the notice provided for in subsection (e) of this section, no runner shall become surety on an undertaking on behalf of a professional bondsman unless that runner has registered his or her current license and a certified copy of his or her power of attorney in the office of the clerk of superior court in the county in which the runner resides and with the clerk of superior court in any other county in which the runner writes bail bonds on behalf of the professional bondsman.

(c1)   On or after the date of the notice provided for in subsection (e) of this section, all licensed professional bail bondsmen, surety bondsmen, and runners shall register in the statewide Electronic Bondsmen Registry in accordance with subsection (e) of this section.

(d)   Professional bondsmen, surety bondsmen, and runners shall file with the clerk of court having jurisdiction over the principal an affidavit on a form furnished by the Administrative Office of the Courts. The affidavit shall include, but not be limited to:

(1)   If applicable, a statement that the bondsman has not, nor has anyone for the bondsman's use, been promised or received any collateral, security, or premium for executing this appearance bond.

(2)   If promised a premium, the amount of the premium promised and the due date.

(3)   If the bondsman has received a premium, the amount of premium received.

(4)   If given collateral security, the name of the person from whom it is received and the nature and amount of the collateral security listed in detail.

(e) On or before October 1, 2006, the Administrative Office of the Courts shall establish a statewide Electronic Bondsmen Registry (Registry) for all licenses, powers of appointment, and powers of attorney requiring registration under this section. When the Registry is established, the Administrative Office of the Courts shall notify the Commissioner and the Commissioner shall notify all licensed professional bondsmen, surety bondsmen, runners, and qualified insurance companies of the Registry. On or after the date of that notice, a person may register as required under this section by maintaining a record of each required license, power of appointment, or power of attorney in the Registry. After a bondsman, surety bondsman, or runner has completed registration in the Registry, he or she is authorized to execute bail bonds pursuant to his or her registered license, power of appointment, or power of attorney in all counties so long as the registered license, power of appointment, or power of attorney remains in effect. (1963, c. 1225, s. 31; 1975, c. 619, s. 1; 1995 (Reg. Sess., 1996), c. 726, s. 19; 2001-269, s. 2.6; 2006-188, s. 1.)

§ 58-71-141. Appointment of bail bondsmen; affidavit required.

(a) Before receiving an appointment, a surety bondsman shall submit to the Commissioner an affidavit, signed under oath, by the surety bondsman and by any former insurer, stating that the surety bondsman does not owe any premium or unsatisfied judgment to any insurer and that the bondsman agrees to discharge all outstanding forfeitures and judgments on bonds previously written. The affidavit shall be in a form prescribed by the Commissioner and shall be submitted by the surety bondsman to the former insurer. If the surety bondsman does not satisfy or discharge all forfeitures or judgments, the former insurer shall submit a notice, with supporting documents, to the appointing insurer, the surety bondsman, and the Commissioner, which states, under oath, that the surety bondsman has failed to satisfy, in a timely manner, the forfeitures and judgments on bonds written by the surety bondsman and that the former insurer has satisfied the forfeiture or judgment from its own funds. The former insurer shall submit the notice and supporting documents to the appointing insurer, the surety bondsman, and the Commissioner within 30 days after the former insurer receives the affidavit from the surety bondsman. Upon receipt of the notice and supporting documents, the appointing insurer shall immediately cancel the surety bondsman's appointment. The surety bondsman may be reappointed only upon certification by the former insurer that all forfeitures and judgments on bonds written by the surety bondsman have been discharged. The appointing insurer or surety bondsman may, within 10 days after receiving the notice and supporting documents from the former insurer, appeal to the Commissioner.

(b)   The Commissioner shall adopt rules, including rules regarding the procedures for appeals and stays of the requirements of this section, to implement this section.

(c)   As used in this section, "former insurer" means the insurer with whom the surety bondsman had a prior appointment and who is responsible for any outstanding bonds written by the surety bondsman. (2003-148, s. 1; 2007-507, s. 13.)

§ 58-71-145. Financial responsibility of professional bondsmen.

Each professional bondsman acting as surety on bail bonds in this State shall maintain a deposit of securities with and satisfactory to the Commissioner of a fair market value of at least one-eighth the amount of all bonds or undertakings written in this State on which he is absolutely or conditionally liable as of the first day of the current month. The amount of this deposit must be reconciled with the bondsman's liabilities as of the first day of the month on or before the fifteenth day of said month and the value of said deposit shall in no event be less than fifteen thousand dollars ($15,000). (1963, c. 1225, s. 29; 1975, c. 619, s. 1; 2000-180, s. 8.)

§ 58-71-150: Repealed by Session Laws 2005-240, s. 4, effective October 1, 2005, and applicable to all notices of applications denied by the Commissioner served on or after that date and to all notices of review outcomes served on or after that date.

§ 58-71-151. Securities held in trust by Commissioner; authority to dispose of same.

The securities deposited by a professional bondsman with the Commissioner shall be held in trust for the protection and benefit of the holder of bail bonds executed by or on behalf of the undersigned bondsman in this State.

Notwithstanding any other provision of law, the Commissioner is authorized to select a bank or trust company as master trustee to hold cash securities to be pledged to the State when deposited with the Commissioner pursuant to statute. Securities may be held by the master trustee in any form that in fact perfects the security interest of the State in the securities. The Commissioner shall by rule establish the manner in which the master trust shall operate. The master trustee may charge the person making the deposit reasonable fees for services rendered in connection with the operation of the trust, and the assets of the account may be used to pay such charges.

A pro rata portion of the securities shall be returned to the bondsman when the Commissioner is satisfied that the deposit of securities is in excess of the amount required to be maintained with the Commissioner by said bondsman; and all the securities shall be returned if the Commissioner is satisfied that the bondsman has satisfied, or satisfactory arrangements have been made to satisfy, the obligations of the bondsman on all the bondsman's bail bonds written in the State.

The Commissioner may sell or transfer any and all of said securities or utilize the proceeds thereof for the purpose of satisfying the liabilities of the professional bondsman on bail bonds given in this State on which the bondsman is liable. (2005-240, s. 3.)

§ 58-71-155. Bondsman to furnish power of attorney with securities.

With the securities deposited with the Commissioner, the professional bondsman shall at the same time deliver to the Commissioner of Insurance a power of attorney, on a form supplied by the Commissioner, executed and acknowledged by the professional bondsman authorizing the sale or transfer of said securities or any part thereof. The power of attorney shall read as follows:

POWER OF ATTORNEY

AUTHORIZING THE COMMISSIONER OF INSURANCE TO

SELL, OR TRANSFER SECURITIES DEPOSITED BY

PROFESSIONAL BONDSMEN IN

NORTH CAROLINA

KNOW ALL MEN BY THESE PRESENTS, That _____, a professional bondsman, located in the County of _____, in the State of _____, has authorized and appointed for himself, his successors, heirs and assigns, the Commissioner of Insurance of the State of North Carolina, in the name and in behalf of said professional bondsman, his true and lawful attorney to sell or transfer any securities deposited or that may be deposited, by said professional bondsman with said Commissioner, under the laws and regulations requiring a deposit of securities to be made by professional bondsmen doing business in the State of North Carolina, insofar as the sale or transfer is deemed necessary by the Commissioner of Insurance to pay any liability arising under a bond which purports to be given by the undersigned bondsman in any county in this State and execution has been issued against said bondsman pursuant to a judgment on the bond and the same has not been satisfied. The securities so deposited are to be held in trust by the Commissioner for the sole protection and benefit of the holder of bail bonds executed by, or on behalf of, the undersigned bondsman. IN WITNESS WHEREOF, I have hereunto set my hand and affixed my seal this _____ day of _____, _____.

_____

Professional Bondsman

Before me, a Notary Public in and for the State of _____ personally appeared _____, a professional bondsman who acknowledged that he executed the foregoing power of attorney.

WITNESS my hand and Notarial Seal, this _____ day of _____, _____.

_____

Notary Public

My Commission Expires: _____

(1975, c. 619, s. 1; 1999-456, s. 59.)

§ 58-71-160. Security deposit to be maintained.

(a) Any professional bondsman, whose security deposits with the Commissioner are, for any reason, reduced in value below the requirements of this Article, shall immediately upon receipt of a notice of deficiency from the Commissioner deposit such additional securities as are necessary to comply with the law. No professional bondsman shall sign, endorse, execute, or become surety on any additional bail bonds, or pledge or deposit any cash, check, or other security of any nature in lieu of a bail bond in any county in North Carolina until the professional bondsman has made such additional deposit of securities as required by the notice of deficiency.

(b) The Commissioner may deny the renewal of any license held by a professional bondsman under this Chapter or may deny the issuance of any license applied for by a professional bondsman under this Chapter if, at the time of the renewal application or license application, the professional bondsman has not complied with a notice of deficiency under subsection (a) of this section. The Commissioner may issue the renewal license or the new license upon compliance by the professional bondsman with the notice of deficiency. (1975, c. 619, s. 1; 2001-269, s. 2.7.)

§ 58-71-165. Report required.

(a) Each professional bail bondsman shall file with the Commissioner a written report in a form prescribed by the Commissioner regarding all bail bonds on which the bondsman is liable as of the first day of each month showing (i) each individual bonded, (ii) the date the bond was given, (iii) the principal sum of the bond, (iv) the State or local official to whom given, and (v) the fee charged for the bonding service in each instance.

(b) Each insurer that appoints surety bondsmen in this State shall file with the Commissioner a written report in a form adopted by the Commissioner regarding all bail bonds on which the insurer is liable as of the last day of each calendar quarter showing the total dollar amount for which the insurer is liable. The report shall be filed on or before the fifteenth day following the end of each calendar quarter.

(c) The reports required by subsection (a) of this section shall be filed on or before the fifteenth day of each month.

(d) Any person who knowingly and willfully falsifies a report required by this section is guilty of a Class I felony. (1975, c. 619, s. 1; 1989, c. 485, s. 43; 1991, c. 644, s. 20; 1993, c. 539, s. 1276; 1994, Ex. Sess., c. 24, s. 14(c); 1998-211, s. 27; 2007-484, s. 44.5; 2007-507, s. 14.)

§ 58-71-167. Portion of bond premium payments deferred.

(a) In any case where the agreement between principal and surety calls for some portion of the bond premium payments to be deferred or paid after the defendant has been released from custody, a written memorandum of agreement between the principal and surety shall be kept on file by the surety with a copy provided to the principal, upon request. The memorandum shall contain the following information:

(1) The amount of the premium payment deferred or not yet paid at the time the defendant is released from jail.

(2) The method and schedule of payment to be made by the defendant to the bondsman, which shall include the dates of payment and amount to be paid on each date.

(3) That the principal is, upon the principal's request, entitled to a copy of the memorandum.

(b) The memorandum must be signed by the defendant and the bondsman, or one of the bondsman's agents, and dated at the time the agreement is made. Any subsequent modifications of the memorandum must be in writing, signed, dated, and kept on file by the surety, with a copy provided to the principal, upon request. (1991, c. 644, s. 22.)

§ 58-71-168. Records to be maintained.

All records related to executing bail bonds, including bail bond registers, monthly reports, receipts, collateral security agreements, and memoranda of agreements, shall be kept separate from records of any other business and must be maintained for not less than three years after the final entry has been made. (1991, c. 644, s. 22.)

§ 58-71-170. Examinations.

(a) Whenever the Commissioner considers it prudent, the Commissioner shall visit and examine or cause to be visited and examined by a competent person appointed by the Commissioner for that purpose any professional bail bondsman, surety bondsman, or runner subject to this Article. For this purpose the Commissioner or person making the examination shall have free access to all records of the licensee that relate to the licensee's business and to the records kept by any of the licensee's agents.

(b) The Commissioner may conduct examinations of surety bondsmen under G.S. 58-2-195 as well as under subsection (a) of this section. (1975, c. 619, s. 1; 1991, c. 644, s. 21; 2001-269, s. 2.8.)

§ 58-71-175. Limit on principal amount of bond to be written by professional bondsman.

No professional bondsman shall become liable on any bond or multiple of bonds for any one individual that totals more than one-fourth of the value of the securities deposited with the Commissioner at that time, until final termination of liability on such bond or multiple of bonds. (1975, c. 619, s. 1; 1987, c. 728, s. 3; 1989, c. 485, s. 42.)

§ 58-71-180. Disposition of fees.

Fees collected by the Commissioner pursuant to this Article shall be credited to the Insurance Regulatory Fund created under G.S. 58-6-25. (1963, c. 1225, s. 32; 1975, c. 619, s. 1; 1991, c. 689, s. 294; 2003-221, s. 9.)

§ 58-71-185. Penalties for violations.

Except as otherwise provided in this Article, any person who violates any of the provisions of this Article is guilty of a Class 1 misdemeanor. (1963, c. 1225, s. 33; 1975, c. 619, s. 1; 1991, c. 644, s. 19; 1993, c. 539, s. 473; 1994, Ex. Sess., c. 24, s. 14(c); 2000-180, s. 9.)

§ 58-71-190. Duplication of regulation forbidden.

No county, city or town in this State shall license or levy a license tax on bail bondsmen nor require such bondsmen to deposit collateral security as a condition for continuing to write bail bonds. (1975, c. 619, s. 1.)

§ 58-71-195. Conflicting laws.

Section 41.1 of Chapter 105 of the General Statutes of North Carolina and all laws and clauses of laws in conflict with the provisions of the Chapter are hereby repealed. Provided, however, that in the event of any conflict between the provisions of this Chapter and those of Chapter 15A of the General Statutes of North Carolina, the provisions of Chapter 15A shall control and continue in full force and effect. (1975, c. 619, s. 2.)

§ 58-71-200. Bondsman access to criminal court records.

(a) In order to assist licensed sureties and their agents in evaluating potential and current clients for the purposes of bail, the Administrative Office of the Courts shall provide any individual with a current license to act as professional bondsman, surety bondsman, or runner with access to search criminal records in the Administrative Office of the Courts' real-time criminal information systems.

(b)   Access granted under subsection (a) of this section shall be limited to information systems containing general criminal case information, as maintained by the clerks of superior court. Access shall not include systems for the production of criminal process by law enforcement officials and judicial officials under G.S. 15A-301.1 or other information not subject to public disclosure.

(c)   Access provided pursuant to subsection (a) of this section shall be without charge for individual searches of the Administrative Office of the Courts' criminal information systems. In order to defray the costs of establishing access, the Administrative Office of the Courts shall charge initial setup fees equivalent to its fees for governmental agencies granted access to its systems to each individual granted access pursuant to subsection (a) of this section.

(d)   All hardware, software, telecommunications charges, or other expenditures required for such access shall be the sole responsibility of the individual bondsman or runner. No State funds may be expended for any such expenses.

(e)   The Commissioner shall coordinate the access granted under subsection (a) of this section by providing all information requested by the Administrative Office of the Courts for the establishment of access. The Administrative Office of the Courts shall not provide access to any bondsman or runner who fails to provide all information requested by the Commissioner.

(f)   The Commissioner shall notify the Administrative Office of the Courts within 24 hours of any action to suspend or revoke a bondsman's or runner's license or authority to act as a bondsman or runner. The Administrative Office of the Courts shall immediately revoke access of the suspended or revoked bondsman or runner to its criminal information systems.

(g)   The Administrative Office of the Courts shall provide to the Commissioner copies of its current policies for access to court information systems for users outside the Judicial Branch. Any bondsman or runner granted access pursuant to subsection (a) of this section shall adhere to all such policies. The Administrative Office of the Courts shall revoke access of any bondsman or runner who violates such policies.

(h)   It is unlawful for any person to willfully do any of the following:

(1) For any person to access information systems of the Administrative Office of the Courts by means of an online identifier, as defined in G.S. 14-208.6(1n), that was assigned to another individual by the Administrative Office of the Courts pursuant to subsection (a) of this section.

(2) For any bondsman or runner granted access pursuant to subsection (a) of this section to allow any other person, directly or indirectly, to make use of access granted to the bondsman or runner pursuant to subsection (a) of this section.

(3) For any bondsman or runner granted access pursuant to subsection (a) of this section to make use of that access at any time when the bondsman or runner knows or has reason to know that his or her license issued under this Article is in a state of suspension or revocation.

(4) For any bondsman or runner granted access pursuant to subsection (a) of this section to distribute, in any medium or manner, information obtained from the information systems of the Administrative Office of the Courts to any person for any reason not directly related to the evaluation of the individual to whom the information pertains for the purposes of bail.

Unless the conduct is covered under some other provision of law providing for a greater punishment, any violation of this subsection shall be a Class H felony. (2011-412, s. 4.1.)

Article 72.

Official Bonds.

§ 58-72-1. Irregularities not to invalidate.

When any instrument is taken by or received under the sanction of the board of county commissioners, or by any person or persons acting under or in virtue of any public authority, purporting to be a bond executed to the State for the performance of any duty belonging to any office or appointment, such instrument, notwithstanding any irregularity or invalidity in the conferring of the office or making of the appointment, or any variance in the penalty or condition of the instrument from the provision prescribed by law, shall be valid and may be put in suit in the name of the State for the benefit of the person injured by a breach of the condition thereof, in the same manner as if the office had been duly conferred or the appointment duly made, and as if the penalty and condition of the instrument had conformed to the provisions of law: Provided, that no action shall be sustained thereon because of a breach of any condition thereof or any part of the condition thereof which is contrary to law. (1842, c. 61; R.C., c. 78, s. 9; 1869-70, c. 169, s. 16; Code, s. 1891; Rev., s. 279; C.S., s. 324.)

§ 58-72-5. Penalty for officer acting without bond.

Every person or officer of whom an official bond is required, who presumes to discharge any duty of his office before executing such bond in the manner prescribed by law, is liable to a forfeiture of five hundred dollars ($500.00) to the use of the State for each attempt so to exercise his office. The clear proceeds of forfeitures provided for in this section shall be remitted to the Civil Penalty and Forfeiture Fund in accordance with G.S. 115C-457.2. (R.C., c. 78, s. 8; Code, s. 1882; Rev., s. 278; C.S., s. 325; 1998-215, s. 91.)

§ 58-72-10. Condition and terms of official bonds.

Every treasurer, sheriff, coroner, register of deeds, surveyor, and every other officer of the several counties who is required by law to give a bond for the faithful performance of the duties of his office, shall give a bond for the term of the office to which such officer is chosen. (1869-70, c. 169; 1876-7, c. 275, s. 5; Code, s. 1874; 1895, c. 207, s. 4; 1899, c. 54, s. 54; Rev., s. 308; C.S., s. 326; 1985, c. 438.)

§ 58-72-15. When county may pay premiums on bonds.

In all cases where the officers or any of them named in G.S. 58-72-10 are required to give a bond, the county commissioners of the county in which said officer or officers are elected are authorized and empowered to pay the premiums on the bonds of any and all such officer or officers. The board of commissioners of any county are further authorized and empowered to require individual or blanket bonds for any or all assistants, deputies or other persons regularly employed in the offices of any such county officer or officers, such bond or bonds to be conditioned upon faithful performance of duty, and, in the event of such requirement, to pay the premiums on such individual or blanket bonds. (1937, c. 440; 1953, c. 799.)

§ 58-72-20. Annual examination of bonds; security strengthened.

The bonds of the officers named in G.S. 58-72-10 shall be carefully examined on the first Monday in December of every year, and if it appears that the security has been impaired, or for any cause become insufficient to cover the amount of money or property or to secure the faithful performance of the duties of the office, then the bond shall be renewed or strengthened, the insufficient security increased within the limits prescribed by law, and the impaired security shall be made good; but no renewal, or strengthening, or additional security shall increase the penalty of said bond beyond the limits prescribed for the term of office. (1869-70, c. 169; 1876-7, c. 275, s. 5; Code, s. 1874; 1895, c. 207, s. 4; 1899, c. 54, s. 54; Rev., s. 308; C.S., s. 327.)

§ 58-72-25. Effect of failure to renew bond.

Upon the failure of any such officer to make such renewal of his bond, it is the duty of the board of commissioners, by an order to be entered of record, to declare his office vacant, and to proceed forthwith to appoint a successor, if the power of filling the vacancy in the particular case is vested in the board of commissioners; but if otherwise, the said board shall immediately inform the proper person having the power of appointment of the fact of such vacancy. (1869-70, c. 169, s. 2; Code, s. 1875; Rev., s. 309; C.S., s. 328.)

§ 58-72-30. Justification of sureties.

Every surety on an official bond required by law to be taken or renewed and approved by the board of commissioners shall take and subscribe an oath before the chairman of the board or some person authorized by law to administer an oath, that he is worth a certain sum (which shall be not less than one thousand dollars ($1,000)) over and above all his debts and liabilities and his homestead and personal property exemptions, and the sum thus sworn to shall in no case be less in the aggregate than the penalty of the bond. But nothing herein shall be construed to abridge the power of the said board of commissioners to require the personal presence of any such surety before the board when the bond is offered, or at such subsequent time as the board may fix, for examination as to his financial condition or other qualifications as surety. (1869-70, c. 169, s. 3; 1879, c. 207; Code, s. 1876; 1889, c. 7; 1891, c. 385; 1901, c. 32; Rev., s. 310; C.S., s. 329.)

§ 58-72-35. Compelling justification before judge; effect of failure.

When oath is made before any judge of the superior court by five respectable citizens of any county within his district that after diligent inquiry made they verily believe that the bond of any officer of such county, which has been accepted by the board of commissioners, is insufficient either in the amount of the penalty or in the ability of the sureties, it is the duty of such judge to cause a notice to be served upon such officer requiring him to appear at some stated time and place and justify his bond by evidence other than that of himself or his sureties. If this evidence so produced fails to satisfy the judge that the bond is sufficient, both in amount and the ability of the sureties, he shall give time to the officer not exceeding 20 days, to give another bond, fixing the amount of the new bond, when there is a deficiency in that particular. And upon failure of the said officer to give a good bond to the satisfaction of the judge within the 20 days, the judge shall declare the office vacant, and if the appointment be with himself, he shall immediately proceed to fill the vacancy; and if not, he shall notify the persons having the appointing power that they may proceed as aforesaid. (1874-5, c. 120; Code, s. 1885; Rev., s. 316; C.S., s. 330.)

§ 58-72-40. Successor bonded; official bonds considered liabilities.

The person so appointed shall give bond before the judge, and the bond so given shall in all respects be subject to the requirements of the law in relation to official bonds; and all official bonds shall be considered debts and liabilities within the meaning of G.S. 58-72-30. (1874-5, c. 120, s. 2; Code, s. 1886; Rev., s. 317; C.S., s. 331.)

§ 58-72-45. Judge to file statement of proceedings with commissioners.

When a vacancy is declared by the judge, he shall file a written statement of all his proceedings with the clerk of the board of commissioners, to be recorded by him. (1874-5, c. 120, s. 3; Code, s. 1887; Rev., s. 318; C.S., s. 332.)

§ 58-72-50. Approval, acknowledgment and custody of bonds.

The approval of all official bonds taken or renewed by the board of commissioners shall be recorded by the clerk to the board. Every such bond shall be acknowledged by the parties thereto or proved by a subscribing witness, before the chairman of the board of commissioners, or before the clerk of the superior court, and the original bond, with the approval of the commissioners endorsed thereon and certified by their chairman, shall be deposited with the clerk of the superior court for safekeeping. Provided that an official bond executed as surety by a surety company authorized to do business in this State need not be acknowledged upon behalf of the surety when such bond is executed under seal in the name of the surety by an agent or attorney-in-fact by authority of a power of attorney duly recorded in the office of the register of deeds of such county. (1869-70, c. 169, s. 4; 1879, c. 207, s. 2; Code, s. 1877; Rev., s. 311; C.S., s. 333; 1957, c. 1011; 2009-570, s. 35; 2012-18, s. 1.9.)

§ 58-72-55. Clerk records vote approving bond; penalty for neglect.

It is the duty of the clerk of the board of commissioners to record in the proceedings of the board the names of those commissioners who are present at the time of the approval of any official bond, and who vote for such approval. Every clerk neglecting to make such record, besides other punishment, shall forfeit his office. Any commissioner may cause his written dissent to be entered on the records of the board. (1790, c. 327, P.R.; 1809, c. 777, P.R.; R.C., c. 78, s. 7; 1869-70, c. 169, s. 8; Code, s. 1881; Rev., s. 314; C.S., s. 336.)

§ 58-72-60. When commissioner liable as surety.

Every commissioner who approves an official bond, which he knows to be, or which by reasonable diligence he could have discovered to have been, insufficient in the penal sum, or in the security thereof, shall be liable as if he were a surety thereto, and may be sued accordingly by any person having a cause of action on said bond. (1869-70, c. 169, s. 6; Code, s. 1879; Rev., s. 313; C.S., s. 335.)

§ 58-72-65. Record of board conclusive as to facts stated.

In all actions under G.S. 58-72-60 a copy of the proceedings of the board of commissioners in the particular case, certified by their clerk under his hand and the seal of the county, is conclusive evidence of the facts in such record alleged and set forth. (1869-70, c. 169, s. 8; Code, s. 1881; Rev., s. 314; C.S., s. 336.)

§ 58-72-70. Person required to approve bond not to be surety.

No member of the board of commissioners, or any other person authorized to take official bonds, shall sign as surety on any official bond upon the sufficiency of which the board of which he is a member may have to pass. (1874-5, c. 120, s. 3; Code, s. 1887; Rev., s. 315; C.S., s. 337.)

Article 73.

Bonds in Surety Company.

§ 58-73-1. State officers may be bonded in surety company.

All persons who are required to give bond to the State of North Carolina to be received by the Governor or by any department of the State government, in lieu of personal security, may give as security for said bond and for the performance of the duties named in the said bond any indemnity or guaranty company authorized to do business in the State of North Carolina, subject to such regulations as the Governor or department may prescribe, and with power in them to demand additional security at any time. Any person presenting any indemnity or guaranty company as surety shall accompany his bond with a statement of the Insurance Commissioner as to the condition of such company as required by law. (1901, c. 754; Rev., s. 272; C.S., s. 338.)

§ 58-73-5. When surety company sufficient surety on bonds and undertakings.

A bond or undertaking by the laws of North Carolina required or permitted to be given by a public official, fiduciary, or a party to an action or proceeding, conditioned for the doing or not doing of an act specified therein, shall be sufficient when it is executed or guaranteed by a corporation authorized in this State to act as guardian or trustee, or to guarantee the fidelity of persons holding places of public or private trust, or to guarantee the performance of contracts, other than insurance policies, or to give or guarantee bonds and undertakings in actions or proceedings.

The bond or undertaking of a corporation having such power shall be sufficient, although the law or regulation in accordance with which it is given requires two or more sureties, or requires the sureties to be residents or freeholders. But the clerk of the superior court may exercise his discretion as to accepting such a corporation's surety on the bonds of fiduciaries or parties to actions or proceedings. (1895, c. 270; 1899, c. 54, s. 45; 1901, c. 706; Rev., s. 273; C.S., s. 339.)

§ 58-73-10. Clerk to notify county commissioners of condition of company.

Each clerk of the superior court shall furnish the chairman of the board of county commissioners of his county with notice of each surety company licensed in this State, and of each surety company whose license has been revoked, in which any officer of the county has been bonded. (Rev., ss. 295, 4803; C.S., s. 340.)

§ 58-73-15. Release of company from liability.

A company executing such bond, obligation or undertaking, may be released from its liability or security on the same terms as are or may be by law prescribed for the release of individuals upon any such bonds, obligations or undertakings. (1899, c. 54, s. 48; Rev., s. 274; C.S., s. 341.)

§ 58-73-20. Company not to plead ultra vires.

Any company which executes any bond, obligation or undertaking under the provisions of this Article is estopped, in any proceeding to enforce the liability which it assumes to incur, to deny its corporate power to execute such instrument or assume such liability. (1899, c. 54, s. 49; 1901, c. 706, s. 1, subsec. 5; Rev., s. 275; C.S., s. 342.)

§ 58-73-25. Failure to pay judgment is forfeiture.

If a surety company against which a judgment is recovered fails to discharge the same within 60 days from the time such final judgment is rendered, it shall forfeit its right to do business in this State, and the Insurance Commissioner shall cancel its license. (1901, c. 706, s. 1, subsec. 5; Rev., s. 275; C.S., s. 343.)

§ 58-73-30. On presentation of proper bond officer to be inducted.

Upon presentation to the person authorized by law to take, accept and file official bonds, of any bond duly executed in the penal sum required by law by the officer chosen to any such office, as principal, and by any surety company, as security thereto, whose insurance or guaranty is accepted as security upon the bonds of United States bonded officials (such insurance company having complied with the insurance laws of the State of North Carolina), or by any other good and sufficient security thereto, such bond shall be received and accepted as sufficient, and the principal thereon shall be inducted into office. (1899, c. 54, s. 53; 1901, c. 706, s. 1, subsec. 5; Rev., s. 276; C.S., s. 344.)

§ 58-73-35. Expense of fiduciary bond charged to fund.

A receiver, assignee, trustee, committee, guardian, executor or administrator, or other fiduciary required by law to give a bond as such, may include as part of his lawful expenses such sums paid to such companies for such suretyship to the extent of bond premiums actually paid per annum on the account of such bonds as the clerk, judge or court may allow. (1901, c. 706, s. 1, subsec. 5; Rev., s. 277; C.S., s. 345; 1939, c. 382.)

Article 74.

Mortgage in Lieu of Bond.

§ 58-74-1. Mortgage in lieu of required bond.

An administrator, executor, guardian, collector or receiver, or an officer required to give an official bond, or the agent or surety of such person or officer, may execute a mortgage on real estate, of the value of the bond required to be given by him to the State of North Carolina, conditioned to the same effect as the bond should be, were the same given, with a power of sale, which power of sale may be executed by the clerk of the superior court, with whom said mortgage shall be deposited, upon a breach of any of the conditions of said mortgage, after advertisement for 30 days. (1874-5, c. 103, s. 2; Code, s. 118; Rev., s. 265; C.S., s. 346.)

§ 58-74-5. Mortgage in lieu of security for appearance, costs, or fine.

Any person required to give a bond or undertaking, or required to enter into a recognizance for his appearance at any court, in any criminal proceeding, or for the security of any costs or fine in any criminal action, may also execute a mortgage on real or personal property of the value of such bond or recognizance, payable to the State of North Carolina, conditioned as such bond or recognizance would be required, with power of sale, which power shall be executed by the clerk in whose court said mortgage is executed, upon a breach of any of the conditions of said mortgage.

No such mortgage on real property executed for the security for costs or fine shall allow a longer time for payment of said costs or fine than six months from the execution thereof, and no mortgage on personal property a longer time than three months, except in cases of appeal, when the time allowed shall be counted from the date of the final decision in the cause.

All legitimate expenses of sale, which shall only be made after due advertisement according to law, shall be paid out of the proceeds of the sale. (1874-5, c. 103, s. 3; Code, s. 120; 1891, c. 425, ss. 1, 2, 3; Rev., s. 266; C.S., s. 347; 1973, c. 108, s. 57.)

§ 58-74-10. Cancellation of mortgage in such proceedings.

Any mortgage given by any person in lieu of bond as administrator, executor, guardian, collector, receiver or as an officer required to give an official bond, or as agent or surety of such person or officer, or in lieu of bond or undertaking or recognizance for his appearance at any court in any criminal proceeding, or for the security of any cost or fine in a criminal action which has been registered, when such party as administrator, executor, guardian, collector, or receiver has filed his final account and when the time required by statute for the bond given by any administrator, executor, guardian, collector, or receiver to remain in force for the purpose of action thereon has expired, or when the officer required to give an official bond has fully complied with the conditions of such bond and the time within which suit is allowed by law to be brought thereon has expired, or when the person giving such mortgage in lieu of bond has made his appearance at the court to which he was bound and did not depart the court without leave, or paid the cost or fine required, may be canceled or discharged by the clerk of the superior court of the county where such action was pending or where the mortgage in lieu of bond is recorded by recording a satisfaction document pursuant to G.S. 45-37(a)(7), and such satisfaction document shall have the effect to discharge and release all the right, title and interest of the State of North Carolina in and to the property described in such mortgage. (1905, c. 106; Rev., s. 267; C.S., s. 348; 1921, c. 29, ss. 1, 2; 1925, c. 252, s. 1; 2011-246, s. 9.)

§ 58-74-15. Validating statute.

All acts heretofore done by the several superior court clerks, cancelling or satisfying any mortgage, or other instruments, herein mentioned and specified are hereby validated. (1925, c. 252, s. 2.)

§ 58-74-20. Clerk of court may give surety by mortgage deposited with register.

In all cases where the clerk of the superior court may be required to give surety, he may deposit a mortgage with the register of deeds, payable to the State, and conditioned, as the bond would have been required, with power of sale. The power of sale shall be executed by the register of deeds, upon a breach of any of the conditions of said mortgage; and the register of deeds shall in all cases immediately register the same, at the expense of the said clerk. (1874-5, c. 103, s. 6; Code, s. 122; Rev., s. 268; C.S., s. 349.)

§ 58-74-25. Mortgage in lieu of bond to prosecute or defend in civil case.

It is lawful for any person desiring to commence any civil action or special proceeding, or to defend the same, his agent or surety, to execute a mortgage on real estate of the value of the bond or undertaking required to be given, at the beginning of said action, or at any stage thereof, to the party to whom the bond or undertaking would be required to be made, conditioned to the same effect as such bond or undertaking, with power of sale, which power of sale may be executed upon a breach of any of the conditions of the said mortgage after advertisement for 30 days. (1874-5, c. 103, s. 1; Code, s. 117; Rev., s. 269; C.S., s. 35.)

§ 58-74-30. Affidavit of value of property required.

In all cases where a mortgage is executed, as hereinbefore permitted, it is the duty of the clerk of the court in which it is executed to require an affidavit of the value of the property mortgaged to be made by at least one witness not interested in the matter, action or proceeding in which the mortgage is given. (1874-5, c. 103, s. 4; Code, s. 121; Rev., s. 270; C.S., s. 351; 1973, c. 108, s. 58.)

§ 58-74-35. When additional security required.

If, from any cause, the property mortgaged in lieu of a bond becomes of less value than the amount of the bond in lieu of which the mortgage is given, and it so appears upon affidavit of any person having any interest in the matter as a security for which the mortgage was given, it is the duty of the mortgagor to give additional security by a deposit of money, or the execution of a mortgage on more property, or justify as required in cases where bond or undertaking is given. (1874-5, c. 103, s. 5; Code, s. 119; Rev., s. 271; C.S., s. 352.)

Article 75.

Deposit in Lieu of Bond.

§ 58-75-1. Deposit of cash or securities in lieu of bond; conditions and requirements.

In lieu of any written undertaking or bond required by law in any matter, before any court of the State, the party required to make such undertaking or bond may make a deposit in cash or securities of the State of North Carolina or of the United States of America, of the amount required by law or, in the case of fiduciaries, of the amount of the trust, in lieu of the said undertaking or bond and such deposit shall be subject to all of the same conditions and requirements as are provided for in written undertakings or bonds, in lieu of which such deposit is made. (1923, c. 58; C.S., s. 352(a); 1947, c. 936.)

Article 76.

Actions on Bonds.

§ 58-76-1. Bonds in actions payable to court officer may be sued on in name of State.

Bonds and other obligations taken in the course of any proceeding at law, under the direction of the court, and payable to any clerk, commissioner, or officer of the court, for the benefit of the suitors in the cause, or others having an interest in such obligation, may be put in suit in the name of the State. (R.C., c. 13, s. 11; Code, s. 51; Rev., s. 280; C.S., s. 353.)

§ 58-76-5. Liability and right of action on official bonds.

Every person injured by the neglect, misconduct, or misbehavior in office of any register, surveyor, sheriff, coroner, county treasurer, or other officer, may institute a suit or suits against said officer or any of them and their sureties upon their respective bonds for the due performance of their duties in office in the name of the State, without any assignment thereof; and no such bond shall become void upon the first recovery, or if judgment is given for the defendant, but may be put in suit and prosecuted from time to time until the whole penalty is recovered; and every such officer and the sureties on the officer's official bond shall be liable to the person injured for all acts done by said officer by virtue or under color of that officer's office. (1793, c. 384, s. 1, P.R.; 1825, c. 9, P.R.; 1833, c. 17; R.C., c. 78, s. 1; 1869-70, c. 169, s. 10; Code, s. 1883; Rev., s. 281; C.S., s. 354; 1973, c. 108, s. 59; 1997-14, s. 2; 2010-96, s. 29.)

§ 58-76-10. Complaint must show party in interest; election to sue officer individually.

Any person who brings suit in manner aforesaid shall state in his complaint on whose relation and in whose behalf the suit is brought, and he shall be entitled to receive to his own use the money recovered; but nothing herein contained shall prevent such person from bringing at his election an action against the officer to recover special damages for his injury. (1793, c. 384, ss. 2, 3, P.R.; R.C., c. 78, s. 2; 1869-70, c. 169, s. 11; Code, s. 1884; Rev., s. 282; C.S., s. 355.)

§ 58-76-15. Summary remedy on official bond.

When a sheriff, coroner, clerk, county or town treasurer, or other officer, collects or receives any money by virtue or under color of his office, and on demand fails to pay the same to the person entitled to require the payment thereof, the person thereby aggrieved may move for judgment in the superior court against such officer and his sureties for any sum demanded; and the court shall try the same and render judgment at the session when the motion shall be made, but 10 days' notice in writing of the motion must have been previously given. (1819, c. 1002, P.R.; R.C., c. 78, s. 5; 1869-70, c. 169, s. 14; 1876-7, c. 41, s. 2; Code, s. 1889; Rev., s. 283; C.S., s. 356; 1973, c. 108, s. 60.)

§ 58-76-20. Officer unlawfully detaining money liable for damages.

When money received as aforesaid is unlawfully detained by any of said officers, and the same is sued for in any mode whatever, the plaintiff is entitled to recover, besides the sum detained, damages at the rate of twelve per centum (12%) per annum from the time of detention until payment. (1819, c. 1002, s. 2, P.R.; R.C., c. 78, s. 9; 1868-9, c. 169; Code, s. 1890; Rev., s. 284; C.S., s. 357.)

§ 58-76-25. Evidence against principal admissible against sureties.

In actions brought upon the official bonds of clerks of courts, sheriffs, coroners, or other public officers, and also upon the bonds of executors, administrators, collectors or guardians, when it may be necessary for the plaintiff to prove any default of the principal obligors, any receipt or acknowledgment of such obligors, or any other matter or thing which by law would be admissible and competent for or toward proving the same as against him, shall in like manner be admissible and competent as presumptive evidence only against all or any of his sureties who may be defendants with or without him in said actions. (1844, c. 38; R.C., c. 44, s. 10; 1881, c. 8; Code, s. 1345; Rev., s. 285; C.S., s. 358; 1973, c. 108, s. 61.)

§ 58-76-30. Officer liable for negligence in collecting debt.

When a claim is placed in the hands of any sheriff or coroner for collection, and he does not use due diligence in collecting the same, he shall be liable for the full amount of the claim notwithstanding the debtor may have been at all times and is then able to pay the amount thereof. (1844, c. 64; R.C., c. 78, s. 3; 1869-70, c. 169, s. 12; Code, s. 1888; Rev., s. 286; C.S., s. 359; 1973, c. 108, s. 62.)

Article 77.

Guaranteed Arrest Bond Certificates of Automobile Clubs and Associations in Lieu of Bond.

§ 58-77-1 through 58-77-5. Repealed by Session Laws 1999-132, s. 12.1, effective June 4, 1999.

Article 78.

State Fire and Rescue Commission.

§ 58-78-1. State Fire and Rescue Commission created; membership.

(a) There is created the State Fire and Rescue Commission of the Department, which shall be composed of 15 voting members to be appointed as follows:

(1) The Commissioner shall appoint 12 members, two from nominations submitted by the North Carolina State Firemen's Association, one from nominations submitted by the North Carolina Association of Fire Chiefs, one from nominations submitted by the Professional Firefighters of North Carolina Association, one from nominations submitted by the North Carolina Society of Fire Service Instructors, one from nominations submitted by the North Carolina

Association of County Fire Marshals, one from nominations submitted by the North Carolina Fire Marshal's Association, two from nominations submitted by the North Carolina Association of Rescue and Emergency Medical Services, Inc., one mayor or other elected city official nominated by the President of the League of Municipalities, one county commissioner nominated by the President of the Association of County Commissioners, and one from the public at large;

(2) The Governor shall appoint one member from the public at large; and

(3) The General Assembly shall appoint two members from the public at large, one upon the recommendation of the Speaker of the House of Representatives pursuant to G.S. 120-121, and one upon the recommendation of the President Pro Tempore of the Senate pursuant to G.S. 120-121.

Public members may not be employed in State government and may not be directly involved in fire fighting or rescue services.

(b) Of the members initially appointed by the Commissioner, the nominees of the North Carolina State Firemen's Association and the nominees of the North Carolina Association of Fire Chiefs and the nominees of the Professional Firefighters of North Carolina Association and of the North Carolina Association of Rescue and Emergency Medical Services, Inc., shall serve three-year terms; the nominees from the North Carolina Society of Fire Service Instructors, the North Carolina Association of County Fire Marshals, and the North Carolina Fire Marshal's Association shall serve two-year terms; and the mayor or other elected city official, the county commissioner, and the member from the public at large shall serve one-year terms. The Governor's initial appointee shall serve a three-year term. The General Assembly's initial appointees shall serve two-year terms. Thereafter all terms shall be for three years.

(c) Vacancies shall be filled by the original appointer in the same manner as the original appointment was made, except that vacancies in the appointments made by the General Assembly shall be filled in accordance with G.S. 120-122.

(d) Appointed members shall serve until their successors are appointed and qualified.

(e) The following State officials, or their designees, shall serve by virtue of their offices as nonvoting members of the Commission: the Commissioner of Insurance, the Commissioner of Labor, the Attorney General, the Secretary of

Public Safety, the Secretary of Environment and Natural Resources, and the President of the Department of Community Colleges.

(f) Members of the Commission shall receive per diem and necessary travel and subsistence allowances in accordance with the provisions of G.S. 138-5 or G.S. 138-6, as appropriate. (1977, c. 1064, s. 1; 1981, c. 791, ss. 1, 2; 1981 (Reg. Sess., 1982), c. 1191, ss. 21, 22; 1983, c. 840, ss. 1, 2; 1985, c. 757, s. 167(b), (d); 1989, c. 727, s. 218; c. 750, s. 1; 1991, c. 720, s. 47; 1993, c. 155, s. 1; 1995, c. 490, s. 20; 1997-116, s. 1; 1997-443, s. 11A.123; 2011-145, s. 19.1(g).)

§ 58-78-5. State Fire and Rescue Commission - Powers and duties.

(a) The Commission shall have the following powers and duties:

(1) To formally adopt a State Fire Education and Training Plan, a State Master Plan for Fire Prevention and Control, a Rescue Training Plan, and a State Master Plan for Rescue Services;

(2) To assist and participate with State and local fire prevention and control agencies in the improvement of fire prevention and control in North Carolina and to work with State and local rescue agencies to improve rescue services in the State;

(3) To increase the professional skills of fire protection and fire-fighting personnel and rescue personnel;

(4) To encourage public support for fire prevention and control and rescue services;

(5) To accept gifts, devises, grants, matching funds, and other considerations from private or governmental sources for use in promoting its work;

(6) To make grants for use in pursuing its objectives, under such conditions as are deemed to be necessary and such other powers as may be necessary to carry out the State's duties with respect to all grants to the State by the United States Fire Administration and the National Fire Academy; and all support

programs brought into the State by these two entities shall be coordinated and controlled by the Commission;

(7)   To make studies and recommendations for the improvement of fire prevention and control and rescue services in the State and to make studies and recommendations for the coordination and implementation of effective fire prevention and control and rescue services and for effective fire prevention and control and rescue services education;

(8)   To set objectives and priorities for the improvement of fire prevention and control and rescue services throughout the State;

(9)   To advise State and local interests of opportunities for securing federal assistance for fire prevention and control and rescue services and for improving fire prevention and control and rescue services administration and planning within the State of North Carolina;

(10)   To assist State agencies and institutions of local government and combinations thereof in the preparation and processing of applications for financial aid and to support fire prevention and control, rescue services, and planning and administration;

(11)   To encourage and assist coordination at the federal, State and local government levels in the preparation and implementation of fire prevention and control and rescue services administrative improvements and crime reduction plans;

(12)   To apply for, receive, disburse and audit the use of funds received from any public and private agencies and instrumentalities for fire prevention and control and rescue services, their administration and plans therefor;

(13)   To enter into monitoring and evaluating the results of contracts and agreements necessary or incidental to the discharge of its assigned responsibilities;

(14)   To provide technical assistance to State and local fire prevention and control and rescue agencies in developing programs for improvement;

(14a)   To serve as a central office for the collection and dissemination of information relative to fire service and rescue service activities and programs in State government. All State government agencies conducting fire service and rescue service related programs and activities shall report the status of these programs and activities to the Commission on a quarterly basis and they shall also report to the Commission any new programs or changes to existing programs as they are implemented;

(14b)   To establish voluntary minimum professional qualifications for all levels of fire service and rescue service personnel;

(14c)   To prepare an annual report to the Governor on its fire prevention and control activities and plans, rescue activities and plans, and to recommend legislation concerning fire prevention and control and rescue services;

(14d)   To reimburse the members of the Commission's certification board, in accordance with G.S. 138-5, for travel and subsistence expenses incurred by them in their duties as certification board officers; and

(15)   To take such other actions as may be deemed necessary or appropriate to carry out its assigned duties and responsibilities.

(16)   To provide workers' compensation benefits under G.S. 58-87-10, to create a Volunteer Safety Workers' Compensation Board to assist it in performing this duty, and to reimburse the members of the Commission's Volunteer Safety Workers' Compensation Board in accordance with G.S. 138-5 for travel and subsistence expenses incurred by them.

(b)   Each State agency involved in fire prevention and control or rescue related activities shall furnish the executive director of the Commission such information as may be required to carry out the intent of this section. (1977, c. 1064, s. 1; 1981, c. 791, ss. 3, 4; 1985, c. 757, s. 167(b); 1989, c. 750, s. 1; 1993, c. 321, s. 41; 1995, c. 507, s. 7.21A(c); 2011-284, s. 58.)

§ 58-78-10. State Fire and Rescue Commission - Organization; rules and regulations; meetings.

(a)   Organization. - The Commission shall elect from its voting members a chairman and vice-chairman to serve as provided by the rules adopted by the Commission.

(b)   Rules and Regulations. - The Commission shall adopt such rules and regulations, not inconsistent with the laws of this State as may be required by the federal government for programs and grants-in-aid for fire protection, firefighting, and rescue purposes which may be made available to the State by the federal government. The Commission shall be the single State agency responsible for establishing policy, planning and carrying out the State's duties with respect to all programs of and grants to the State by the United States Fire Administration, Federal Emergency Management Agency. In respect to such programs and grants, the Commission shall have authority to review, approve and maintain general oversight to the State plan and its implementation, including subgrants and allocations to local units of government and local fire prevention and control and rescue agencies.

All actions taken by the Commission in the performance of its duties shall be implemented and administered by the Department.

(c)   Meetings. - The Commission shall meet quarterly. Seven members shall constitute a quorum. All meetings shall be open to the public. (1977, c. 1064, s. 1; 1981, c. 791, s. 5; 1983, c. 840, s. 3; 1985, c. 757, s. 167(b), (c), (e), (f); 1989, c. 750, s. 1.)

§ 58-78-15. State Fire and Rescue Commission; staff.

(a)   There shall be an executive director nominated by the Commission with direct responsibilities to the Commission, who shall be appointed by the Commissioner.

(b)   Personnel of the Department shall serve as staff to the Commission. The Department shall provide the clerical and professional services required by the Commission and, at the direction of the Commission, shall develop and administer the State Master Plan for Fire Prevention and Control, the State Fire Education and Training Plan, the Rescue Training Plan, the State Master Plan for Rescue Services, and any additional related programs as may be established by, or assigned to, the Commission. (1977, c. 1064, s. 1; 1985, c. 757, s. 167(b), (i); 1989, c. 750, s. 1.)

§ 58-78-20. State Fire and Rescue Commission - Fiscal affairs.

All funds for the operation of the Commission and its staff shall be appropriated to the Department. All such funds shall be held in a separate or special account on the books of the Department with a separate financial designation or code number to be assigned by the Department of Administration or its agent. Expenditures for staff salaries and operating expenses shall be made in the same manner as expenditures of any other Department funds. The Department may hire such additional personnel as may be necessary to handle the work of the Commission, within the limits of funds appropriated to it by the State and made available to it by the federal government. (1957, c. 269, s. 1; 1977, c. 1064, s. 1; 1985, c. 757, s. 167(b), (c); 1989, c. 750, s. 1.)

Article 79.

Investigation of Fires and Inspection of Premises.

§ 58-79-1. Fires investigated; reports; records.

The Attorney General, through the State Bureau of Investigation, and the chief of the fire department, or chief of police where there is no chief of the fire department, in municipalities and towns, and the county fire marshal and the sheriff of the county and the chief of the rural fire department where such fire occurs outside of a municipality, are hereby authorized to investigate the cause, origin, and circumstances of every fire occurring in such municipalities or counties in which property has been destroyed or damaged, and shall specially make investigation whether the fire was the result of carelessness or design. A preliminary investigation shall be made by the chief of fire department or chief of police, where there is no chief of fire department in municipalities, and by the county fire marshal and the sheriff of the county or the chief of the rural fire department where such fire occurs outside of a municipality, and must be begun within three days, exclusive of Sunday, of the occurrence of the fire, and the Attorney General, through the State Bureau of Investigation, shall have the right to supervise and direct the investigation when he deems it expedient or necessary.

The officer making the investigation of fires shall forthwith notify the Attorney General, and must within one week of the occurrence of the fire furnish to the

Attorney General a written statement of all facts relating to the cause and origin of the fire, the kind, value and ownership of the property destroyed, and such other information as is called for by the forms provided by the Attorney General. Departments capable of submitting the required information by the utilization of computers and related equipment, by means of an approved format of standard punch cards, magnetic tapes or an approved telecommunications system, may do so in lieu of the submission of the written statement as provided for in this section. The Attorney General shall keep in his office a record of all reports submitted pursuant to this section. These reports shall at all times be open to public inspection. (1899, c. 58; 1901, c. 387; 1903, c. 719; Rev., s. 4818; C.S., s. 6074; 1943, c. 170; 1969, c. 894; 1977, c. 596, s. 1.)

§ 58-79-5. Attorney General to make examination; arrests and prosecution.

It is the duty of the Attorney General to examine, or cause examination to be made, into the cause, circumstances, and origin of all fires occurring within the State to which his attention has been called in accordance with the provisions of G.S. 58-79-1, or by interested parties, by which property is accidentally or unlawfully burned, destroyed, or damaged, whenever in his judgment the evidence is sufficient, and to specially examine and decide whether the fire was the result of carelessness or the act of an incendiary. The Attorney General shall, in person, by deputy or otherwise, fully investigate all circumstances surrounding such fire, and, when in his opinion such proceedings are necessary, take or cause to be taken the testimony on oath of all persons supposed to be cognizant of any facts or to have means of knowledge in relation to the matters as to which an examination is herein required to be made, and shall cause the same to be reduced in writing. If the Attorney General or any deputy appointed to conduct such investigations, is of the opinion that there is evidence to charge any person or persons with the crime of arson, or other willful burning, or fraud in connection with the crime of arson or other willful burning, he may arrest with warrant or cause such person or persons to be arrested, charged with such offense, and prosecuted, and shall furnish to the district attorney of the district all such evidence, together with the names of witnesses and all other information obtained by him, including a copy of all pertinent and material testimony taken in the case. (1899, c. 58, s. 2; 1901, c. 387, s. 2; 1903, c. 719; Rev., s. 4819; C.S., s. 6075; 1943, c. 170; 1955, c. 642, s. 1; 1959, c. 1183; 1973, c. 47, s. 2; 1977, c. 596, s. 2.)

§ 58-79-10. Powers of Attorney General in investigations.

The Attorney General, or his deputy appointed to conduct such examination, has the powers of a trial justice for the purpose of summoning and compelling the attendance of witnesses to testify in relation to any matter which is by provisions of this Article a subject of inquiry and investigation, and may administer oaths and affirmations to persons appearing as witnesses before them. False swearing in any such matter or proceeding is perjury and shall be punished as such. The Attorney General or his deputy has authority at all times of the day or night, in performance of the duties imposed by the provisions of this Article, to enter upon and examine any building or premises where any fire has occurred, and other buildings and premises adjoining or near the same. All investigations held by or under the direction of the Attorney General or his deputy may, in their discretion, be private, and persons other than those required to be present by the provisions of this Article may be excluded from the place where the investigation is held, and witnesses may be kept apart from each other and not allowed to communicate with each other until they have been examined. (1899, c. 58, s. 3; 1901, c. 387, s. 3; Rev., s. 4820; C.S., s. 6076; 1943, c. 170; 1977, c. 596, s. 2.)

§ 58-79-15. Failure to comply with summons or subpoena.

The failure of a person to comply with a summons or subpoena of the Attorney General or his deputy under G.S. 58-79-10 shall be brought before a court of record and punished as for contempt in the same manner as if he had failed to appear and testify before said court of record. (1955, c. 642, s. 2; 1977, c. 596, s. 2.)

§ 58-79-20. Inspection of premises; dangerous material removed.

The Commissioner of Insurance, or the chief of fire department or chief of police where there is no chief of fire department, or the city or county building inspector, electrical inspector, heating inspector, or fire prevention inspector has the right at all reasonable hours, for the purpose of examination, to enter into and upon all buildings and premises in their jurisdiction. When any of such officers find in any building or upon any premises overcrowding in violation of occupancy limits established pursuant to the North Carolina State Building Code, combustible material or inflammable conditions dangerous to the safety of such building or premises they shall order the same to be removed or remedied, and this order shall be forthwith complied with by the owner or occupant of such buildings or premises. The owner or occupant may, within twenty-four hours, appeal to the Commissioner of Insurance from the order, and the cause of the complaint shall be at once investigated by his direction, and unless by his authority the order of the officer above named is revoked it remains in force and must be forthwith complied with by the owner or occupant. The Commissioner of Insurance, fire chief, or building inspector, electrical inspector, heating inspector, or fire prevention inspector shall make an immediate investigation as to the presence of combustible material or the existence of inflammable conditions in any building or upon any premises under their jurisdiction upon complaint of any person having an interest in such building or premises or property adjacent thereto. The Commissioner may, in person or by deputy, visit any municipality or county and make such inspections alone or in company with the local officer. The Commissioner shall submit annually, as early as consistent with full and accurate preparation, and not later than the first day of June, a detailed report of his official action under this Article, and it shall be embodied in his report to the General Assembly. (1899, c. 58, s. 4; 1901, c. 387, s. 4; 1903, c. 719; Rev., s. 4821; C.S., s. 6077; 1943, c. 170; 1969, c. 1063, s. 3; 1977, c. 596, s. 4; 1985, c. 576, s. 2.)

§ 58-79-22. Door lock exemption permit.

Any business entity licensed to sell automatic weapons as a federal firearms dealer that is in the business of selling firearms or ammunition and that operates a firing range which rents firearms and sells ammunition that desires to be exempt from the door lock requirements of Chapter 10 of Volume 1 of the North Carolina State Building Code may apply for a permit to do so with the Department in accordance with G.S. 143-143.4 and rules adopted by the Department. The Department shall charge a permit fee of five hundred dollars ($500.00) for the issuance of a permit issued pursuant to G.S. 143-143.4. (2001-324, s. 2.)

§ 58-79-25. Deputy investigators.

It shall be the duty of the Attorney General to appoint two or more persons as deputies, whose particular duty it shall be to investigate forest fires and endeavor to ascertain the persons guilty of setting such fires and cause prosecution to be instituted against those who, as a result of such investigation, are deemed guilty. (1899, c. 58, s. 6; 1901, c. 387, s. 6; 1903, c. 719, s. 2; Rev., s. 4823; 1915, c. 109, s. 2; 1919, c. 186, s. 7; C.S., s. 6078; Ex. Sess. 1924, c. 119; 1943, c. 170; 1977, c. 596, s. 2.)

§ 58-79-30. Repealed by Session Laws 1999-456, s. 66.

§ 58-79-35. Fire prevention and Fire Prevention Day.

It is the duty of the Commissioner of Insurance, the Superintendent of Public Instruction and the State Board of Education to provide a pamphlet containing printed instructions for properly conducting fire drills in all schools and auxiliary school buildings and the principal of every public and private school shall conduct at least one fire drill every month during the regular school session in each building in his charge where children are assembled. The fire drills shall include all children and teachers and the use of various ways of egress to assimilate evacuation of said buildings under various conditions, and such other regulations as prescribed by the Commissioner of Insurance, Superintendent of Public Instruction and State Board of Education.

The Commissioner of Insurance and Superintendent of Public Instruction shall further provide for the teaching of "Fire Prevention" in the colleges and schools of the State, and to arrange for a textbook adapted to such use. The ninth day of October of every year shall be set aside and designated as "Fire Prevention Day," and the Governor shall issue a proclamation urging the people to a proper observance of the day, and the Commissioner of Insurance shall bring the day and its observance to the attention of the officials of all organized fire departments of the State, whose duty it shall be to disseminate the materials and to arrange suitable programs to be followed in its observance. (1915, c. 166, s. 5; C.S., s. 6080; 1925, c. 130; 1943, c. 170; 1947, c. 781; 1957, c. 845.)

§ 58-79-40. Insurance company to furnish information.

(a) The chief of any municipal fire or police department, county fire marshal or sheriff, or special agent of the State Bureau of Investigation may request any insurance company investigating a fire loss of real or personal property to release any information in its possession relative to that loss. The company shall release the information and cooperate with any official authorized to request such information pursuant to this section. The information shall include, but is not limited to:

(1) Any insurance policy relevant to a fire loss under investigation and any application for such a policy;

(2) Policy premium payment records;

(3) History of previous claims made by the insured for fire loss;

(4) Material relating to the investigation of the loss, including statements of any person, proof of loss, and any other relevant evidence.

(b) If an insurance company (or insurance agency) has reason to suspect that a fire loss to its insured's real or personal property was caused by incendiary means, the company shall furnish the State Bureau of Investigation with all relevant material acquired during its investigation of the fire loss, cooperate with and take such action as may be requested of it by any law-enforcement agency, and permit any person ordered by a court to inspect any of its records pertaining to the policy and the loss.

(c) In the absence of fraud or malice, no insurance company (or insurance agency), or person who furnishes information on its behalf, shall be liable for damages in a civil action or subject to criminal prosecution for any oral or written statement made or any other action that is necessary to supply information required pursuant to this section.

(d) The officials and departmental and agency personnel receiving any information furnished pursuant to this section shall hold the information in confidence until such time as its release is required pursuant to a criminal or civil proceeding.

(e) Any official referred to in subsection (a) of this section may be required to testify as to any information in his possession regarding the fire loss of real or personal property in any civil action in which any person seeks recovery under a policy against an insurance company for the fire loss. (1977, c. 520, s. 1.)

§ 58-79-45. Fire incident reports.

(a) Whenever a fire department responds to a fire, the chief of that department shall complete or cause to be completed a fire incident report, which report shall be on a form prescribed by the Department of Insurance. When such report is made without fraud, bad faith, or actual malice, the person making the report is not subject to liability for libel or slander.

(b) The fire department shall forward a copy of the completed form to the fire marshal of the county in which the fire occurred. If there is no fire marshal in that county, the fire department shall forward a copy of the report to the county commissioners. The fire department shall retain the original of the report. The fire department and the fire marshal or county commissioners to whom reports are sent shall retain the reports for a period of five years.

(c) At the request of any person, the county fire marshal or county commissioners shall provide such person, for a reasonable copying charge, a certified copy of the report. (1989 (Reg. Sess., 1990), c. 1054, s. 7.)

Article 80.

State Volunteer Fire Department.

§ 58-80-1. Purpose of Article; meaning of "State Fire Marshal".

The purpose of this Article shall be the creation of a State Volunteer Fire Department to provide protection for property lying outside the boundaries of municipalities, and to render assistance anywhere within the State of North Carolina, in municipalities or counties, in emergencies caused by fire, floods, tornadoes, or otherwise, in the manner and subject to the conditions provided in this Article. As used in this Article and elsewhere in the General Statutes, "State

Fire Marshal" means the Commissioner of Insurance of the State of North Carolina. (1939, c. 364, s. 1; 1985, c. 666, s. 66.)

§ 58-80-5. Personnel.

The personnel of the North Carolina State Volunteer Fire Department shall consist of all active members of the organized fire departments, who are members of the North Carolina State Firemen's Association, of municipalities whereof the governing bodies shall subscribe to and endorse this Article. (1939, c. 364, s. 2.)

§ 58-80-10. Organization.

The North Carolina State Fire Marshal shall be chief of the State Volunteer Fire Department; regular municipal fire chiefs shall be assistant chiefs; assistant chiefs shall be deputy chiefs; battalion chiefs, captains; lieutenants and privates shall hold the same position that they occupy in their municipal companies. When engaged in rendering assistance at the scene of any emergency, the ranking officer of the first department arriving at the scene of the emergency shall have complete charge of all operations until the arrival of a superior officer. All subordinate officers and men shall act under the direction of such ranking officer. Whenever present at the scene of an emergency, the chief shall have full and complete control and authority over operations of all members of the Department. (1939, c. 364, s. 3.)

§ 58-80-15. Acceptance by municipalities.

Any municipality having an organized fire department and desiring to participate in the establishment of the State Volunteer Fire Department, may do so by a resolution of the governing body accepting and endorsing the provisions of this Article: Provided, that acceptance shall not be compulsory. (1939, c. 364, s. 4.)

§ 58-80-20. Withdrawal.

Any municipality which has accepted the provisions of this Article may withdraw its fire departments from membership in the State Volunteer Fire Department by resolution of the governing body thereof. Notice of such withdrawal shall be given to the State Fire Marshal and withdrawal shall not become effective until 60 days after his receipt thereof. (1939, c. 364, s. 5.)

§ 58-80-25. Dispatching firemen and apparatus from municipalities.

Municipalities endorsing this Article shall retain full and complete control and authority in sending or permitting firemen and apparatus to go beyond the limits of the municipality. The governing bodies of such municipalities shall designate and authorize a person, and at least two alternates, who shall have authority to grant or deny permission to firemen and apparatus to leave the municipality in all cases where request is made for assistance beyond its corporate limits, and the municipality shall, through the office of its municipal fire chief, furnish to the office of the State Commissioner of Insurance, and to the secretary of the North Carolina State Firemen's Association, a list of the persons so authorized by the municipality. The secretary of the State Firemen's Association shall furnish to all municipalities and counties accepting this Article a list of all such persons so designated in all municipalities within the State. (1939, c. 364, s. 6; 1943, c. 170.)

§ 58-80-30. No authority in State Volunteer Fire Department to render assistance to nonaccepting counties.

The State Volunteer Fire Department shall not have authority to render assistance in any emergency occurring within a county which has not accepted the terms and conditions of this Article by resolution of the board of county commissioners: Provided, that nothing in this Article shall be construed to prevent any municipality from voluntarily permitting its fire department to render assistance in any emergency, notwithstanding that it may arise in a county which has failed to accept this Article. (1939, c. 364, s. 7.)

§ 58-80-35. Acceptance by counties.

Any county desiring to accept the benefits of this Article may do so by resolution of the board of county commissioners. Any such county may thereupon make agreements and enter into contracts with respect to payment for services rendered by the State Volunteer Fire Department within its boundaries in the following manner:

The county may contract with any municipality which has accepted the terms of this Article, whether within or without said county, to pay to such municipality an annual fee as a consideration for the municipality providing equipment and carrying compensation insurance which will enable it to respond to calls from within the county so contracting, and to pay an additional sum per truck for each mile traveled from the station house to the scene of the emergency, and to pay an additional sum per truck per hour or fraction thereof for the use of its water or chemical pumping equipment. Said sums shall be paid to the city within 30 days after such services have been performed: Provided, that nothing in this section shall be construed to prevent the county and municipality from adopting a different schedule of fees in cases where those provided above shall be considered excessive or inadequate: Provided, that if the emergency shall occur within the limits of another city or town, such city or town and not the county wherein it lies shall be responsible for the payments and shall assume all liabilities as provided in this section. (1939, c. 364, s. 8; 1973, c. 803, s. 5.)

§ 58-80-40. Municipalities not to be left unprotected.

At no time shall the entire personnel or equipment of any municipal fire department be absent from the municipality in response to a call to another municipality, or other place lying at a distance exceeding two miles from the corporate limits, but there shall remain within the municipal limits such personnel and equipment as in the judgment of the local fire chief might provide sufficient protection during the absence of the remainder. (1939, c. 364, s. 9.)

§ 58-80-45. Rights and privileges of firemen; liability of municipality.

When responding to a call and while working at a fire or other emergency outside the limits of the municipality by which they are regularly employed or in volunteer fire service, all members of the State Volunteer Fire Department shall have the same authority, rights, privileges and immunities which are afforded them while responding to calls within their home municipality. In permitting its fire department or equipment to attend an emergency or answer a call beyond the municipal limits, whether under the terms of this Article or otherwise, a municipality shall be deemed in exercise of a governmental function, and shall hold the privileges and immunities attendant upon the exercise of such functions within its corporate limits. (1939, c. 364, s. 10.)

§ 58-80-50. Relief in case of injury or death.

In case of injury or death of any member of the State Volunteer Fire Department arising out of and in the course of the performance of his duties, while such member is assisting at any emergency arising beyond the limits of the municipality with which he is connected, or while going to or returning from the scene of such emergency, such fireman shall be entitled to compensation under the terms of the North Carolina Workers' Compensation Act, and the municipality with which he is connected shall be liable for the compensation provided under that Act. (1939, c. 364, s. 11; 1991, c. 636, s. 3.)

§ 58-80-55. Local appropriations.

Each county and municipality is authorized to make appropriations for the purposes of this Article and to fund them by levy of property taxes pursuant to G.S. 153A-149 and 160A-209 and by the allocation of other revenues whose use is not otherwise restricted by law. Sanitary districts are authorized to make appropriations for the purposes of this Article and to fund them by annual levy of a tax on property having a situs in the district under the rules and according to the procedures prescribed in the Machinery Act (Chapter 105, Subchapter II) and by the allocation of other revenues whose use is not otherwise restricted by law. (1973, c. 803, s. 4.)

§ 58-80-60. Sums from contingent fund of State made available for administration of Article.

In order to assist in carrying out the purposes of the Article the Governor may, from time to time, make provisions for assistance to the North Carolina State Firemen's Association in a sum not to exceed two thousand five hundred dollars ($2,500), in any one year, out of the contingent fund appropriated in the General Appropriation Act. One half of the amount so provided shall, in each instance, go to the State Firefighters' Relief Fund, and one half to the expenses of the said Association incurred in carrying out the provisions of this Article. (1939, c. 364, s. 12; 2007-246, s. 2.)

Article 81.

Hotels; Safety Provisions.

§ 58-81-1: Repealed by Session Laws 1995, c. 517, s. 33.

§ 58-81-5. Careless or negligent setting of fires.

Any person who in any fashion or manner negligently or carelessly sets fire to any bedding, furniture, draperies, house or household furnishings or other equipment or appurtenances in or to any hotel or other building of like occupancy shall be guilty of a Class 1 misdemeanor. (1947, c. 1066; 1993, c. 539, s. 474; 1994, Ex. Sess., c. 24, s. 14(c).)

§ 58-81-10. Penalty for noncompliance.

Any owner, owners, proprietor or keeper of any hotel or other building of like occupancy who fails to comply with any of the foregoing provisions of this Article shall be guilty of a Class 3 misdemeanor and punished only by a fine of not less than ten dollars ($10.00) nor more than fifty dollars ($50.00). Each day of noncompliance herewith shall constitute a separate offense. (1947, c. 1066; 1993, c. 539, s. 475; 1994, Ex. Sess., c. 24, s. 14(c).)

§ 58-81-15. Construction of Article.

Nothing in this Article shall be construed to limit powers granted to and duties imposed upon the chiefs of fire departments and building inspectors by Article 11, Chapter 160 of the General Statutes of North Carolina, but the powers granted in this Article shall be in addition thereto. (1947, c. 1066.)

Article 82.

Authority and Liability of Firemen.

§ 58-82-1. Authority of firemen; penalty for willful interference with firemen.

Members and employees of county, municipal corporation, fire protection district, sanitary district or privately incorporated fire departments shall have authority to do all acts reasonably necessary to extinguish fires and protect life and property from fire. Any person, including the owner of property which is burning, who shall willfully interfere in any manner with firemen engaged in the performance of their duties shall be guilty of a Class 1 misdemeanor. (1965, c. 648; 1993, c. 539, s. 476; 1994, Ex. Sess., c. 24, s. 14(c).)

§ 58-82-5. Liability limited.

(a) For the purpose of this section, a "rural fire department" means a bona fide fire department incorporated as a nonprofit corporation which under schedules filed with or approved by the Commissioner of Insurance, is classified as not less than Class "9" in accordance with rating methods, schedules, classifications, underwriting rules, bylaws, or regulations effective or applied with respect to the establishment of rates or premiums used or charged pursuant to Article 36 or Article 40 of this Chapter and which operates fire apparatus of the value of five thousand dollars ($5,000) or more.

(b) A rural fire department or a fireman who belongs to the department shall not be liable for damages to persons or property alleged to have been sustained and alleged to have occurred by reason of an act or omission, either of the rural fire department or of the fireman at the scene of a reported fire, when that act or omission relates to the suppression of the reported fire or to the direction of traffic or enforcement of traffic laws or ordinances at the scene of or in connection with a fire, accident, or other hazard by the department or the fireman unless it is established that the damage occurred because of gross negligence, wanton conduct or intentional wrongdoing of the rural fire department or the fireman.

(c)   Any member of a volunteer fire department or rescue squad who receives no compensation for his services as a fire fighter or emergency medical care provider, who renders first aid or emergency health care treatment at the scene of a fire to a person who is unconscious, ill, or injured as a result of the fire shall not be liable in civil damages for any acts or omissions relating to such services rendered, unless such acts or omissions amount to gross negligence, wanton conduct or intentional wrongdoing. (1983, c. 520, s. 1; 1985, c. 611, s. 1; 1987, c. 146, s. 2.)

Article 82A.

Pyrotechnics Training and Permitting.

§ 58-82A-1. State Fire Marshal establish pyrotechnic safety guidelines.

(a)   Guidelines. - The Commissioner of Insurance through the Office of the State Fire Marshal, in consultation with the State Fire and Rescue Commission, must establish guidelines, testing, and training requirements for the following:

(1)   Individuals who assist a display operator with the exhibition, use, handling, or discharge of pyrotechnics in connection with a concert or public exhibition authorized under Article 54 of Chapter 14 of the General Statutes.

(2)   Individuals seeking to obtain a display operator license, proximate audience display operator license, or assistant display operator license under this Article.

(b)   Definitions. - The definitions in G.S. 14-410 apply in this Article.

(c) Rule making. - The Commissioner may adopt rules to implement this Article. (2009-507, s. 3; 2010-22, s. 1.)

§ 58-82A-1.1. Definitions.

The following definitions apply in this Article:

(1) Assistant display operator. - An individual who, under the supervision of the display operator, assists with the safety, setup, and discharge of a pyrotechnic display and who is licensed pursuant to this Article.

(2) Event employee. - An individual who works under the supervision of the display operator and who assists with the safety, setup, and discharge of a pyrotechnic display but does not handle the pyrotechnic materials.

(3) Outdoor pyrotechnics display. - A pyrotechnic display that is outdoors and uses 1.4G, 1.3G, 1.2G, and 1.1G pyrotechnics and is a minimum of 75 feet from the audience in accordance with NFPA 1123.

(4) Proximate audience display. - A display of pyrotechnics that occurs within a building or structure or that occurs outside before an audience within 75 feet of the pyrotechnics in accordance with NFPA 1126.

(5) Proximate audience display operator. - An individual who is responsible for the safety, setup, and discharge of the proximate audience display and who is licensed under this Article.

(6) Pyrotechnics. - All fireworks not exempted by G.S. 14-414 and that are used for professional outdoor displays and classified as fireworks by UN0333 (1.1G), UN0334 (1.2G), UN0335 (1.3G), or UN0336 (1.4G) by the United States Department of Transportation under 49 C.F.R. § 172.101.

(7) Pyrotechnics display operator. - An individual who is responsible for the safety, setup, and discharge of the pyrotechnic display, who is responsible for the supervision of personnel at the pyrotechnic display, and who is licensed under this Article.

(8) Supervision. - The direction and management of the activities of personnel in the safety, setup, handling, and display of an outdoor pyrotechnic display, a proximate audience display, or a flame effect display. (2010-22, s. 2.)

§ 58-82A-1.5. Commissioner of Insurance to administer Article; rules; employees; evidence of Commissioner's action.

(a) The Commissioner shall have full power and authority to administer the provisions of this Article, which establishes guidelines for the use, handling, exhibiting, or discharge of pyrotechnics in connection with a concert or public exhibition, as allowed under Article 54 of Chapter 14 of the General Statutes, and to license and regulate pyrotechnic operators. The Commissioner shall adopt any rules necessary to enforce the purposes and provisions of this Article.

(b) Any written instrument purporting to be a copy of any action, proceeding, or finding of fact by the Commissioner, or any record of the Commissioner authenticated under the head of the Commissioner by the seal of the Commissioner's office, shall be accepted by all courts of this State as prima facie evidence of the contents thereof. (2010-22, s. 3.)

§ 58-82A-2. Individual training requirements.

An individual may not use, handle, exhibit, or discharge pyrotechnics in connection with a concert or public exhibition, as allowed under Article 54 of Chapter 14 of the General Statutes, unless the individual successfully completes the training approved or offered by the Commissioner of Insurance through the Office of State Fire Marshal or meets all of the following conditions:

(1) Is an active member in good standing with a local fire or rescue department and has experience in pyrotechnics or explosives, as verified by the State Fire Marshal.

(2) Possesses the professional qualifications required by the State Fire Marshal or the professional qualifications required by the jurisdiction where permitting is being sought, whichever is greater. The professional qualifications set by the State Fire Marshal may not be less than the voluntary minimum professional qualifications for all levels of fire service and rescue service

personnel established by the State Fire and Rescue Commission under G.S. 58-78-5. (2009-507, s. 3.)

§ 58-82A-2.1. Require licenses.

(a) No person shall obtain a pyrotechnics permit under Article 54 of Chapter 14 of the General Statutes unless the person possesses the appropriate license, as provided by this Article.

(b) An applicant for a license authorized by this Article shall apply on forms supplied by the Commissioner. The Commissioner shall inquire as to the applicant's qualifications and other matters relative to the applicant's fitness to be licensed or to continue to be licensed.

(c) When a license is issued under this section, the Commissioner shall issue to the licensee an identification card approved by the Commissioner. Each licensee must carry this card at all times when working in the scope of the licensee's employment. A licensee whose license terminates or is terminated shall surrender the identification card to the Commissioner, when requested by the Commissioner. The Commissioner may contract directly with persons for the processing and issuance of identification cards required by this section and may charge a reasonable fee in addition to the license fee in an amount that offsets the cost of the service, including the costs associated with the contract authorized by this subsection. Contracts entered into under this subsection shall not be subject to Article 3 of Chapter 143 of the General Statutes. (2010-22, s. 4.)

§ 58-82A-2.5. Terms of licenses.

A license issued to a pyrotechnics display operator, a proximate audience display operator, or an assistant display operator under this Article authorizes the licensee to act in that capacity until the license is suspended, revoked, or not renewed. Upon the suspension or revocation of a license, or the failure to renew a license, the licensee shall return the license to the Commissioner. A pyrotechnics display operator's license, a proximate audience display operator's license, and an assistant display operator's license is valid for three years unless suspended or revoked and may be renewed every three years from the date of issuance upon payment of the applicable renewal fee. (2010-22, s. 5.)

§ 58-82A-3. Pyrotechnics display operator license.

(a) License Required. - A display operator license issued by the Commissioner is required for an individual to obtain the necessary authorization under Article 54 of Chapter 14 of the General Statutes to exhibit, use, handle, manufacture, or discharge pyrotechnics at a concert or public exhibition in this State. A license issued under this section is valid for three years unless it is revoked by the Commissioner.

(b) Requirements. - The Commissioner may issue a display operator license to an individual if all of the following conditions are met:

(1) The individual is at least 21 years of age.

(2) The individual has assisted a display operator as an assistant display operator in the exhibition, use, or display of pyrotechnics at a concert or public exhibition, as allowed under Article 54 of Chapter 14 of the General Statutes, on at least three occasions.

(3) The individual successfully completes the minimum training requirements established by the State Fire Marshal.

(4) The individual successfully passes an examination approved by the State Fire Marshal that demonstrates the individual has the knowledge to safely handle, store, and exhibit Class 1.4g, 1.3g, 1.2g, and 1.1g pyrotechnics or provides satisfactory evidence of current certification by a third party acceptable to the State Fire Marshal.

(5) Repealed by Session Laws 2010-22, s. 6, effective October 1, 2010.

(6) The individual has no violations of any provision of this Article or of any similar provision of any other state and submits an "Employer Possessor Letter of Clearance" issued to the individual by the Bureau of Alcohol, Tobacco and Firearms pursuant to 18 U.S.C. Chapter 40.

(b1) The Commissioner may issue a Limited Pyrotechnic Operator license to an individual meeting all the requirements of subsection (b) of this section with the exception of the "Employer Possessor Letter of Clearance" required by subdivision (6) of subsection (b) of this section if the individual signs a statement provided by the Commissioner affirming that the individual has not been convicted of violating 18 U.S.C. Chapter 40, Section 842(i), and is not otherwise prohibited from possessing pyrotechnic materials by any provision of 18 U.S.C. Chapter 40, Section 842(i).

(c),   (d) Repealed by Session Laws 2010-22, s. 6, effective October 1, 2010.

(e) Public exhibitions consisting of materials exempted by G.S. 14-414 are exempt from the operator license requirements. (2009-507, s. 3; 2010-22, s. 6; 2013-275, s. 3.)

§ 58-82A-10. Proximate audience display operator license.

A proximate audience display operator license issued by the Commissioner is required for an individual to obtain the necessary authorization under Article 54 of Chapter 14 of the General Statutes to exhibit, use, handle, manufacture, or discharge pyrotechnics at a concert or public exhibition with a proximate audience display of pyrotechnics in this State. The Commissioner may issue a proximate audience display operator license to an individual who meets all of the following requirements:

(1) Is at least 21 years of age at the time of application.

(2) Completes the training program approved by the Commissioner for pyrotechnic proximate audience display operators or another program which the Commissioner determines to be substantially equivalent.

(3) Successfully passes the written examination provided by the Commissioner.

(4) Submits evidence of active participation as a display operator in the safe performance of at least three displays or as an assistant display operator in the safe performance of at least three displays under the direct supervision of a display operator.

(5) Has no violations of any provision of this Article or of any similar provision of any other state and submits an "Employer Possessor Letter of Clearance" issued to the individual by the Bureau of Alcohol, Tobacco and Firearms pursuant to 18 U.S.C. Chapter 40 or, if the Bureau of Alcohol, Tobacco and Firearms has not issued a Letter of Clearance to the individual, the individual signs a statement provided by the Commissioner affirming that the individual has not been convicted of violating 18 U.S.C. Chapter 40, Section 842(i). (2010-22, s. 7.)

§ 58-82A-15. Assistant display operator license.

(a) No person shall assist a pyrotechnics display operator or a proximate audience display operator with the exhibition, use, handling, or discharge of pyrotechnics or pyrotechnic effects in connection with a concert or public exhibition authorized under Article 54 of Chapter 14 of the General Statutes without an assistant display operator's license issued by the Commissioner.

(b) The Commissioner may issue an assistant display operator license to an individual who meets all of the following requirements:

(1) Is at least 18 years of age.

(2) Signs a statement provided by the Commissioner affirming that the individual has read and understands the pyrotechnics safety guidelines established by the Office of the State Fire Marshal.

(3) Successfully passes the written examination provided by the Commissioner.

(4) Has no violations of any provision of this Article or of any similar provision of any other state and submits an "Employer Possessor Letter of Clearance" issued to the individual by the Bureau of Alcohol, Tobacco and Firearms pursuant to 18 U.S.C. Chapter 40 or, if the Bureau of Alcohol, Tobacco and Firearms has not issued a Letter of Clearance to the individual, the individual signs a statement provided by the Commissioner affirming that the individual has not been convicted of violating 18 U.S.C. Chapter 40 Section 842(i). (2010-22, s. 7.)

§ 58-82A-20. License fees.

(a) A nonrefundable license fee of one hundred dollars ($100.00) shall be paid by the applicant to the Commissioner at the time of each application for a pyrotechnics display operator license.

(b) A nonrefundable license fee of one hundred dollars ($100.00) shall be paid by the applicant to the Commissioner at the time of each application for a license as a proximate audience display operator license.

(c) A nonrefundable license fee of thirty dollars ($30.00) shall be paid to the Commissioner by the applicant with each application for a license as an assistant display operator. (2010-22, s. 7.)

§ 58-82A-25. Qualifications for event employees.

Notwithstanding the provisions of this Article, the Commissioner or the fire code official for the jurisdiction issuing the pyrotechnics permit under G.S. 14-413 may certify an individual as an event employee if the individual meets the following requirements:

(1) Is at least 18 years of age.

(2) Possesses and provides a valid drivers license or other state-issued identification card.

(3) Correctly passes an on-site examination, administered by the Office of the State Fire Marshal or fire code official for the jurisdiction issuing the permit under G.S. 14-413, of a minimum of five questions to test basic pyrotechnic safety knowledge.

(4) Provides written confirmation from the licensed display operator or proximate audience display operator that the event employee is working under the supervision of the operator and that the event employee will not be in the presence of the pyrotechnic materials without signing a statement provided by the Commissioner affirming that the individual has not been convicted of violating 18 U.S.C. Chapter 40, Section 842(i), or is not otherwise prohibited from possessing pyrotechnic materials by any provision of 18 U.S.C. Chapter

40, Section 842(i). The event employee shall not be allowed to discharge or be in the presence of the pyrotechnic materials unless under direct supervision of a licensed pyrotechnic operator or an on-site representative as provided in G.S. 14-410(a1)(2). An event employee certification is valid only for the concert or public exhibition listed on the pyrotechnic permit and cannot be renewed. (2010-22, s. 7; 2013-275, s. 4.)

§ 58-82A-30. Examination fees.

(a) Each applicant for a license as a pyrotechnic display operator, a proximate audience display operator, or assistant display operator shall take a written examination approved by the Commissioner. The Commissioner may contract with a person to process, administer, and grade the examination in the same manner as for agent examinations under Article 33 of this Chapter. The Commissioner may charge a fee to offset the costs of the contract for examination services.

(b) The fee for the examination is ten dollars ($10.00). The examination fee is nonrefundable. (2010-22, s. 7.)

§ 58-82A-35. Renewal fees.

(a) To renew a license as a pyrotechnics display operator, a proximate audience display operator, or an assistant display operator, a licensee shall make application to the Commissioner upon the renewal application form provided by the Commissioner and attest that the statements made in the application are true, correct, and complete to the best of the individual's knowledge and belief. Failure to provide the attestation or providing untrue, incorrect, or incomplete statements shall be grounds for denial, suspension, or revocation of the license.

(b) Before approving the application for renewal, the Commissioner shall find that the licensee:

(1) Has not committed any act which is grounds for denial, suspension, nonrenewal, or revocation under this Article.

(2) Has not had administrative action taken against a pyrotechnics display operator's license or the equivalent by this or any other state.

(3) Has on at least three occasions participated in the use, handling, exhibiting, or discharge of pyrotechnics in connection with a concert or public exhibition pursuant to the terms of the license.

(4) Has paid the applicable fees set forth in this Article.

(5) Has completed a minimum of 12 hours of continuing education during the previous three-year period.

(c) The renewal fee for a pyrotechnics display operator license and a proximate audience display operator license is sixty dollars ($60.00) for each license renewed. The renewal fee for an assistant display operator license is thirty dollars ($30.00). (2010-22, s. 7.)

§ 58-82A-40. Dual license holding.

If any individual holds more than one license issued under this Article simultaneously, all licenses are considered one license for the purpose of disciplinary actions involving suspension, revocation, or nonrenewal under this Article. Separate fees must be paid for each license. (2010-22, s. 7.)

§ 58-82A-45. Reciprocity.

The Commissioner may issue a license under this Article to an individual who holds a comparable valid permit, license, or certification issued by another state, provided the minimum requirements of that state are at least equal to the minimum requirements under this Article for the specific license issued and the person pays the application fee required under this Article. (2010-22, s. 7.)

§ 58-82A-50. Discipline.

The Commissioner may deny, suspend, revoke, or refuse to renew any license under this Article if any of the following apply:

(1)   The licensee violates any provision of this Article.

(2)   The applicant or licensee violates any requirement of a permit issued under G.S. 14-413.

(3)   The licensed display operator or proximate audience display operator fails to provide direct supervision and control over individuals who assist the licensee in handling, using, exhibiting, or displaying pyrotechnics.

(4)   The licensed display operator, proximate audience display operator, or assistant display operator is convicted of a crime under Article 54 of Chapter 14 of the General Statutes.

(5)   Another state revokes the permit, license, or certification issued to the licensee by that state.

(6)   A material misstatement, misrepresentation, or fraud was committed in obtaining a license under this Article.

(7)   Cheating on an examination required by this Article.

(8)   Knowingly aiding or abetting others to evade or violate the provisions of this Article.

(9)   Any existing cause for which the issuance of the license could have been denied had it been known to the Commissioner at the time of issuance. (2010-22, s. 7.)

§ 58-82A-55. License sanction and denial procedures.

(a)   The suspension or revocation of, or refusal to renew, any license under this Article may be contested in accordance with the provisions of Article 3A of Chapter 150B of the General Statutes.

(b)   Whenever the Commissioner denies an initial application for a license or an application for a reissuance of a license, the Commissioner shall notify the applicant and advise the applicant, in writing, of the reasons for the denial of the license. The application may also be denied for any reason for which a license may be suspended or revoked or not renewed under this Article. In order for an applicant to be entitled to a review of the Commissioner's action, the applicant must make a written demand upon the Commissioner for a review no later than 30 days after the service of the notification upon the applicant. The review shall be completed without undue delay, and the applicant shall be notified promptly in writing of the outcome of the review. In order for an applicant who disagrees with the outcome of the review to be entitled to a hearing under Article 3A of Chapter 150B of the General Statutes, the applicant must make a written demand upon the Commissioner for a hearing no later 30 days after service upon the applicant of the Commissioner's decision. (2010-22, s. 7.)

Article 83.

Mutual Aid between Fire Departments.

§ 58-83-1. Authority to send firemen and apparatus beyond territorial limits; privileges and immunities.

A county, municipal corporation, fire protection district, sanitary district or incorporated fire department shall have full authority to send, or to decline to send, firemen and apparatus beyond the territorial limits which it normally serves.

When responding to a call and while working at a fire or other emergency outside the territorial limits which it normally serves, members and employees of county, municipal corporation, fire protection district, sanitary district and incorporated fire departments shall have all authority, rights, privileges and immunities including coverage under the Workers' Compensation Laws, as they have when responding to a call and while working at a fire or other emergency inside the territorial limits normally served.

A county, municipal corporation, fire protection district, sanitary district, or incorporated fire department, in attending an emergency or answering a call outside the limits of the county, municipal corporation, fire protection district, sanitary district, or other area normally served, shall have all authority, rights, privileges, and immunities that it would have in attending an emergency or answering a call inside the territorial limits normally served. (1965, c. 707; 1991, c. 636, s. 3.)

Article 84.

Fund Derived from Insurance Companies.

§ 58-84-1: Repealed by Session Laws 2006-196, s. 6, effective January 1, 2008, and applicable to proceeds credited to the Department of Insurance on or after that date.

§ 58-84-5. Definitions.

The following definitions apply in Articles 84 through 88 of this Chapter:

(1) City. - A fire district.

(2) Clerk. - The clerk of a fire district or, if there is no clerk, the person so designated by the governing body of the fire district.

(3) Fire district. - Any political subdivision of the State that meets all of the following conditions:

a. It has an organized fire department under the control of its governing body.

b. Its fire department has apparatus and equipment that is in serviceable condition for fire duty and is valued at one thousand dollars ($1,000) or more.

c. It enforces the fire laws to the satisfaction of the Commissioner.

(4) Town. - A fire district. (1951, c. 1032, s. 1; 1995 (Reg. Sess., 1996), c. 747, s. 5.)

§§ 58-84-10 through 58-84-20: Repealed by Session Laws 1995 (Regular Session, 1996), c. 747, s. 6.

§ 58-84-25. Disbursement of funds by Insurance Commissioner.

(a)   Distribution. - The Insurance Commissioner shall deduct the sum of three percent (3%) from the tax proceeds credited to the Department pursuant to G.S. 105-228.5(d)(3) and pay the same over to the treasurer of the State Firemen's Association for general purposes. The Insurance Commissioner shall deduct the sum of one percent (1%) from the tax proceeds and retain the same in the budget of the Department of Insurance for the purpose of administering the disbursement of funds by the board of trustees in accordance with the provisions of G.S. 58-84-35. The Insurance Commissioner shall, pursuant to G.S. 58-84-50, credit the amount forfeited by nonmember fire districts to the North Carolina State Firemen's Association. The Insurance Commissioner shall distribute the remaining tax proceeds to the treasurer of each fire district as provided in subsections (b) and (c) of this section.

(b)   Allocation to Counties. - The Insurance Commissioner shall allocate to each county an amount of tax proceeds based upon the amount allocated to it in the previous year. If the amount allocable in the current year is less than the amount allocated in the previous year, then the Commissioner shall reduce the amount allocated to each county. The amount of the reduction is equal to the difference in the amount allocated in the previous year and the amount allocable in the current year multiplied by a fraction, the numerator of which is the population of the county and the denominator of which is the population of the State. If the amount allocable in the current year is greater than the amount allocated in the previous year, then the Commissioner shall increase the amount allocated to each county. The amount of the increase is equal to the excess proceeds multiplied by a fraction, the numerator of which is the population of the county and the denominator of which is the population of the State.

(c)   Distribution to Fire Districts. - Once the Insurance Commissioner has allocated the tax proceeds to a county under subsection (b) of this section, the Commissioner shall distribute those allocations to the fire districts in that county. The amount distributed to each fire district is equal to the total amount allocated to the county multiplied by a fraction, the numerator of which is the tax value of the property located in the fire district and the denominator of which is the tax value of all property located in any fire district in that county. A county shall provide the Commissioner with the tax value of property located in each fire district in that county by January 1 of each year. If a county does not submit information that the Commissioner needs to make a distribution by the date the information is due, the Commissioner shall distribute the allocation based on the most recent information the Commissioner has.

(d) Administration. - These funds shall be held by the treasurer of a fire district as a separate and distinct fund. The fire district shall immediately pay the funds to the treasurer of the local board of trustees upon the treasurer's election and qualification, for the use of the board of trustees of the firemen's local relief fund in each fire district, which board shall be composed of five members, to be used by it for the purposes provided in G.S. 58-84-35. (1907, c. 831, s. 5; C.S., s. 6067; 1925, c. 41; 1985 (Reg. Sess., 1986), c. 1014, s. 168; 1989, c. 485, s. 63; 1995 (Reg. Sess., 1996), c. 747, s. 7; 2006-196, s. 7; 2007-250, s. 2; 2012-45, s. 1; 2013-360, s. 20.2(c).)

§ 58-84-30. Trustees appointed; organization.

For each county, town or city complying with and deriving benefits from the provisions of this Article, there shall be appointed a local board of trustees, known as the trustees of the Firefighters' Relief Fund, to be composed of five members, two of whom shall be elected by the members of the local fire department who are qualified as beneficiaries of such fund, two of whom shall be elected by the mayor and board of aldermen or other local governing body, and one of whom shall be named by the Commissioner of Insurance. Their selection and term of office shall be as follows:

(1) The members of the fire department shall hold an election each January to elect their representatives to above board. In January 1950, the firefighters shall elect one member to serve for two years and one member to serve for one year, then each year in January thereafter, they shall elect only one member and his term of office shall be for two years. Members elected pursuant to this section shall be either (i) residents of the fire district or (ii) active or retired members of the fire department.

(2) The mayor and board of aldermen or other local governing body shall appoint, in January 1950, two representatives to above board, one to hold office

for two years and one to hold office for one year, and each year in January thereafter they shall appoint only one representative and his term of office shall be for two years. Members appointed pursuant to this section shall be residents of the fire district.

(3) The Commissioner of Insurance shall appoint one representative to serve as trustee and he shall serve at the pleasure of the Commissioner. The member appointed pursuant to this section shall be either (i) a resident of the fire district or (ii) an active or retired member of the fire department.

All of the above trustees shall hold office for their elected or appointed time, or until their successors are elected or appointed, and shall serve without pay for their services. They shall immediately after election and appointment organize by electing from their members a chairman and a secretary and treasurer, which two last positions may be held by the same person. The treasurer of said board of trustees shall give a good and sufficient surety bond in a sum equal to the amount of moneys in his hand, to be approved by the Commissioner of Insurance. The cost of this bond may be deducted by the Insurance Commissioner from the receipts collected pursuant to G.S. 58-84-10 before distribution is made to local relief funds. If the chief or chiefs of the local fire departments are not named on the board of trustees as above provided, then they shall serve as ex officio members without privilege of voting on matters before the board. (1907, c. 831, s. 6; C.S., s. 6068; 1925, c. 41; 1945, c. 74, s. 1; 1947, c. 720; 1949, c. 1054; 1973, c. 1365; 1985, c. 666, s. 64; 1987, c. 174, ss. 1, 5; 2007-246, s. 3; 2012-45, s. 2.)

§ 58-84-35. Disbursement of funds by trustees.

The board of trustees shall have entire control of the funds derived from the provisions of this Article, and shall disburse the funds only for the following purposes:

(1) To safeguard any fireman in active service from financial loss, occasioned by sickness contracted or injury received while in the performance of his duties as a fireman.

(2) To provide a reasonable support for those actually dependent upon the services of any fireman who may lose his life in the fire service of his town, city, or State, either by accident or from disease contracted or injury received by

reason of such service. The amount is to be determined according to the earning capacity of the deceased.

(2a) To provide assistance, upon approval by the Secretary of the State Firemen's Association, to a destitute member fireman who has served honorably for at least five years.

(3) Repealed by Session Laws 1985, c. 666, s. 61.

(4) To provide for the payment of any fireman's assessment in the Firemen's Fraternal Insurance Fund of the State of North Carolina if the board of trustees finds as a fact that said fireman is unable to pay the said assessment by reason of disability.

(5) To provide for benefits of supplemental retirement, workers compensation, and other insurance and pension protection for firefighters otherwise qualifying for benefits from the Firefighters' Relief Fund as set forth in Article 85 of this Chapter.

(6) To provide for educational benefits to firemen and their dependents who otherwise qualify for benefits from the Firefighters' Relief Fund as set forth in Article 85 of this Chapter.

Notwithstanding any other provisions of law, no expenditures shall be made pursuant to subsections (5) and (6) of this section unless the State Firemen's Association has certified that such expenditures will not render the Fund actuarially unsound for the purposes of providing the benefits set forth in subsections (1), (2), and (4) of this section. If, for any reason, funds made available for subsections (5) and (6) of this section shall be insufficient to pay in full any benefits, the benefits pursuant to subsections (5) and (6) shall be reduced pro rata for as long as the amount of insufficient funds exists. No claim shall accrue with respect to any amount by which a benefit under subsections (5) and (6) shall have been reduced. (1907, c. 831, s. 6; 1919, c. 180; C.S., s. 6069; Ex. Sess. 1921, c. 55; 1923, c. 22; 1925, c. 41; 1945, c. 74, s. 2; 1985, c. 666, s. 61; 1987, c. 174, ss. 2, 3; 1997-456, s. 27; 2007-246, s. 4; 2008-187, s. 13.)

§ 58-84-40. Trustees to keep account and file certified reports.

(a) Each local board of trustees shall keep a correct account of all moneys received and disbursed by them. On a form prescribed by the North Carolina State Firemen's Association, each local board shall certify by October 31 of each year the following to the Association: the balance of the local fund, proof of sufficient bonding, a full accounting of the previous year's expenditures, and a full accounting of membership qualifications. Such certification shall be made concurrently with the local unit's statement of Fire Readiness.

(b) In turn, the State Firemen's Association shall certify to the Department of Insurance by January 1 of each year on a form prescribed by the Department, the local units which have complied with the requirements of subsection (a) of this section.

(c) In the event that any board of trustees in any of the towns and cities benefited by this Article shall neglect or fail to perform their duties, or shall willfully misappropriate the funds entrusted in their care by obligating or disbursing such funds for any purpose other than those set forth in G.S. 58-84-35, then the Insurance Commissioner shall withhold any and all further payments to such board of trustees, or their successors, until the matter has been fully investigated by an official of the State Firemen's Association, and adjusted to the satisfaction of the Insurance Commissioner.

(d) In the event that any local relief fund provided for in this Article becomes impaired, then the Firefighters' Relief Fund may in the discretion of its board of trustees assist the local unit administering the fund in providing for relief to injured firefighters and their dependents or survivors; provided, however, that any funds so provided to such impaired units shall be repaid in full at the statutory rate of interest from future local unit receipts if the impairment resulted from violations of this Article. (1907, c. 831, s. 7; C.S., s. 6070; 1925, c. 41; 1985, c. 666, s. 63; 2007-246, s. 5.)

§ 58-84-45: Repealed by Session Laws 2000-67, s. 26.21(a).

§ 58-84-46. Certification to Commissioner.

On or before October 31 of each year the clerk or finance officer of each city or county that has a local board of trustees under G.S. 58-84-30 shall file a certificate of eligibility with the Commissioner. The certificate shall contain information prescribed by administrative rule adopted by the Commissioner. If the certificate is not filed with the Commissioner on or before January 31 in the ensuing year:

(1)   The city or county that failed to file the certificate shall forfeit the payment next due to be paid to its board of trustees.

(2)   The Commissioner shall pay over that amount to the treasurer of the North Carolina State Firemen's Association.

(3)   That amount shall constitute a part of the Firefighters' Relief Fund. (2000-67, s. 26.21(b); 2001-421, s. 3; 2007-246, s. 6.)

§ 58-84-50. Fire departments to be members of State Firemen's Association.

For the purpose of supervision and as a guaranty that provisions of this Article shall be honestly administered in a businesslike manner, it is provided that every department enjoying the benefits of this law shall be a member of the North Carolina State Firemen's Association and comply with its constitution and bylaws. If the fire department of any city, town or village shall fail to comply with the constitution and bylaws of said Association, said city, town or village shall forfeit its right to the next annual payment due from the funds mentioned in this Article, and the Commissioner of Insurance shall pay over said amount to the treasurer of the North Carolina State Firemen's Association and same shall constitute a part of the Firefighters' Relief Fund. (1907, c. 831, s. 9; 1919, c. 180; C.S., s. 6072; 1925, c. 41; c. 309, s. 2; 1965, c. 624; 2007-246, s. 7.)

§ 58-84-55. No discrimination on account of race.

The local boards of trustees of the Firefighters' Relief Fund shall make no discrimination based upon race in the payment of benefits. (1907, c. 831, s. 10; C.S., s. 6073; 1985, c. 666, s. 62; 2007-246, s. 8.)

§ 58-84-60. Immunity.

A person serving on a local board of trustees of the Firefighters' Relief Fund shall be immune individually from civil liability for monetary damages, except to the extent covered by insurance, for any act or failure to act arising out of this service, except where the person:

(1)   Was not acting within the scope of that person's official duties;

(2)   Was not acting in good faith;

(3)   Committed gross negligence or willful or wanton misconduct that resulted in the damages or injury;

(4)   Derived an improper personal financial benefit, either directly or indirectly, from the transaction; or

(5)   Incurred the liability from the operation of a motor vehicle. (2007-54, s. 1; 2007-246, s. 8.1.)

Article 85.

State Appropriation.

§ 58-85-1. Application of fund.

The money paid into the hands of the treasurer of the North Carolina State Firemen's Association shall be known and remain as the "Firefighters' Relief Fund" of North Carolina, and shall be used as a fund for the relief of firefighters and county fire marshals, who are members of this Association, who may be injured or rendered sick by disease contracted in the actual discharge of duty as firefighters or county fire marshals, and for the relief of surviving spouses, children, and if there be no surviving spouse or children, then dependent mothers of the firefighters and county fire marshals killed or dying from disease so contracted in the discharge of duty; to be paid in the manner and in the sums to the individuals of the classes herein named and described as may be provided for and determined upon in accordance with the constitution and bylaws of the Association, and any provisions and determinations made under the constitution and bylaws shall be final and conclusive as to the persons entitled to benefits and as to the amount of benefit to be received, and no action at law shall be maintained against the Association to enforce any claim or recover any benefit under this Article or under the constitution and bylaws of the Association; but if any officer or committee of the Association omit or refuse to perform any duty imposed upon the officer or them, nothing herein contained shall be construed to prevent any proceedings against that officer or committee to compel the officer or them to perform that duty. No firefighter or county fire marshal shall be entitled to receive any benefits under this section until the firefighters' relief fund of his city or town has been exhausted. Notwithstanding the above provisions, the Executive Board of the North Carolina State Firemen's Association is hereby authorized to grant educational scholarships to members and the children of members, to subsidize premium payments of members over 65 years of age to the Firemen's Fraternal Insurance Fund of the North Carolina State Firemen's Association, and to provide accidental death and dismemberment insurance for members of those fire departments not eligible for benefits pursuant to standards of certification adopted by the State Firemen's Association for the use of local relief funds. (1891, c. 468, s. 3; Rev., s. 4393; C.S., s. 6058; 1925, c. 41; 1981 (Reg. Sess., 1982), c. 1215; 1987, c. 174, s. 4; 1993 (Reg. Sess., 1994), c. 678, s. 33; 2004-199, s. 22(a); 2007-246, s. 1.)

§ 58-85-5: Reserved for future codification purposes.

§ 58-85-10. Treasurer to file report and give bond.

The treasurer of the North Carolina State Firemen's Association shall make a detailed report to the State Treasurer of the yearly expenditures of the appropriation under Articles 84 through 88 of this Chapter on or before the end of the fiscal year, showing the total amount of money in his hands at the time of the filing of the report, and shall give a bond to the State of North Carolina with good and sufficient sureties to the satisfaction of the Treasurer of the State of North Carolina in a sum not less than the amount of money on hand as shown by said report. (1891, c. 468, s. 4; Rev., s. 4394; C.S., s. 6059; 1925, c. 41.)

§ 58-85-15. Who shall participate in the fund.

The line of duty entitling one to participate in the fund shall be so construed as to mean actual fire duty only, and any actual duty connected with the fire department or county fire marshal office when directed to perform the same by an officer in charge. (1891, c. 468, s. 5; Rev., s. 4395; C.S., s. 6060; 1925, c. 41; 2004-199, s. 22(b).)

§ 58-85-20. Who may become members.

Any organized fire company in North Carolina, holding itself ready for duty, may, upon compliance with the requirements of its constitution and bylaws, become a member of the North Carolina State Firemen's Association, and any fireman of good moral character in North Carolina, and belonging to an organized fire company, who complies with the requirements of the constitution and bylaws of the North Carolina State Firemen's Association, may become a member of the Association. Any county fire marshal office may, upon compliance with the requirements of its constitution and bylaws, become a member of the North Carolina Firemen's Association, and any employee of a county fire marshal office of good moral character whose sole duty is to act as a fire marshal, deputy fire marshal, assistant fire marshal, or firefighter of the county, who complies with the requirements of its constitution and bylaws, may become a member of the North Carolina Firemen's Association. (1891, c. 468, s. 6; Rev., s. 4396; C.S., s. 6061; 1925, c. 41; 2004-199, s. 22(c).)

§ 58-85-25. Applied to members of regular fire company.

G.S. 58-85-1, 58-85-10, 58-85-15, 58-85-20, and 58-85-25 shall apply to any fireman or fire marshal who is a member of a regularly organized fire company or county fire marshal office, and is a member in good standing of the North Carolina State Firemen's Association. (1891, c. 468, s. 7; Rev., s. 4397; C.S., s. 6062; 1925, c. 41; 2004-199, s. 22(d).)

§ 58-85-30. Treasurer to pay fund to Volunteer Firemen's Association.

(a) The treasurer of the North Carolina State Firemen's Association shall pay to the treasurer of the North Carolina State Volunteer Firemen's Association one sixth of the funds arising from the three percent (3%) paid the treasurer of the North Carolina State Firemen's Association by the Commissioner each year to be used by the North Carolina State Volunteer Firemen's Association for the purposes set forth in G.S. 58-84-35.

(b) Local units of the North Carolina State Volunteer Firemen's Association shall maintain records and report to the North Carolina State Firemen's Association in accordance with G.S. 58-84-40, and shall be subject to the sanctions in G.S. 58-84-40. (1925, c. 41; 1985, c. 666, s. 65; 2003-221, s. 11.)

Article 85A.

State Fire Protection Grant Fund.

§ 58-85A-1. Creation of Fund; allocation to local fire districts and political subdivisions of the State.

(a) There is created in the Department of Insurance the State Fire Protection Grant Fund. The purpose of the Fund is to compensate local fire districts and political subdivisions of the State for providing local fire protection to State-owned buildings and their contents.

(b) The Department of Insurance shall develop and implement an equitable and uniform statewide method for distributing any funds to the State's local fire districts and political subdivisions.

(c) It is the intent of the General Assembly to appropriate annually to the State Fire Protection Grant Fund up to four million one hundred eighty thousand dollars ($4,180,000) from the General Fund, one hundred fifty-eight thousand dollars ($158,000) from the Highway Fund, and one million three hundred forty-five thousand dollars ($1,345,000) from University of North Carolina receipts. Funds received from the General Fund shall be allocated only for providing local fire protection for State-owned property supported by the General Fund; funds received from the Highway Fund shall be allocated only for providing local fire protection for State-owned property supported by the Highway Fund; and funds received from University of North Carolina receipts shall be allocated only for providing local fire protection for State-owned property supported by University of North Carolina receipts. (1997-443, s. 23(a); 2000-140, s. 93.1(a); 2001-424, s. 12.2(b); 2007-323, ss. 23.4(a), 23.4(b); 2008-107, s. 22.2; 2011-145, s. 25.1.)

Article 86.

North Carolina Firefighters' and Rescue Squad Workers' Pension Fund.

§ 58-86-1. Fund established; administration by board of trustees; rules and regulations.

For the purpose of furthering the general welfare and police powers and obligations of the State with respect to the protection of all its citizens from the consequences of loss or damage by fire and of injury by serious accident or illness, of increasing the protection of life and property against loss or damage by fire, of improving firefighting and life saving techniques, of increasing the potential of fire departments, rescue squads, organizations and groups, of fostering increased and more widely spread training of personnel of these organizations and groups, and of providing incentive and inducement to participate in fire prevention, firefighting and rescue squad activities and for the establishment of new, improved or extended fire departments, rescue squads, organizations and groups to the end that ultimately all areas of the State and all of its citizens will receive the benefits of fire protection and rescue squads' activity and a resulting reduction of loss or damage to life and property by fire hazard or injury by serious accident or illness, and in recognition of the public service rendered to the State of North Carolina and its citizens by "eligible firefighters and rescue squad workers," as defined by this Article, there is created in this State a fund to be known, and designated as "The North Carolina Firefighters' and Rescue Squad Workers' Pension Fund" to be administered as provided in this Article.

The North Carolina Firefighters' and Rescue Squad Workers' Pension Fund is established to provide pension allowances and other benefits for eligible firefighters and rescue squad workers in the State who elect to become members of the fund. The board of trustees created by this Article shall have authority to administer the fund and shall make necessary rules and regulations to carry out the provisions of this Article. (1957, c. 1420, s. 1; 1959, c. 1212, s. 1; 1961, c. 980; 1981, c. 1029, s. 1; 2013-284, s. 1(a).)

§ 58-86-2. Definitions.

The following words and phrases as used in this Article, unless a different meaning is plainly required by the context, shall have the following meanings:

(1)   "Board" means the Board of Trustees of the Local Governmental Employees' Retirement System.

(2)   "Chair" means the chair of the Board of Trustees of the Local Governmental Employees' Retirement System.

(3)   "Director" means the Director of the Retirement Systems Division of the North Carolina Department of State Treasurer. The Director shall promptly transmit to the State Treasurer all moneys collected on behalf of members, which moneys shall be deposited by the State Treasurer into the fund.

(4)   "Eligible fire department" means a bona fide fire department which is certified to the Commissioner of Insurance by the governing body thereof, and determined as classified as not less than class "9S," and said fire department holds training sessions not less than four hours monthly.

(5)   "Eligible firefighter" means all persons 18 years of age or older who are firefighters of the State of North Carolina or any political subdivision thereof, including those performing such functions in the protection of life and property through firefighting within a county or city governmental unit. "Eligible firefighter" shall also mean an employee of a county whose sole duty is to act as fire marshal, deputy fire marshal, assistant fire marshal, or firefighter of the county. "Eligible firefighter" shall also mean those persons meeting the other qualifications of this Article, not exceeding 25 volunteer firefighters plus one additional volunteer firefighter per 100 population in the area served by their respective departments.

(6)   "Eligible rescue or emergency medical services squad" means organized rescue squad units eligible for membership in the North Carolina Association of Rescue and Emergency Medical Services, Inc.

(7) "Eligible rescue squad worker" means all persons 18 years of age or older who are members of a rescue or emergency medical services squad that is eligible for membership in the North Carolina Association of Rescue and Emergency Medical Services, Inc. "Eligible rescue squad worker" shall also mean those persons meeting the other qualifications of this Article.

(8) "Fully credited service" means a period of time for which the Board has received certification that a member has met all eligibility requirements for participation in the Pension Fund and for which the Board has received timely monthly payments under G.S. 58-86-35 or G.S. 58-86-40. In lieu of monthly payments under G.S. 58-86-35 or G.S. 58-86-40, a member may purchase fully credited service for any period of service as set forth in G.S. 58-86-45.

(9) "Inactive member" means a member of the fund who is not on a leave of absence under G.S. 58-86-95 and who is not making timely monthly payments under G.S. 58-86-35 or G.S. 58-86-40.

(10) "Member" means an eligible firefighter or eligible rescue squad worker who has elected to participate in the North Carolina Firefighters' and Rescue Squad Workers' Pension Fund.

(11) "Pension Fund" means the North Carolina Firefighters' and Rescue Squad Workers' Pension Fund.

(12) "Training sessions" for eligible rescue squad workers means sessions in which attendance will result in the preparation of, or knowledge gained by, the member in the area of rescue, emergency medical services, injury prevention, or protection of life and property. Such drill or training sessions held by the eligible rescue squad unit to meet the requirements of this Article shall be held for the purpose of providing a learning or preparation experience for the members.

(13) "Training sessions" for eligible firefighters means sessions in which attendance will result in the preparation of, or knowledge gained by, the member in the area of fire prevention, fire suppression, or protection of life and property. Such drill or training sessions held by the eligible fire department to meet the requirements of this Article shall be held for the purpose of providing a learning or preparation experience for the members. (2013-284, s. 1(a).)

§ 58-86-5: Repealed by Session Laws 2013-284, s. 1(a), effective July 1, 2013.

§ 58-86-6. Firefighters' and Rescue Squad Workers' Pension Fund Advisory Panel.

There is created an advisory panel to be known as the Firefighters' and Rescue Squad Workers' Pension Fund Advisory Panel, hereinafter referred to as "the advisory panel."

The advisory panel shall consist of seven persons:

(1)   The Director of the Retirement Systems Division of the North Carolina Department of State Treasurer or his or her designee, who shall act as chair.

(2)   A designee of the State Insurance Commissioner.

(3)   Five members to be appointed by the Board of Trustees of the Local Governmental Employees' Retirement System: one paid firefighter, one volunteer firefighter, one paid rescue squad worker, one volunteer rescue squad worker, and one representing the public at large, for terms of four years each. One member of the advisory panel appointed by the Board of Trustees of the Local Governmental Employees' Retirement System must be a member of that Board. Members of the advisory panel may succeed themselves if reappointed by the Board of Trustees of the Local Governmental Employees' Retirement System.

The persons serving on the Board of Trustees of the Firefighters' and Rescue Squad Workers' Pension Fund on June 30, 2013, may serve as members of the advisory panel until the expiration of their current terms. No member of the advisory panel shall receive any salary, compensation, or expenses other than that provided in G.S. 138-6 for each day's attendance at duly and regularly called and held meetings of the advisory panel. (2013-284, s. 1(a).)

§ 58-86-10. Powers and duties of the board.

The Board of Trustees of the North Carolina Local Governmental Employees' Retirement System shall administer the Pension Fund. The board shall request appropriations out of the general fund for administrative expenses and to provide for the financing of this pension fund, employ necessary clerical assistance, determine all applications for pensions, provide for the payment of pensions, make all necessary rules and regulations not inconsistent with law for the governance of this fund, prescribe rules and regulations of eligibility of persons to receive pensions, expend funds in accordance with the provisions of this Article, and generally exercise all other powers necessary for the administration of the fund created by this Article. (1957, c. 1420, s. 1; 1959, c. 1212, s. 1; 1981, c. 1029, s. 1; 2013-284, s. 1(a).)

§ 58-86-11. Powers and duties of the advisory panel.

The advisory panel shall meet at least once annually upon call of the chair. The advisory panel shall have no administrative authority but shall prepare an annual report to the Board of Trustees of the North Carolina Local Governmental Employees' Retirement System regarding the status and needs of the North Carolina Firefighters' and Rescue Squad Workers' Pension Fund. (2013-284, s. 1(a).)

§ 58-86-15: Repealed by Session Laws 2013-284, s. 1(a), effective July 1, 2013.

§ 58-86-20. State Treasurer to be custodian of fund; appropriations; contributions to fund; expenditures.

The State Treasurer shall be the custodian of the North Carolina Firefighters' and Rescue Squad Workers' Pension Fund and shall invest its assets in accordance with the provisions of G.S. 147-69.2 and G.S. 147-69.3. The appropriations made by the General Assembly out of the general fund to provide money for administrative expenses shall be handled in the same manner as any other general fund appropriation. One-fourth of the appropriation made out of the general fund to provide for the financing of the pension fund shall be transferred quarterly to a special fund to be known as the North Carolina Firefighters' and Rescue Squad Workers' Pension Fund. There shall be set up in the State Treasurer's office a special fund to be known as the North Carolina

Firefighters' and Rescue Squad Workers' Pension Fund, and all contributions made by the members of this pension fund shall be deposited in the special fund. All expenditures for refunds, investments or benefits shall be in the same manner as expenditures of other special funds. (1957, c. 1420, s. 1; 1959, c. 1212, s. 1; 1961, c. 980; 1971, c. 30; 1979, c. 467, s. 10; 1981, c. 1029, s. 1; 2013-284, s. 1(a).)

§ 58-86-25. Determination and certification of eligible firefighters.

Eligible firefighters must attend 36 hours of training sessions in each calendar year. Each eligible fire department shall annually determine and report the names of those firefighters meeting the eligibility qualifications of this Article to its respective governing body, which upon determination of the validity and accuracy of the qualification shall promptly certify the list to the North Carolina State Firemen's Association. The Firemen's Association shall provide a list of those persons meeting the eligibility requirements of this Article to the State Treasurer by January 31 of each year. For the purposes of the preceding sentence, the governing body of a fire department operated: by a county is the county board of commissioners; by a city is the city council; by a sanitary district is the sanitary district board; by a corporation, whether profit or nonprofit, is the corporation's board of directors; and by any other entity is that group designated by the board. An "eligible firefighter" may not also qualify as an "eligible rescue squad worker" in order to receive double benefits available under this Article. (1957, c. 1420, s. 1; 1959, c. 1212, s. 1; 1981, c. 1029, s. 1; 1983, c. 416, s. 7; 1985, c. 241; 2000-67, s. 26.22; 2001-222, s. 1; 2003-362, s. 1; 2009-66, s. 2(b); 2013-284, s. 1(a).)

§ 58-86-30. Determination and certification of "eligible rescue squad worker."

Eligible rescue squad workers must attend at least 36 hours of training sessions in each calendar year. Each rescue or emergency medical services squad eligible for membership in the North Carolina Association of Rescue and Emergency Medical Services, Inc., must file a roster certified by the secretary of the association of those rescue or emergency medical services squad workers meeting the requirements of this section with the State Treasurer by January 31 of each calendar year.

An "eligible rescue squad worker" may not qualify also as an "eligible firefighter" in order to receive double benefits available under this Article. (1981, c. 1029, s. 1; 1991 (Reg. Sess., 1992), c. 833, s. 3; 1995, c. 507, s. 7.21A(h); 2009-66, s. 2(c); 2013-284, s. 1(a).)

§ 58-86-35. Firefighters' application for membership in fund; monthly payments by members; payments credited to separate accounts of members; termination of membership.

Those firefighters who are eligible pursuant to G.S. 58-86-25 may apply to the board for membership. Each firefighter upon becoming a member of the fund shall pay the director of the fund the sum of ten dollars ($10.00) per month; each payment shall be made no later than March 31 subsequent to the end of the calendar year in which the month occurred. The Pension Fund shall not award fully credited service based on payments received later than March 31 subsequent to the end of the calendar year in which the month occurred unless the payment is applied as provided in G.S. 58-86-45(a1). The monthly payments shall be credited to the separate account of the member and shall be kept by the custodian so it is available for payment on withdrawal from membership or retirement.

A member may elect to terminate membership in the fund at any time and request the refund of payments previously made to the fund. However, a member's delinquency in making the monthly payments required by this section does not result in the termination of membership without such an election by the member. (1957, c. 1420, s. 1; 1959, c. 1212, s. 1; 1981, c. 1029, s. 1; 1995, c. 507, s. 7.21A(d); 2005-91, s. 14; 2005-281, s. 1.2; 2009-66, s. 2(d); 2013-284, s. 1(a).)

§ 58-86-40. Rescue squad worker's application for membership in funds; monthly payments by members; payments credited to separate accounts of members; termination of membership.

Those rescue squad workers eligible pursuant to G.S. 58-86-30 may apply to the board for membership. Each eligible rescue squad worker upon becoming a member shall pay the director of the fund the sum of ten dollars ($10.00) per month; each payment shall be made no later than March 31 subsequent to the end of the calendar year in which the month occurred. The Pension Fund shall not award fully credited service based on payments received later than March 31 subsequent to the end of the calendar year in which the month occurred unless the payment is applied as provided in G.S. 58-86-45(a1). The monthly payments shall be credited to the separate account of the member and shall be kept by the custodian so it is available for payment on withdrawal from membership or retirement.

A member may elect to terminate membership in the fund at any time and request the refund of payments previously made to the fund. However, a member's delinquency in making the monthly payments required by this section does not result in the termination of membership without such an election by the member. (1981, c. 1029, s. 1; 1983, c. 500, s. 1; 1991 (Reg. Sess., 1992), c. 833, s. 4; 1995, c. 507, s. 7.21A(e); 2005-91, s. 15; 2005-281, s. 1.3; 2009-66, s. 2(e); 2013-284, s. 1(a).)

§ 58-86-45. Additional retroactive membership.

(a) Repealed by Session Laws 2013-284, s. 1(a), effective July 1, 2013.

(a1) Any firefighter or rescue squad worker who is a current or former member of a fire department or rescue squad chartered by the State of North Carolina may purchase credit for any periods of service to any chartered fire department or rescue squad not otherwise creditable by making a lump sum payment to the Annuity Savings Fund equal to the full liability of the service credits calculated on the basis of the assumptions used for purposes of the actuarial valuation of the system's liabilities, which payment shall take into account the retirement allowance arising on account of the additional service credit commencing at the earliest age at which the member could retire on a retirement allowance, as determined by the board of trustees upon the advice of the consulting actuary, plus an administrative fee to be set by the board of trustees. This provision for the payment of a lump sum for service "not otherwise creditable" shall apply, inter alia, to all purchases of service credits for months as to which timely payments were not previously made pursuant to G.S. 58-86-35 or G.S. 58-86-40, whichever is applicable.

(b) An eligible firefighter or rescue squad worker who is not yet 35 years old may apply to the board of trustees for membership in the fund at any time. Upon becoming a member, the worker may make a lump sum payment of ten dollars

($10.00) per month retroactively to the time the worker first became eligible to become a member, plus interest at an annual rate to be set by the board upon advice from actuary for each year of retroactive payments. Upon making this lump sum payment, the worker shall be given credit for all prior service in the same manner as if the worker had applied for membership upon first becoming eligible.

A member who is not yet 35 years old may receive credit for the prior service upon making a lump sum payment of ten dollars ($10.00) for each month since the worker first became eligible, plus interest at an annual rate to be set by the board for each year of retroactive payments. Upon making this lump sum payment, the date of membership shall be the same as if the worker had applied for membership upon first becoming eligible. (1985 (Reg. Sess., 1986), c. 1014, s. 49.1(a); 1989, c. 693; 1993, c. 429, s. 1; 1995, c. 507, s. 7.21A(f); 2000-67, s. 26.17(a); 2009-66, s. 2(f); 2013-284, s. 1(a).)

§ 58-86-50: Repealed by Session Laws 2009-66, s. 2.(g), effective July 1, 2009.

§ 58-86-55. Monthly pensions upon retirement.

Any member who has served 20 years as an "eligible firefighter" or "eligible rescue squad worker" in the State of North Carolina, as provided in G.S. 58-86-25 and G.S. 58-86-30, and who has attained the age of 55 years is entitled to be paid a monthly pension from this fund. The monthly pension shall be in the amount of one hundred seventy dollars ($170.00) per month. Any retired firefighter receiving a pension shall, effective July 1, 2008, receive a pension of one hundred seventy dollars ($170.00) per month.

Members shall pay ten dollars ($10.00) per month as required by G.S. 58-86-35 and G.S. 58-86-40 for a period of no longer than 20 years. No "eligible rescue squad member" shall receive a pension prior to July 1, 1983. No member shall be entitled to a pension hereunder until the member's official duties as a fireman or rescue squad worker for which the member is paid compensation shall have been terminated and the member shall have retired as such according to standards or rules fixed by the board of trustees.

A member who is totally and permanently disabled while in the discharge of the member's official duties as a result of bodily injuries sustained or as a result of extreme exercise or extreme activity experienced in the course and scope of those official duties and who leaves the fire or rescue squad service because of this disability shall be entitled to be paid from the fund a monthly benefit in an amount of one hundred seventy dollars ($170.00) per month beginning the first month after the member's fifty-fifth birthday. All applications for disability are subject to the approval of the board who may appoint physicians to examine and evaluate the disabled member prior to approval of the application, and annually thereafter. Any disabled member shall not be required to make the monthly payment of ten dollars ($10.00) as required by G.S. 58-86-35 and G.S. 58-86-40.

A member who is totally and permanently disabled for any cause, other than line of duty, who leaves the fire or rescue squad service because of this disability and who has at least 10 years of service with the pension fund, may be permitted to continue making a monthly contribution of ten dollars ($10.00) to the fund until the member has made contributions for a total of 240 months. The member shall upon attaining the age of 55 years be entitled to receive a pension as provided by this section. All applications for disability are subject to the approval of the board who may appoint physicians to examine and evaluate the disabled member prior to approval of the application and annually thereafter.

A member who, because the member's residence is annexed by a city under Part 2 or Part 3 of Article 4A of Chapter 160A of the General Statutes, or whose department is closed because of an annexation by a city under Part 2 or Part 3 of Article 4A of Chapter 160A of the General Statutes, or whose volunteer department is taken over by a city or county, and because of such annexation or takeover is unable to perform as a firefighter or rescue squad worker of any status, and if the member has at least 10 years of service with the pension fund, may be permitted to continue making a monthly contribution of ten dollars ($10.00) to the fund until the member has made contributions for a total of 240 months. The member upon attaining the age of 55 years and completion of such contributions shall be entitled to receive a pension as provided by this section. Any application to make monthly contributions under this section shall be subject to a finding of eligibility by the Board of Trustees upon application of the member.

The pensions provided shall be in addition to all other pensions or benefits under any other statutes of the State of North Carolina or the United States, notwithstanding any exclusionary provisions of other pensions or retirement systems provided by law. (1957, c. 1420, s. 1; 1959, c. 1212, s. 1; 1961, c. 980; 1971, c. 336; 1977, c. 926, s. 1; 1981, c. 1029, s. 1; 1983, c. 500, s. 2; c. 636, s. 24; 1985 (Reg. Sess., 1986), c. 1014, s. 49.1(b); 1987 (Reg. Sess., 1988), c. 1099, s. 1; 1991, c. 720, s. 48; 1993 (Reg. Sess., 1994), c. 653, s. 1; 1995, c. 507, s. 7.21A(g); 1997-443, s. 33.25(a); 1998-212, s. 28.21(a); 2000-67, s. 26.18; 2002-113, s. 1; 2002-126, s. 28.7; 2003-284, s. 30.19; 2004-124, s. 31.18; 2005-276, s. 29.26; 2006-66, s. 22.19; 2007-323, s. 28.21; 2008-107, s. 26.25; 2013-284, s. 1(a).)

§ 58-86-60. Payments in lump sums.

The board shall direct payment in lump sums from the fund in the following cases:

(1) To any firefighter or rescue squad worker upon the attaining of the age of 55 years, who, for any reason, is not qualified to receive the monthly retirement pension and who was enrolled as a member of the fund, an amount equal to the amount paid into the fund by him. This provision shall not be construed to preclude any active firefighter or rescue squad worker from completing the requisite number of years of active service after attaining the age of 55 years necessary to entitle the firefighter or rescue squad worker to the pension.

(2) If any firefighter or rescue squad worker dies before attaining the age at which a pension is payable to the firefighter or rescue squad worker under the provisions of this Article, there shall be paid to his or her surviving spouse, or if there be no surviving spouse, to the person responsible for his or her child or children, or if there be no surviving spouse or children, then to his or her heirs at law as may be determined by the board or to his or her estate, if it is administered and there are no heirs, an amount equal to the amount paid into the member's separate account by or on behalf of the said firefighter or rescue squad worker.

(3) If any firefighter or rescue squad worker dies after beginning to receive the pension payable to the firefighter or rescue squad worker by this Article, and before receiving an amount equal to the amount paid into the fund by him or her, there shall be paid to his or her surviving spouse, or if there be no surviving spouse, then to the person responsible for his or her child or children, or if there be no surviving spouse or children, then to his or her heirs at law as may be

determined by the board or to his or her estate, if it is administered and there are no heirs, an amount equal to the difference between the amount paid into the member's separate account by or on behalf of the said firefighter or rescue squad worker and the amount received by him or her as a pensioner.

(4) Any member who withdraws from the fund shall, upon proper application, be paid all moneys without accumulated earnings on the payments after the time they were made. A member may not purchase time under G.S. 58-86-45 for which he or she has received a refund. (1957, c. 1420, s. 1; 1959, c. 1212, s. 1; 1977, c. 926, s. 2; 1981, c. 1029, s. 1; 1987, c. 667, s. 1; 2009-66, s. 2(h); 2009-365, s. 1; 2013-284, s. 1(a).)

§ 58-86-65. Pro rata reduction of benefits when fund insufficient to pay in full.

If, for any reason, the fund created and made available for any purpose covered by this Article shall be insufficient to pay in full any pension benefits, or other charges, then all benefits or payments shall be reduced pro rata, for as long as the deficiency in amount exists. No claim shall accrue with respect to any amount by which a pension or benefit payment shall have been reduced. (1957, c. 1420, s. 1; 1959, c. 1212, s. 1; 1981, c. 1029, s. 1.)

§ 58-86-70. Provisions subject to future legislative change.

These pensions shall be subject to future legislative change or revision, and no member of the fund, or any person, is deemed to have acquired any vested right to a pension or other payment provided by this Article. (1957, c. 1420, s. 1; 1959, c. 1212, s. 1; 1981, c. 1029, s. 1.)

§ 58-86-75. Determination of creditable service; information furnished by applicants for membership.

The board shall determine by appropriate rules and regulations the number of years' credit for service of firefighters and rescue squad workers. Firefighters and rescue squad workers who are now serving as such shall furnish the board with information upon applying for membership as to previous service.

Notwithstanding any other provisions of this Article, the Board may grant qualified prior service credits to eligible firemen [firefighters] and rescue squad workers under such terms and conditions that the Board may adopt when the Board determines that an eligible firefighter or rescue squad worker has been denied such service credits through no fault of his or her own. (1957, c. 1420, s. 1; 1959, c. 1212, s. 1; 1981, c. 1029, s. 1; 1987 (Reg. Sess., 1988), c. 1086, s. 29; 2013-284, s. 1(a).)

§ 58-86-80. Length of service not affected by serving in more than one department or squad; transfer from one department or squad to another.

A firefighter's or rescue squad worker's length of service shall not be affected by the fact that he or she may have served with more than one department or squad, and upon transfer from one department or squad to another, notice of the fact shall be given to the board. (1957, c. 1420, s. 1; 1959, c. 1212, s. 1; 1981, c. 1029, s. 1; 2013-284, s. 1(a).)

§ 58-86-85: Repealed by Session Laws 2005-91, s. 13, effective July 1, 2005, and Session Laws 2005-281, s. 1.1, effective August 18, 2005.

§ 58-86-90. Exemptions of pensions from attachment; rights nonassignable.

Except for the applications of the provisions of G.S. 110-136, and in connection with a court-ordered equitable distribution under G.S. 50-20, the pensions provided are not subject to attachment, garnishments or judgments against the firefighter or rescue squad worker entitled to them, nor are any rights in the fund or the pensions or benefits assignable. (1957, c. 1420, s. 1; 1959, c. 1212, s. 1; 1969, c. 486; 1981, c. 1029, s. 1; 1985, c. 402; 1989, c. 792, s. 2.1; 2013-284, s. 1(a).)

§ 58-86-91: Repealed by Session Laws 2013-284, s. 1(a), effective July 1, 2013.

§ 58-86-95. Leaves of absence; inactive membership.

(a)   Any member who resigns as an eligible firefighter or an eligible rescue squad worker, whichever is applicable, may withdraw from the fund and seek a refund under G.S. 58-86-60 or take a leave of absence as provided by G.S. 58-86-95, or he or she will be considered an inactive member.

(b)   In order to take a leave of absence, any member not on active military service must provide the office of the director with written notice that the member is taking a leave of absence. Any member not on active military service on leave of absence for more than five years in any six-year period shall be considered an inactive member.

(c)   A member is not eligible for service credit for the time he or she is on leave of absence and is not required to make monthly payments for that time. During the time a member is on leave of absence he or she is not eligible for benefits from the pension fund. A member who has taken a leave of absence may subsequently withdraw from the pension fund and seek a refund under G.S. 58-86-60. If a member dies while he or she is on leave of absence, the appropriate person or persons may seek a refund under G.S. 58-86-60.

(d)   Any member not on active military service who does not make contributions for two consecutive years and has not taken a leave of absence shall be considered an inactive member.

(e)   The director of the pension fund shall communicate annually with each eligible fire department and eligible rescue or emergency medical services squad and transmit a list of those persons on a leave of absence. The director may consult with eligible fire departments and eligible rescue or emergency medical services squads with regard to the presumed status of members.

(f)   The director of the pension fund shall maintain records of all inactive members of the fund, including dates of termination of service at an eligible fire department and eligible rescue or emergency medical services squad, and may consult with eligible fire departments and eligible rescue or emergency medical services squads with regard to the presumed status of members.

(g)   Members on active military service must notify the director prior to commencement of active military service and subsequent to return from active duty and shall be granted a leave of absence for the entire time of the military service.

(h)   If a member who is in service and has not received 20 years of fully credited service in this System on December 1, 2013, is convicted of an offense listed in G.S. 58-86-100 for acts committed after December 1, 2013, then that member shall forfeit all benefits under this System, except for a return of member contributions. If a member who is in service and has not received 20 years of fully credited service in this System on December 1, 2013, is convicted of an offense listed in G.S. 58-86-100 for acts committed after December 1, 2013, then that member is not entitled to any fully credited service that accrued after December 1, 2013. (2013-284, s. 1(a); 2013-284, ss. 1(a), 2(c).)

§ 58-86-100. Forfeiture of retirement benefits for certain felonies that would bring disrepute on a fire department or rescue squad.

(a)   Except as provided in G.S. 58-86-95(h), the Board of Trustees shall not pay any retirement benefits or allowances, except for a return of member contributions, to any member who is convicted of any felony under federal law or the laws of this State if all of the following apply:

(1)   The offense is committed while the member is not yet 55 years of age or has not yet received 20 years of fully credited service or while the member is 55 years of age or older and has 20 years of fully credited service but is still serving as a participant in an eligible fire department or eligible rescue squad.

(2)   The conduct resulting in the member's conviction is directly related to service as a firefighter or rescue squad worker and brings disrepute on a fire department or rescue squad.

(b)   Subdivision (2) of subsection (a) of this section shall apply to felony convictions where the court finds under G.S. 15A-1340.16(d)(9a) or other applicable State or federal procedure that the offense is directly related to service as a firefighter or rescue squad worker.

(c)   If a member or former member whose benefits under the System were forfeited under this section, except for the return of member contributions, subsequently receives an unconditional pardon of innocence or the conviction is vacated or set aside for any reason, then the member or former member may seek a reversal of the benefit forfeiture by presenting sufficient evidence to the State Treasurer. If the State Treasurer determines a reversal of the benefit forfeiture is appropriate, then all benefits will be restored upon repayment of all accumulated contributions. Repayment of all accumulated contributions that have been received by the individual under the forfeiture provisions of this section must be made in a total lump-sum payment. An individual receiving a reversal of benefit forfeiture must receive reinstatement of the service credit forfeited. (2013-284, s. 2(a).)

Article 87.

Volunteer Safety Workers Assistance.

§ 58-87-1. Volunteer Fire Department Fund.

(a) Fund. - The Volunteer Fire Department Fund is created as an interest-bearing, nonreverting fund in the Department to provide matching grants to volunteer fire departments to purchase equipment and make capital improvements. The Commissioner shall administer the Fund. Up to one percent (1%) of the Fund may be used for additional staff and resources to administer the Fund in each fiscal year.

(a1) Grant Program. - An eligible fire department may apply to the Commissioner for a grant under this section. In awarding grants under this section, the Commissioner must, to the extent possible, select applicants from all parts of the State based upon need. The Commissioner must award the grants on May 15 of each year subject to the following limitations:

(1) The size of a grant may not exceed thirty thousand dollars ($30,000).

(2) The applicant shall match the grant on a dollar-for-dollar basis.

(3) The grant may be used only for equipment purchases, payment of highway use taxes on those purchases, or capital expenditures necessary to provide fire protection services.

(4) An applicant may receive no more than one grant per fiscal year.

(b) Eligible Fire Department. - A fire department is eligible for a grant under this section if it meets all of the conditions of this subsection. No fire department may be declared ineligible for a grant solely because it is classified as a municipal fire department.

(1) It serves a response area of 12,000 or less in population. In making the population determination, the Department must use the most recent annual population estimates certified by the State Budget Officer.

(2) It consists entirely of volunteer members, with the exception that the unit may have paid members to fill the equivalent of six full-time paid positions.

(3) It has been certified by the Department of Insurance.

(c) Report. - The Commissioner must submit a written report to the General Assembly within 60 days after the grants have been made. This report must contain the amount of the grant and the name of the recipient. (1987, c. 709, s. 1; 1987 (Reg. Sess., 1988), c. 1062, ss. 6-9; 1989, c. 770, s. 30; 1995, c. 507, s. 7.21A(k); 1998-212, s. 25(a); 1999-319, s. 1; 2004-203, s. 5(c); 2006-196, s. 8; 2007-250, s. 3; 2013-360, s. 20.2(b).)

§ 58-87-5. Volunteer Rescue/EMS Fund.

(a) There is created in the Department of Insurance the Volunteer Rescue/EMS Fund to provide grants to volunteer rescue units providing rescue or rescue and emergency medical services to purchase equipment and make capital improvements. An eligible rescue or rescue/EMS unit may apply to the Department of Insurance for a grant under this section. The application form and criteria for grants shall be established by the Department. The North Carolina Association of Rescue and Emergency Medical Services, Inc., shall provide the Department with an advisory priority listing for rescue equipment eligible for funding, and the Department of Health and Human Services shall provide the Department with an advisory priority listing of EMS equipment eligible for funding. The State Treasurer shall invest the Fund's assets according to law, and the earnings shall remain in the Fund. On December 15 of each year, the Department shall make grants to eligible rescue or rescue/EMS units subject to all of the following limitations:

(1) A grant to an applicant who is required to match the grant with non-State funds may not exceed twenty-five thousand dollars ($25,000), and a grant to an applicant who is not required to match the grant with non-State funds may not exceed three thousand dollars ($3,000).

(2) An applicant whose liquid assets, when combined with the liquid assets of any corporate affiliate or subsidiary of the applicant, are more than one thousand dollars ($1,000) shall match the grant on a dollar-for-dollar basis with non-State funds.

(3) The grant may be used only for equipment purchases or capital expenditures.

(4) An applicant may receive no more than one grant per fiscal year.

In awarding grants under this section, the Department shall to the extent possible select applicants from all parts of the State based upon need. Up to two percent (2%) of the Fund may be used for additional staff and resources to administer the Fund in each fiscal year. In addition, notwithstanding G.S. 58-78-20, up to four percent (4%) of the Fund may be used for additional staff and resources for the North Carolina Fire and Rescue Commission.

(b) A rescue, emergency medical services, or rescue/EMS unit is eligible for a grant under this section if it meets all of the following conditions:

(1) Repealed by Session Laws 1989 (Regular Session, 1990), c. 1066, s. 33(a).

(2) It consists entirely of volunteer members, with the exception that the unit may have paid members to fill the equivalent of 10 full-time paid positions.

(3) It has been recognized by the Department as an organization that provides rescue, emergency medical services, or rescue and emergency medical services. A unit that provides emergency medical services only is eligible for grant funding only after all those eligible rescue or rescue and emergency medical services units that are approved have been funded each grant year. A unit that only provides emergency medical services may be funded up to the level of emergency medical services that the unit is approved to provide by the authority having jurisdiction.

(4) It satisfies the eligibility criteria established by the Department under subsection (a) of this section.

(c) For the purpose of this section and Article 88 of this Chapter, "rescue" means the removal of individuals facing external, nonmedical, and nonpatient related peril to areas of relative safety. A "rescue unit" or "rescue squad" means a group of individuals who are not necessarily trained in emergency medical services, fire fighting, or law enforcement, but who expose themselves to an external, nonmedical, and nonpatient related peril to effect the removal of individuals facing the same type of peril to areas of relative safety. The unit or squad must comply with existing State statutes and with eligibility criteria established by the North Carolina Association of Rescue and Emergency Medical Services, Inc. (1987 (Reg. Sess., 1988), c. 1062, s. 2; 1989, c. 115; c. 534, s. 2; 1989 (Reg. Sess., 1990), c. 1066, s. 33(a); 1991 (Reg. Sess., 1992), c. 943, s. 2; 1995, c. 507, s. 7.21A(l); 1997-443, s. 11A.20; 1998-212, s. 25(b); 1999-319, s. 2; 2005-283, s. 1.)

§ 58-87-7. Oversight and accountability of grant awards.

To increase accountability and to expedite receipt of certain grant awards, notwithstanding any other provision, the Office of the State Fire Marshal and other employees of the Department of Insurance may in their discretion conduct on-site examinations of fire, rescue, and EMS equipment and supplies purchased with funds awarded from either the Volunteer Fire Department Fund or the Volunteer Rescue/EMS Fund. The on-site examinations may include the inspection of equipment purchased from prior grants and may be conducted prior to or simultaneous with the delivery of the grant awards. The on-site examination shall document what equipment and supplies have been purchased by the volunteer fire department or volunteer rescue/EMS department and whether those items were received by the department and visually reviewed by the on-site examiner. Items that have already been distributed or put in the field shall be noted by the on-site examiner. The Office of the State Fire Marshal shall maintain records of on-site inspections and provide them, or a summary thereof, in reports to the State Auditor or the Office of State Budget and Management. (2010-22, s. 11.)

§ 58-87-10. Workers' Compensation Fund for the benefit of volunteer safety workers.

(a) Definition. - As used in this section, the term "eligible unit" means a volunteer fire department or volunteer rescue/EMS unit that is not part of a unit of local government and is exempt from State income tax under G.S. 105-130.11.

(b) Creation. - The Workers' Compensation Fund is created in the Department of Insurance as an expendable trust fund. Accordingly, interest and other investment income earned by the Fund accrues to it, and revenue in the Fund at the end of a fiscal year remains in the Fund and does not revert.

(c) Use. - Revenue in the Workers' Compensation Fund shall be used to provide workers' compensation benefits to members of eligible units. Chapter 97 of the General Statutes governs the payment of benefits from the Fund. Benefits are payable for compensable injuries or deaths that occur on or after July 1, 1996.

(d) Administration. - The State Fire and Rescue Commission, established under G.S. 58-78-1, shall administer the Workers' Compensation Fund and shall perform this duty by contracting with a third-party administrator. The contracting procedure is not subject to Article 3C of Chapter 143 of the General Statutes. The reasonable and necessary expenses incurred by the Commission in administering the Fund shall be paid out of the Fund by the State Treasurer. The Commission may adopt rules to implement this section.

(e) Revenue Source. - Revenue is credited to the Workers' Compensation Fund from a portion of the proceeds of the tax levied under G.S. 105-228.5(d)(3). In addition, every eligible unit that elects to participate shall pay into the Fund an amount set annually by the State Fire and Rescue Commission to ensure that the Fund will be able to meet its payment obligations under this section. The amount shall be set as a per capita fixed dollar amount for each member of the roster of the eligible unit.

The payment shall be made to the State Fire and Rescue Commission on or before July 1 of each year. The Commission shall remit the payments it receives to the State Treasurer, who shall credit the payments to the Fund.

(f) (Effective until April 1, 2016) The amount of the tax imposed by G.S. 105-228.5(d)(3) credited to the Workers' Compensation Fund shall be the maximum allowed under that statute.

(f) (Effective April 1, 2016) Funding Study. - The Department of Insurance shall conduct a periodic actuarial study to calculate the amount required to meet the needs of the Fund. The study shall be based on a revenue amount that is the greater of the amount paid by members of the Fund as determined under subsection (e) of this section for the fiscal year to which the study applies or the amount paid by members of the Fund as determined under subsection (e) of this section for fiscal year 2012-2013. The study shall be reviewed by the Office of State Budget and Management. On or before March 1 of each year, the Office of State Budget and Management, in consultation with the Department of Insurance, must notify the Secretary of Revenue of the amount required to meet the needs of the Fund, as determined by the study, for the upcoming fiscal year. The Secretary of Revenue shall remit that amount, subject to the twenty percent (20%) limitation in G.S. 105-228.5(d)(3), to the Fund. (1995, c. 507, s. 7.21A(a); 1999-132, s. 1.2; 2013-360, s. 20.2(d), (e).)

Article 88.

Rescue Squad Workers' Relief Fund.

§ 58-88-1. Definitions.

As used in this Article:

(1) "Association" means the North Carolina Association of Rescue and Emergency Medical Services, Inc.

(2) "Board" means the Board of Trustees of the Fund.

(3) "EMS" means emergency medical services.

(4) "Fund" means the Rescue Squad Workers' Relief Fund.

(5) "Secretary-Treasurer" means the Secretary-Treasurer of the Association. (1987, c. 584, s. 5.)

§ 58-88-5. Rescue Squad Workers' Relief Fund; trustees; disbursement of funds.

(a) The "Rescue Squad Workers' Relief Fund" is created. It consists of the revenue credited to the Fund under G.S. 20-183.7(c) and shall be used for the purposes set forth in this Article.

(b) The Executive Committee of the Association shall be the Board of Trustees of the Fund. The Board shall consist of the Commander, Vice-Commander, Secretary-Treasurer, and two past Commanders of the Association. The Commander shall be the Chairman of the Board. The Commander, Vice-Commander, and Secretary-Treasurer shall appoint the two past Commanders of the Association, who shall serve at the pleasure of the appointing officers.

(c) The Commissioner of Insurance has exclusive control of the Fund and shall disburse revenue in the Fund to the Association only for the following purposes:

(1) To safeguard any rescue or EMS worker in active service from financial loss, occasioned by sickness contracted or injury received while in the performance of his or her duties as a rescue or EMS worker.

(2) To provide a reasonable support for those persons actually dependent upon the services of any rescue or EMS worker who may lose his or her life in the service of his or her town, county, city, or the State, either by accident or from disease contracted or injury received by reason of such service. The amount is to be determined according to the earning capacity of the deceased.

(3) To award scholarships to children of members, deceased members or retired members in good standing, for the purpose of attending a two year or four year college or university, and for the purpose of attending a two year course of study at a community college or an accredited trade or technical school, any of which is located in the State of North Carolina. Continuation of the payment of educational benefits for children of active members shall be

conditioned on the continuance of active membership in the rescue or EMS service by the parent or parents.

(4)   To pay death benefits to those persons who were actually dependent upon any member killed in the line of duty.

(4a)   To pay additional benefits approved by the Board of Trustees of the Fund to rescue and EMS workers who are eligible pursuant to G.S. 58-88-10 and who are members of the Association.

(5)   Notwithstanding any other provision of law, no expenditures shall be made pursuant to subdivisions (1), (2), (3), (4), and (4a) of this subsection unless the Board has certified that the expenditures will not render the Fund actuarially unsound for the purpose of providing the benefits set forth in subdivisions (1), (2), (3), (4), and (4a). If, for any reason, funds made available for subdivisions (1), (2), (3), (4), and (4a) are insufficient to pay in full any benefit, the benefits pursuant to subdivisions (1), (2), (3), (4), and (4a) shall be reduced pro rata for as long as the amount of insufficient funds exists. No claims shall accrue with respect to any amount by which a benefit under subdivisions (1), (2), (3), (4), and (4a) has been reduced. (1987, c. 584, s. 5; 1987 (Reg. Sess., 1988), c. 1062, s. 10; 1989 (Reg. Sess., 1990), c. 1066, s. 33(c); 1995, c. 421, s. 1.)

§ 58-88-10. Membership eligibility.

(a)   Any member of a rescue squad or EMS service who is eligible for membership in the Association and who has attended a minimum of 36 hours of training and meetings in the last calendar year; and each rescue squad or EMS service whose members are eligible for membership in the Association who has filed a roster certifying to the Secretary-Treasurer who certifies to the Commissioner of Insurance by January 1 of each calender year that all eligible members have met the requirements, shall be eligible for the Fund. Any eligible member who, in the actual discharge of his or her duties as rescue or EMS personnel, is (1) made sick by disease contracted or (2) becomes disabled, shall be entitled to the benefits from the Fund.

(b)   Any organized rescue squad or EMS service in North Carolina holding itself ready for duty may, upon compliance with the requirements of the constitution and by-laws of the Association, be eligible for membership in the Fund.

(c)   The line of duty entitling one to participate in the Fund shall be so construed as to mean actual rescue or EMS duty only. (1987, c. 584, s. 5.)

§ 58-88-15. Accounting; reports; audits.

The Board shall keep a correct account of all monies received and disbursed by the Board; and shall annually file a report with the Commissioner of Insurance at such time and in such form prescribed by the Commissioner of Insurance and the State Auditor. The Board shall be bonded by the sum of any money total for which it is responsible. The books, records, and operations of the Board shall be subject to the oversight of the State Auditor pursuant to Article 5A of Chapter 147 of the General Statutes. (1987, c. 584, s. 5; 1993, c. 257, s. 3.)

§ 58-88-20. Justification of claim.

The eligibility of the claimant and the justification of each claim shall be certified by the chief or chief officer of the local department before a magistrate, notary public, or other officer authorized to administer oaths, on a form furnished by the Secretary-Treasurer. This form must be accompanied by a certificate of the attending physician on a form also to be furnished by the Secretary-Treasurer. Each person receiving benefits from the Fund shall file an annual justification of claim form with the Secretary-Treasurer stating that the need for the claim still exists. (1987, c. 584, s. 5.)

§ 58-88-25. Application for benefits.

Applications for benefits from the Fund shall be made to the Secretary-Treasurer under the following conditions and procedure: Within 30 days after the contracting of a disease or the occurrence of accident for which benefits are sought, the chief or chief officer of the local department shall notify the Secretary-Treasurer in writing that the person applying for benefits is a member of the Fund and request the necessary forms from the Secretary-Treasurer's office to be submitted for the benefits. (1987, c. 584, s. 5.)

§ 58-88-30. Administration costs.

The Association shall withhold twelve percent (12%) from the money received pursuant to G.S. 20-183.7(c) for the administration of the Fund. The Commissioner of Insurance shall withhold two percent (2%) from the money received pursuant to G.S. 20-183.7(c) for the administration of the Fund. (1987, c. 584, s. 5; 1989 (Reg. Sess., 1990), c. 1066, s. 33(d); 1991 (Reg. Sess., 1992), c. 943, s. 3; 2008-107, s. 29.9(a).)

Article 89.

Repealed.

§§ 58-89-1 through 58-89-30: Repealed by Session Laws 2004-162, s. 1, effective January 1, 2005.

Article 89A.

North Carolina Professional Employer Organization Act.

Part 1. In General.

§ 58-89A-1. Title.

This Article shall be known and may be cited as the "North Carolina Professional Employer Organization Act". (2002-168, s. 8; 2004-162, s. 1.)

§ 58-89A-5. Definitions.

In this Article:

(1) "Applicant" means a person applying for a license or a group license under this Article.

(2) "Assigned employee" means an employee who is performing services for a client company under a contract between a licensee and a client company in which employment responsibilities are shared or allocated. "Assigned employee" does not include a temporary employee. Individuals who are directors, shareholders, partners, and managers of a client company are assigned employees to the extent the licensee and the client have agreed that those individuals are assigned employees and provided that those individuals meet the criteria of this subdivision and act as operational managers or perform reviews for the client company.

(3) "Audited GAAP financial statement" means a financial statement that is audited by an independent certified public accountant and presented in accordance with generally accepted accounting principles.

(4) "Client company" or "client" means a person that contracts with a licensee and is assigned employees by the licensee under that contract.

(5) "Control", including the terms "controlling", "controlled by", and "under common control with" means the direct or indirect possession of the power to direct or cause the direction of the management and policies of a person, whether through the ownership of voting securities, by contract other than a commercial contract for goods or nonmanagement services, or otherwise. Control is presumed to exist if any natural person directly or indirectly owns, controls, holds with the power to vote, or holds proxies representing ten percent (10%) or more of the voting securities of any other person. This presumption may be rebutted by a showing made in the manner provided by rule of the Commissioner. The Commissioner may determine, after furnishing all persons in interest notice and opportunity to be heard and making specific findings of fact to support such determination, that control exists in fact, notwithstanding the absence of a presumption to that effect.

(6) "Financial responsibility" means the current and expected future condition of financial solvency sufficient to support a reasonable expectation

that an applicant or licensee can successfully conduct its business without jeopardizing the interests of its assigned employees, client companies, or the public.

(7)   "Good moral character" means a personal history of honesty, trustworthiness, fairness, a good reputation for fair dealings, and respect for the rights of others and for state and federal laws.

(8)   Repealed by Session Laws 2013-413, s. 11.1(a), effective October 1, 2013.

(9)   "Licensee" means a person licensed under this Article to provide professional employer services. The term includes a professional employer organization group licensed under G.S. 58-89A-35(b). Unless specifically stated otherwise in this Article, "licensee" includes persons who are licensed under this Article pursuant to alternative licensing procedures as set forth in G.S. 58-89A-76.

(10)   "Managed services" means services provided by an organization that is the sole employer of employees whom it supplies to staff and manage a specific portion of a company's workforce or a specific facility within a company on an ongoing basis. The managed services organization has responsibility for ensuring the capabilities and skills of the employees it supplies or provides, for all employer functions, for supervisory responsibility over the employees, and for management accountability of the facility or function.

(11)   "PEO agreement" means a written contract by and between a client company and a professional employer organization that provides:

a.   For the allocation and sharing between the client company and the licensee of the responsibilities of employers with respect to the assigned employees, including hiring, firing, and disciplining of employees; and

b.   That the licensee and the client company assume the responsibilities required by this Article.

(12)   "Person" has the same meaning as in G.S. 58-1-5(9).

(13)   "Personnel placement service" means a job placement service offered through an organization that assists persons seeking employment to find a job with companies that are seeking employees. Companies that hire persons

through a personnel placement service are the sole employers of the persons hired, and the personnel placement service does not have any responsibility as an employer.

(14) "Professional employer organization" or "PEO" means a person that offers professional employer services and includes "staff leasing services companies", "employee leasing companies", "staff leasing companies", and "administrative employers" who offer or propose to offer professional employer services in this State.

(15) "Professional employer organization group" or "PEO group" means a combination of professional employer organizations that operates under a group license issued under this Article or is otherwise subject to group licensure requirements under G.S. 58-89A-35(b).

(16) "Professional employer services" means an arrangement by which employees of a licensee are assigned to work at a client company and in which employment responsibilities are in fact shared by the licensee and the client company in accordance with G.S. 58-89A-100, the employee's assignment is intended to be of a long-term or continuing nature, rather than temporary or seasonal in nature. "Professional employer services" does not include services that provide temporary employees or independent contractors, a personnel placement service, managed services, payroll services that do not involve employee staffing or leasing, the sharing of employees by commonly owned companies within the meaning of section 414(b) and (c) of the Internal Revenue Code of 1986, as amended, or similar groups that do not meet the requirements of this subdivision.

(17) "Temporary employees" means persons employed under an arrangement by which an organization hires its own employees and assigns them to a client company to support or supplement the client's workforce in a special work situation, including:

a. An employee absence;

b. A temporary skill shortage;

c. A seasonal workload; or

d. A special assignment or project. (2002-168, s. 8; 2004-162, s. 1; 2007-127, s. 12; 2013-413, s. 11.1(a).)

§ 58-89A-10: Repealed by Session Laws 2008-124, s. 7.3, effective October 1, 2008.

§ 58-89A-15. Rules.

(a)   The Commissioner may adopt rules necessary to implement, administer, and enforce the provisions of this Article.

(b)   Each licensee and each person subject to licensure requirements under this Article are subject to the provisions of this Article and to the rules adopted by the Commissioner.

(c)   Nothing in this Article preempts the existing statutory or rule-making authority of any other State agency or entity to regulate professional employer services in a manner consistent with the statutory authority of that State agency or entity. (2002-168, s. 8; 2004-162, s. 1.)

§ 58-89A-20. Interagency cooperation.

A State agency, in performing duties under other law that affects the regulation of professional employer services, shall cooperate with the Commissioner as necessary to implement, administer, and enforce this Article. (2004-162, s. 1.)

§ 58-89A-25. Effect of other law on client companies and assigned employees.

(a)   This Article does not exempt a client company of a licensee, or any assigned employee, from any other license requirements imposed under local, State, or federal law.

(b)   An employee who is licensed, registered, or certified under law and who is assigned to a client company is considered to be an employee of the client company for the purpose of that license, registration, or certification.

(c) A licensee is not engaged in the unauthorized practice of an occupation, trade, or profession that is licensed, certified, or otherwise regulated by a State agency or other political subdivision of the State, including a county or city, by entering into a PEO agreement with a client company and assigned employees.

(d) With respect to a bid, contract, purchase order, program, or agreement entered into with the State or a political subdivision of the State, or State program or benefit otherwise available to a client company, a client company's status, certification, or qualification pursuant to the bid, contract, benefit, program, agreement, or State program shall not be affected because the client company has entered into an agreement with a licensee or utilizes the services of a licensee.

(e) Nothing in this Article or in any PEO agreement or other professional employer services contract shall affect, modify, or amend any collective bargaining agreement or the rights or obligations of any client company, professional employer organization, or any assigned employee under the National Labor Relations Act, 29 U.S.C. § 151, et seq. (2004-162, s. 1.)

§ 58-89A-30. Other provisions of this chapter.

G.S. 58-2-45, 58-2-50, 58-2-55, 58-2-60, 58-2-65, 58-2-69, 58-2-70, 58-2-75, 58-2-100, 58-2-155, 58-2-163, 58-2-180, 58-2-185, 58-2-200, 58-2-240, and 58-3-100 shall apply to all persons licensed under this Article and all persons subject to licensure requirements under this Article. (2004-162, s. 1; 2007-127, s. 13.)

§ 58-89A-31. Tax credits and other incentives.

For purposes of determination of tax credits and other economic incentives provided by the State or a political subdivision and based on employment, covered employees are considered employees solely of the client. A client shall be entitled to the benefit of any tax credit, economic incentive, or other benefit arising as the result of the employment of covered employees of the client. Each professional employer organization must provide, upon request by a client, employment information that is required by any agency or department of the

State or a political subdivision responsible for administration of any tax credit or economic incentive and that is necessary to support a request, claim, application, or other action by a client seeking the tax credit or economic incentive. For purposes of this section, the term "political subdivision" has the same meaning as in G.S. 162A-65(a)(8). (2004-162, s. 1; 2009-552, s. 4.)

Part 2. License Requirements and Limitations.

§ 58-89A-35. License required; professional employer organization groups.

(a) No person shall engage in or offer professional employer services in this State unless the person holds a license issued under this Article.

(b) Two or more professional employer organizations that are controlled by the same ultimate parent, entity, or persons may be licensed as a professional employer organization group. A professional employer organization group may satisfy the reporting and financial requirements of this Article on a consolidated basis. As a condition of licensure as a professional employer organization group, each professional employer organization that is a member of the group shall guarantee payment of all financial obligations of every other member. Notwithstanding the definition of "person" in this Article, whenever two or more entities combine to seek issuance of a single license under this Article, the requirements for group licensure under this subsection shall be met before issuance of a license and any license issued will be a group license issued pursuant to this subsection. (2002-168, s. 8; 2004-162, s. 1.)

§ 58-89A-40. Qualifications for controlling person.

(a) To be qualified to serve as a controlling person of a licensee under this Article, the controlling person shall be at least 18 years of age, be of good moral character, and have educational, managerial, or business experience relevant to:

(1) Operation of a professional employer organization; or

(2) Service as a controlling person of a professional employer organization.

(b) This section does not apply to persons who are licensed pursuant to the alternative licensing procedures set forth in G.S. 58-89A-76 or to entities that are controlling persons. (2004-162, s. 1.)

§ 58-89A-45. Reserved.

§ 58-89A-50. Surety bond; letter of credit; other deposits.

(a) An applicant for licensure shall file with the Commissioner a surety bond, or other items as set forth in subsection (f) of this section, in the amount of one hundred thousand dollars ($100,000) for the benefit of the Commissioner. An applicant whose current assets do not exceed current liabilities pursuant to G.S. 58-89A-60(b) shall file an additional surety bond or other items set forth in subsection (f) of this section equal to or in excess of current liabilities less current assets.

(b) The surety bond required by this section shall be in a form acceptable to the Commissioner, issued by an insurer authorized by the Commissioner to write surety business in this State, and maintained in force while the license remains in effect or any obligations or liabilities of the applicant, licensee or PEO previously licensed by this State remain outstanding.

(c) The surety bond required by this section may be exchanged or replaced with another surety bond if (i) the surety bond applies to obligations and liabilities that arose during the period of the original surety bond, (ii) the surety bond meets the requirements of this section, and (iii) 90 days' advance written notice is provided to the Commissioner.

(d) Repealed by Session Laws 2013-413, s. 11.2(b), effective October 1, 2013.

(e) Notice of cancellation or nonrenewal of the surety bond required by this section shall be provided to the Commissioner in writing at least 45 days before cancellation or nonrenewal.

(e1) A surety bond may be cancelled by the issuer of the bond with respect to future obligations or liabilities upon proper notice pursuant to this section and without regard to approval or acceptance of the Commissioner.

(f) In lieu of the surety bond required by this section, an applicant may submit to the Commissioner an irrevocable letter of credit in a form acceptable to the Commissioner issued by a financial institution, the deposits of which are insured by the Federal Deposit Insurance Corporation, or may maintain on deposit with the Commissioner an amount equal to the amount required under subsection (a) of this section in cash or in value of securities of the kind specified in G.S. 58-5-20.

(g) This section does not apply to persons who are licensed pursuant to the alternative licensing procedures set forth in G.S. 58-89A-76 or to persons who are de minimis registrants pursuant to G.S. 58-89A-75.

(h) The license of any licensee that fails to provide and maintain a surety bond, letter of credit, cash, or securities pursuant to this section shall be automatically and immediately suspended, and the licensee shall tender its license to the Commissioner within three days of failure to satisfy this requirement. (2004-162, s. 1; 2005-124, s. 1; 2008-124, ss. 7.1, 7.2; 2009-552, s. 1; 2013-413, s. 11.1(b).)

§ 58-89A-55. Reserved.

§ 58-89A-60. License application.

(a) Every applicant for licensure shall file with the Commissioner, on a form prescribed by the Commissioner, the following information:

(1) The name, organizational structure, and date of organization of the applicant, the addresses of the principal office and of all offices in this State, the name of the contact person, the type of operations within this State, and the taxpayer or employer identification number.

(2) A list by jurisdiction of each name under which the applicant has operated in the preceding five years, including any alternative names, names of

predecessors, and, if known, names of successor business entities. The list required by this subdivision shall include the parent company name and any trade name, trademark, or service mark of the applicant.

(3)   A list of all officers and controlling persons of the applicant, their biographical information, including their management background, and an affidavit from each attesting to his or her good moral character and management competence.

(4)   The location of the business records of the applicant.

(5)   An attestation, executed by the chief financial officer and chief executive officer of the applicant, that the applicant is current as of the date the application is submitted with respect to all of its obligations for payroll, payroll-related taxes, workers' compensation insurance, and employee benefits. If any such obligations are in dispute with a client as of the date the application is submitted and the disputed amount is material when considered in the context of the applicant's most recent audited financial statement, then the applicant shall disclose the nature of the dispute causing the obligations to be unpaid and the amount of money in controversy.

(6)   Any other information the Commissioner deems necessary and requires by rule to establish that the applicant and the officers and controlling persons are of good moral character, have business integrity, and have financial responsibility.

(b)   Every applicant shall file with the Commissioner an audited GAAP financial statement, prepared as of a date not more than 90 days before the date of application that demonstrates that the applicant or licensee's current assets exceed current liabilities and attached to which is a separate document signed by the chief executive and the chief financial officer certifying that (i) each has reviewed the financial statement; (ii) based on each signatory's knowledge, the financial statement does not contain any untrue or misleading statement of material fact or omit a fact with respect to the period covered by the financial statement; and (iii) based on each signatory's knowledge, the financial statement fairly presents in all material respects the financial condition of the licensee as of, and for, the period presented in the financial statement.

Notwithstanding the requirements of this subsection, the Commissioner may, in the Commissioner's discretion, accept an audited GAAP financial statement that has been prepared more than 90 days before submission to the Commissioner if the Commissioner deems such acceptance appropriate. The Commissioner may, in the Commissioner's discretion, impose conditions upon such acceptance of financial statements prepared more than 90 days prior to submission.

The audited GAAP financial statement shall be prepared in accordance with generally accepted accounting principles and audited by an independent certified public accountant licensed to practice in the jurisdiction in which such accountant is located and shall be without qualification as to the going concern status of the PEO. A PEO group may submit combined or consolidated audited financial statements to meet the requirements of this section, except that a PEO that has not had sufficient operating history to have audited financial statements based upon at least 12 months of operating history must meet the financial capacity requirements of this subsection and present financial statements reviewed by a certified public accountant.

(c)   Every applicant shall submit to the Commissioner the application fee pursuant to G.S. 58-89A-65.

(d)   Every applicant shall furnish the Commissioner a complete set of fingerprints and a recent photograph in a form prescribed by the Commissioner of each officer, director, and controlling person. Each set of fingerprints shall be certified by an authorized law enforcement officer.

Upon request by the Department, the Department of Justice shall provide to the Department from the State and National Repositories of Criminal Histories the criminal history of any applicant and the officer, director, and controlling person of any applicant. Along with the request, the Department shall provide to the Department of Justice the fingerprints of the person that is the subject of the request, a form signed by the person that is the subject of the request consenting to the criminal record check and use of fingerprints and other identifying information required by the State and National Repositories, and any additional information required by the Department of Justice. The person's fingerprints shall be forwarded to the State Bureau of Investigation for a search of the State's criminal history record file, and the State Bureau of Investigation may forward a set of fingerprints to the Federal Bureau of Investigation for a national criminal history record check. The Department shall keep all information obtained pursuant to this subsection confidential. The Department of Justice may charge a fee to offset the cost incurred by it to conduct a criminal record check under this section. The fee shall not exceed the actual cost of locating, editing, researching, and retrieving the information.

In the event that an applicant has secured a professional employer organization license in another state in which the professional employer organization's controlling persons have completed a criminal background investigation within 12 months of this application, a certified copy of the report from the appropriate authority of that state may satisfy the requirement of this subsection. This subsection also applies to a change in a controlling party of a professional employer organization. For purposes of investigation under this subsection, the Commissioner shall have all the power conferred by G.S. 58-2-50 and other applicable provisions of this Chapter.

(e) An application for licensure of a professional employer organization group shall contain the information and submissions required by this section for each member of the group.

(f) No application is complete until the Commissioner has received all information and submissions required under subsections (a) through (e) of this section. Subsections (a) through (e) of this section do not apply to persons who are licensed pursuant to the alternative licensing procedures set forth in G.S. 58-89A-76.

(g) The Commissioner may deny the license of an applicant under this Article if, after notice to the applicant and an opportunity for a hearing, the Commissioner finds that a controlling person has:

(1) Made any untrue material statement regarding the background or experience of any controlling person;

(2) Violated, or failed to comply with, any professional employer services law or any rule or order of the Commissioner or of any other State official responsible for the regulation of professional employer services;

(3) Obtained or attempted to obtain the license through misrepresentation or fraud;

(4) Been convicted of a felony;

(5) Been found in a final judgment or administrative proceeding to have committed fraud or an unfair trade practice; or

(6) Been a controlling person in another professional employer organization that has had its license or registration suspended, terminated, or revoked by any state.

(h) If the Commissioner finds that the applicant has not fully met the requirements for licensure, the Commissioner shall refuse to issue the license and shall notify the applicant in writing of the denial, stating the grounds for the denial. The application may also be denied for any reason for which a license may be suspended or terminated under G.S. 58-89A-155. To obtain a review to determine the reasonableness of the Commissioner's denial, the applicant shall make written demand upon the Commissioner within 30 days after notice is given under G.S. 150B-38(c). The review shall be completed without undue delay, and the applicant shall be notified promptly in writing as to the outcome of the review. If the applicant disagrees with the outcome of the review and seeks a hearing, under Article 3A of Chapter 150B of the General Statutes, on the outcome of the review, the applicant shall make a written demand upon the Commissioner for the hearing within 30 days after notice of the outcome of the review is given under G.S. 150B-38(c).

(i) Removal, demotion, or discharge of a controlling person in response to an order of the Commissioner of the alleged unsuitability of that person is an affirmative defense to any claim by that individual based on the removal, demotion, or discharge.

(j) The Commissioner may, in the Commissioner's discretion, waive the required evaluation of an officer, director or controlling person if that officer, director or controlling person has been evaluated previously under this Article.

(k) After denial, suspension, or termination of a license, and before issuing a new license or reinstating a license, the Commissioner shall review and consider:

(1) The extent to which the applicant or licensee has adequately corrected any problems; and

(2) Whether the applicant or licensee has demonstrated that the applicant or licensee had exercised due diligence to avoid the reason or reasons for the denial or termination.

The applicant or licensee bears the burden of proof with respect to subdivisions (1) and (2) of this subsection. (2002-168, s.8; 2004-162, s. 1; 2013-413, s. 11.1(c).)

§ 58-89A-65. Fees.

(a) Each applicant for a professional employer organization license or de minimis registration shall pay to the Commissioner, before the issuance of the license, a nonrefundable application fee of one thousand dollars ($1,000).

(b) Each licensee shall pay to the Commissioner when filing the information required under G.S. 58-89A-70(d) an annual filing fee of one thousand dollars ($1,000).

(c) Each applicant for alternative licensing under G.S. 58-89A-76 and each applicant for renewal of a license provided under G.S. 58-89A-76 shall pay to the Commissioner, before issuance or renewal of the license, a fee of five hundred dollars ($500.00).

(d) When the Commissioner finds that a licensee has committed an act that is a ground for disciplinary violation under G.S. 58-89A-155 or that a licensee has committed a prohibited act in violation of G.S. 58-89A-170, and such decision becomes final following the conclusion of all administrative or judicial proceedings, the Commissioner may charge an applicant or licensee reasonable fees to recover the Department's costs associated with investigations, inspections, examinations, and any other administrative or enforcement responsibilities created under this Article.

(e) Fees collected by the Commissioner under this Article shall be deposited in the Insurance Regulatory Fund under G.S. 58-6-25 and shall be used to implement this Article. (2002-168, s. 8; 2004-162, s. 1; 2005-124, s. 2.)

§ 58-89A-70. License issuance and maintenance.

(a) The Commissioner shall issue a license to an applicant whom the Commissioner determines has satisfied the requirements of this Article not later than the 90th day after the date on which the completed application is filed with the Commissioner. The Commissioner shall notify an applicant of any deficiency in the application not later than the 60th day after the date on which the Commissioner receives the application.

(b)   A license issued by the Commissioner under this Article shall remain in effect until revoked, suspended, surrendered, or otherwise terminated.

(c)   By obtaining licensure under this Article, the controlling persons of a licensee certify, under penalty of law, their compliance with the requirements of licensure and of operation as a professional employer organization pursuant to this Article.

(d)   Within 120 days after the end of each fiscal year, each licensee shall file with the Commissioner all of the following information:

(1)   Evidence of "financial responsibility" as set forth in G.S. 58-89A-60(b).

(2)   Any information required by G.S. 58-89A-60(a) for which there has been a change since the last or initial filing. Any change of controlling persons may subject the licensee to a background investigation of those controlling persons as required by G.S. 58-89A-60.

(3)   The annual filing fee, pursuant to G.S. 58-89A-65.

(4)   Any other information the Commissioner determines is needed for the review of a licensee.

(e)   In order to maintain licensure, each licensee may be required to file with the Commissioner no later than 45 days after the end of each quarter of the fiscal year:

(1)   A financial statement for the preceding quarter that is not audited but is set forth in a format similar to the annual audited GAAP financial statement; and

(2)   An attestation, executed by the chief financial officer and the chief executive officer of the licensee, that the licensee is current with respect to all of its obligations for payroll, payroll-related taxes, workers' compensation insurance, and employee benefits. If any of the obligations listed in this subdivision are in dispute with a client and the disputed amount is material when considered in the context of the licensee's most recent audited financial statement, then the licensee shall disclose the nature of the dispute causing the

obligations to be unpaid and the amount of money in controversy. (2004-162, s. 1.)

§ 58-89A-75. De minimis registration.

(a) A person who seeks to offer limited professional employer services in this State shall be eligible for de minimis registration status upon compliance with this section and may operate as a de minimis registrant in this State upon notification pursuant to this section. A person shall satisfy the requirements for a de minimis registration only if the professional employer organization:

(1) Does not maintain a physical professional employer organization office located in this State;

(2) Does not employ salespersons who reside or direct their sales activities in this State;

(3) Does not employ directly or in common control with another person, as defined in G.S. 58-89A-5(12), more than 50 assigned employees in this State;

(4) Does not advertise through any media outlet physically located in this State;

(5) Is a licensed or registered professional employer organization in at least one other state of the United States; and

(6) Is operated by and under the control of persons of good moral character.

A professional employer organization operating under a de minimis registration shall be subject to all of the responsibilities and authority of a licensee under this Article except for G.S. 58-89A-50, 58-89A-60 and 58-89A-70(c), (d), and (e).

(b) A person seeking de minimis registration status shall notify the Commissioner, on a form prescribed by the Commissioner, attesting that the professional employer organization meets all of the eligibility requirements for de minimis registration status under this section and additionally provide, at a minimum, the following information:

(1) The name of the professional employer organization, the address of its principal office, the name of the contact person, and the taxpayer or employer identification number;

(2) A list by jurisdiction of each name under which the registrant has operated in the preceding five years, including any alternative names, names of predecessors, and, if known, successor business entities;

(3) A list of all officers, directors, and controlling person(s) of the registrant and their biographical information in a form to be determined by the Commissioner; and

(4) The location of the business records of the person.

(c) If the Commissioner finds that the person seeking de minimis registration has not fully met the requirements for de minimis registration, the person shall not be eligible for de minimis registration status, and the Commissioner shall notify the person in writing. Within 30 days after service of the notification, the person may make a written demand upon the Commissioner for a review to determine the reasonableness of the Commissioner's action. The review shall be completed without undue delay, and the person shall be notified promptly in writing as to the outcome of the review. Within 30 days after service of the notification as to the outcome, the person may make a written demand upon the Commissioner for a hearing under Article 3A of Chapter 150B of the General Statutes if the person disagrees with the outcome.

(d) If the Commissioner determines that the notification of eligibility for de minimis registration is incomplete, the Commissioner shall notify the person of the deficiency, and the registrant shall be allowed time, not to exceed 30 days from the date of the notice, to correct the deficiency. Failure of the person to correct the deficiency within the 30-day time period shall result in the de minimis being deemed denied. Except as otherwise provided in this section, a person notified of a deficiency under this section may continue to operate while the deficiency is being corrected unless the Commissioner determines that the person is ineligible for de minimis registration status or is otherwise not authorized to operate in this State.

(e) After a de minimis registrant's initial notification, a de minimis registrant shall annually notify the Commissioner of its continuing eligibility for de minimis registration status no earlier than January 1 and no later than January 15 of each year. The annual notification shall include the attestation of eligibility for de minimis registration and any change in the information previously provided to the Commissioner under this section.

(f) A person operating under a de minimis registration to engage in professional employer services in North Carolina that ceases to satisfy any of the requirements for de minimis registration under this section shall apply for a professional employer organization license. The de minimis registrant may continue to operate in North Carolina pending approval of the registrant's application for a license provided the application is filed with the Commissioner no later than 30 days after the professional employer organization becomes ineligible for de minimis registration. If the application for licensure is denied or is not filed as prescribed in this section, the de minimis registrant must cease engaging in professional employer services in North Carolina. (2004-162, s. 1; 2005-124, s. 3; 2007-127, s. 14; 2009-570, s. 9.)

§ 58-89A-76. Alternative licensing.

The Commissioner, by rule, may provide for the acceptance of an affidavit by a bonded, independent, and qualified assurance organization that has been approved by the Commissioner certifying the qualifications of a professional employer organization for licensing under this Article in lieu of the requirements of G.S. 58-89A-40 through G.S. 58-89A-60. A professional employer organization licensed under this section shall be exempt from the provisions of G.S. 58-89A-70(c), (d), and (e). (2004-162, s. 1.)

§ 58-89A-80. License not assignable; change of name or location.

(a) A licensee shall not conduct business under any name other than that specified in the license. A license issued under this Article is not assignable. A licensee shall not conduct business under any fictitious or assumed name without prior written authorization from the Commissioner. The Commissioner shall not authorize the use of a name that is so similar to that of a public office or agency or to that of another licensee that the public may be confused or misled by the name's use. A licensee shall not conduct business under more than one name unless the licensee has obtained a separate license for each name or the licensee is operating under a group license pursuant to G.S. 58-89A-35.

(b) Except as provided in this subsection, a licensee may change the licensee's licensed name only once in a calendar year by notifying the Commissioner and paying a fee for the change of name. The fee for a name change shall be fifty dollars ($50.00). A licensee may change the licensee's name without the payment of the name change fee if the name change is submitted with the information required by G.S. 58-89A-70(d). If a licensee has changed its name once during a calendar year, the licensee shall not change its name again unless the name change is approved by the Commissioner.

(c) A licensee shall notify the Commissioner in writing within 30 days of any change in the status of the licensee, including:

(1) Any change in the location of the licensee's primary business office;

(2) The addition of or change in the location of any other business offices providing professional employer services in this State; and

(3) A change in the location of business records maintained by the licensee.

(d) A licensee may advertise in this State using only the name that is on the license issued by the Commissioner.

(e) Each written proposal provided to a prospective client company and each PEO agreement between a licensee and a client company or assigned employee shall clearly identify the name of the licensee. (2004-162, s. 1.)

§ 58-89A-85. Supervision; rehabilitation; liquidation.

If at any time the Commissioner determines, after notice and an opportunity for the licensee to be heard, that a licensee (i) has been or will be unable, in such a manner as may endanger the ability of the licensee, to fully perform its obligations pursuant to this Article or (ii) is bankrupt, the Commissioner may either (i) commence a supervision proceeding pursuant to Article 30 of this Chapter or (ii) apply to the Superior Court of Wake County or to the federal bankruptcy court that has previously taken jurisdiction over the licensee, if applicable, for an order directing the Commissioner or authorizing the Commissioner to rehabilitate or to liquidate a licensee in accordance with Article 30 of this Chapter. (2004-162, s. 1; 2013-413, s. 11.1(d).)

§ 58-89A-90. Reserved.

Part 3. Licensee Duties and Responsibilities.

§ 58-89A-95. Agreement.

(a) A licensee shall establish the terms of a PEO agreement by a written contract between the licensee and the client company.

(b) The licensee shall give written notice of the agreement, by agreement or otherwise, as it affects assigned employees to each employee assigned to a client company work site.

(c) Repealed by Session Laws 2013-413, s. 11.1(e), effective October 1, 2013. (2004-162, s. 1; 2013-413, s. 11.1(e).)

§ 58-89A-100. Contract requirements.

A contract between a licensee and a client company shall provide:

(1) Unless otherwise expressly agreed by a professional employer organization and a client company in a PEO agreement, the client company retains the exclusive right of direction and control over the assigned employees as is necessary to conduct the client company's business and without which the client company would be unable to conduct its business, to discharge any fiduciary responsibility that it may have, or to comply with any applicable licensure, regulatory, or statutory requirement of the client company or an assigned employee. The PEO agreement shall provide that employment responsibilities not allocated to the licensee by the PEO agreement or this section remain with the client company.

(2) That the licensee assumes responsibility for the payment of wages to the assigned employees as agreed to in the PEO agreement.

(3) That the licensee assumes responsibility for the payment of payroll taxes and collection of taxes from payroll on assigned employees.

(4) That the licensee shall have a right to hire, discipline, and terminate an assigned employee as may be necessary to fulfill the licensee's responsibilities under this Chapter and a PEO agreement. The client company shall have a right to hire, discipline, and terminate an assigned employee.

(5) That the licensee retains a right of direction and control over the adoption of employment policies and the management of workers' compensation claims, claim filings, and related procedures in accordance with applicable federal laws and the laws of this State.

(6) That responsibility to obtain workers' compensation coverage for assigned employees, from an entity authorized to do business in this State and otherwise in compliance with all applicable requirements, shall be specifically allocated in the PEO agreement to either the client company or the licensee. If the responsibility is allocated to the licensee under any such agreement, that agreement shall require that the licensee maintain and provide to the client company, at the termination of the agreement if requested by the client company, records regarding the loss experience related to workers' compensation insurance provided to assigned employees pursuant to the agreement. (2004-162, s. 1; 2013-413, s. 11.1(f).)

§ 58-89A-105. Employee benefit plans; required disclosure; other reports.

(a) A licensee may sponsor and maintain employee benefit plans for the benefit of assigned employees. Any health insurance plan sponsored and maintained by a licensee shall only be fully insured by one of the following:

(1) A licensed insurance company that is authorized to write accident and health insurance, as defined in G.S. 58-7-15(3).

(2) A service corporation organized and licensed under Article 65 of this Chapter.

(3) A health maintenance organization organized and licensed under Article 67 of this Chapter.

(a1) A client company may sponsor and maintain employee benefit plans for the benefit of assigned employees.

(b),(c) Repealed by Session Laws 2008-124, s. 7.4, effective October 1, 2008.

(d) For the purposes of this section, a health insurance plan is fully insured only if all of the benefits provided under the plan are covered by an approved policy issued by one or more of the entities specified in subsection (a) of this section. A health insurance plan is not fully insured if the plan is any form of stop-loss insurance or any other form of reinsurance.

(e) Existing licensees shall comply with subsection (a) of this section by October 1, 2009. If on October 1, 2009, an existing licensee sponsors and maintains any health insurance plan that is not fully insured by one or more of the entities specified in subsection (a) of this section, the licensee may continue to sponsor and maintain the health insurance plan if it complies with G.S. 58-89A-106. (2004-162, s. 1; 2008-124, s. 7.4; 2009-552, s. 2.)

§ 58-89A-106. Health insurance plan requirements.

(a) In order for a licensee to sponsor and maintain a health benefit plan that is not fully insured by one or more of the entities specified in subsection (a) of G.S. 58-89A-105 on and after October 1, 2009, as authorized by subsection (e) of that section, the licensee shall meet all of the requirements listed in this subsection. A health benefit plan developed under this section is not required to provide coverage that meets the requirements of other provisions of this Chapter that mandate either coverage or the offer of coverage by the type or level of health care services or health care provider. The licensee shall:

(1) Use a third-party administrator licensed or registered under Article 56 of this Chapter.

(2) Hold all health insurance plan assets, including participant contributions, in a separate trust account for use only with the health benefit plan.

(3) Provide sound reserves for the health benefit plan that are determined on an annual basis by an actuary who is a member in good standing of the American Academy of Actuaries. The Commissioner may establish, by rule, a process for approving plan reserves.

(4)   Maintain the health benefit plan for only employees of the licensee or employees of the client company and neither offer nor advertise the health insurance benefit plan to the public generally.

(5)   Issue to each covered employee a policy, contract, certificate, summary plan description, or other evidence of the benefits and coverages provided. The evidence of benefits and coverages provided shall contain, in boldface print in a conspicuous location, the following statement: "THE BENEFITS UNDER THIS PLAN MAY NOT BE EQUAL TO THE MANDATED BENEFITS REQUIRED OF FULLY INSURED PLANS. THE BENEFITS AND COVERAGES DESCRIBED HEREIN ARE PROVIDED THROUGH A SELF-FUNDED HEALTH BENEFIT PLAN ESTABLISHED BY [name of PEO]. EXCESS INSURANCE IS PROVIDED BY AN AUTHORIZED INSURANCE COMPANY TO COVER HIGH AMOUNT MEDICAL CLAIMS. THE HEALTH BENEFIT PLAN IS NOT PROTECTED BY ANY INSURANCE GUARANTY ASSOCIATION. OTHER RELATED FINANCIAL INFORMATION IS AVAILABLE FROM YOUR EMPLOYER OR FROM THE [name of PEO]." Any statement required by this subsection is not required on identification cards issued to covered employees or other insureds.

(6)   File all contracts with third-party administrators with the Commissioner and report any changes to those contracts to the Commissioner before their implementation.

(7)   Obtain and maintain stop-loss insurance from an insurer authorized to write insurance in this State and that meets the following requirements:

a.   If individual stop-loss insurance, it is actuarially appropriate for the size of the group, surplus, and the expected losses, as determined by a qualified actuary and approved by the Commissioner.

b.   If aggregate stop-loss insurance, it is actuarially appropriate for the size of the group, surplus, and the expected losses as determined by a qualified actuary and approved by the Commissioner. If the licensee is unable to obtain aggregate stop-loss insurance that is actuarially appropriate, the licensee shall maintain at least a thirty percent (30%) lag reserve above expected losses, as determined by a qualified actuary.

c.   If prescribed by the Commissioner, by rule, it satisfies net retention levels in accordance with a PEO's surplus and expected claims.

(8) File with the Commissioner for information the summary plan description and the evidence of the benefits and coverages provided under the health benefit plan that is issued to the person covered by the health benefit plan.

(9) Establish and maintain a written plan of operation for the health benefit plan.

(10) File with the Commissioner the plan of operation for the health benefit plan and any updates to the plan of operation within 30 days of implementation.

(11) Upon request of the Commissioner, provide information that summarizes paid and incurred expenses and contributions or premiums received and any additional evidence that the PEO's health benefit plan is actuarially sound.

(b) Notwithstanding Chapter 132 of the General Statutes, all documents filed by a licensee under this section are confidential, are not open for public inspection, and are not discoverable or admissible in evidence in a civil action brought by a party other than the Department against a person regulated by the Department, its directors, officers, or employees, unless the court finds that the interests of justice require that the documents be discoverable or admissible in evidence. The Commissioner, however, may use the contracts filed under this subsection in the furtherance of any regulatory or legal action brought as part of the Commissioner's official duties. (2009-552, s. 3; 2010-96, s. 11.)

§ 58-89A-107. Examinations of self-funded health benefit plans.

(a) The Commissioner may conduct an examination of a licensee's self-funded employee benefit plan as often as the Commissioner considers appropriate.

(b) An examination under this Article shall be conducted in accordance with the Examination Law of this Chapter, G.S. 58-2-131 through G.S. 58-2-133.

(c) In lieu of an examination of any foreign or alien licensee's self-funded employee benefit plan, the Commissioner may, in the Commissioner's discretion, accept an examination report on the licensee's self-funded employee benefit plan prepared by the appropriate regulator for the licensee's state of domicile.

(d)   When making an examination under this section, the Commissioner may retain attorneys, appraisers, independent actuaries, independent certified public accountants, or other professionals and specialists as examiners, the reasonable cost of which shall be borne by the licensee that is the subject of the examination.

(e)   The amount paid by a PEO for an examination of its health benefit plan under this section shall not exceed sixty thousand dollars ($60,000), unless the PEO and the Commissioner agree on a higher amount. The State Treasurer shall deposit all funds received under this section in the Insurance Regulatory Fund established under G.S. 58-6-25. Funds received under this section shall be used by the Department for offsetting the actual expenses incurred by the Department for examinations under this section. (2009-552, s. 3.)

§ 58-89A-110. Workers' compensation insurance.

(a)   A licensee or the licensee's client company shall provide workers' compensation insurance coverage through a licensed insurance carrier or a licensed self-insurance plan for the licensee's assigned employees as provided in Chapter 97 of the General Statutes, the Workers' Compensation Act. To the extent that the licensee secures and maintains workers' compensation coverage for assigned employees, the carrier may elect to provide such coverage to the licensee pursuant to either the multiple coordinated policy method, as set forth in subsection (b) of this section, or the single policy method, as set forth in subsection (c) of this section.

(b)   If the licensee provides workers' compensation coverage pursuant to the multiple coordinated policy method, the licensee shall secure a separate policy for each client company of the licensee. Each policy shall identify the name of the client company and the licensee. The licensee shall be named as the insured and identify the client company. The licensee shall specify that it is the labor contractor for the client company by using the designation "L/C/F" on the policy.

Each policy shall expire on the same date. The policy shall not include coverage for nonleased employees of the client company or employees solely employed by the licensee. Only the licensee, as the first-named insured under such a policy, may request the insurer to cancel the policy. Each policy shall be sent to the licensee as the named insured.

The client company of a licensee shall have a continuing obligation to provide coverage as required by Chapter 97 of the General Statutes, the Workers' Compensation Act, for any employees of the client company who are not assigned employees and not otherwise covered under a policy described in this subsection.

If a client company of a licensee leases employees from more than one licensee, there shall be a separate policy for the assigned employees of each licensee.

The workers' compensation carrier also shall issue a policy covering the internal employees of the licensee unless they are otherwise covered.

All policies written in accordance with this subsection by the same insurance carrier that reference the same licensee as labor contractor shall be combined for premium discount purposes.

When policies written in accordance with this subsection are written by the same insurance carrier, the carrier and licensee may agree to a retrospective rating program or any other permitted pricing program.

Whenever a policy written in accordance with this subsection is cancelled, the insurance company writing the policy shall provide individual notices of cancellation as required by this Chapter to the licensee and the client company of the licensee.

(c) If the licensee provides workers' compensation coverage pursuant to the single policy method, the insurer shall issue to the licensee a single policy covering all assigned employees in this State in accordance with Chapter 97 of the General Statutes, the Workers' Compensation Act, and any other applicable laws or rating plans of this State.

As a condition of issuing a single policy, the licensee shall provide to the insurer of the policy all of the following information regarding each client company of the licensee with assigned employees in this State:

(1) The correct legal name, any fictitious names, and the federal identification number.

(2) The name and address of the president and chief executive officer.

(3) The business mailing address.

(4) The business telephone number and facsimile number.

The licensee shall also provide to the insurer the name and address of the insurance agent or broker responsible for securing the policy of insurance on behalf of the licensee.

The insurer shall issue to each client company of the licensee a certificate of insurance on the single policy. The certificate of insurance shall require that the insurer provide notice of cancellation to the licensee and the client company of the licensee.

Whenever a policy written in accordance with this subsection is cancelled, the insurance company writing the policy shall provide individual notices of cancellation as required by this Chapter to the licensee and the client company of the licensee.

If the insurer fails to provide individual notices of cancellation to the licensee and the client company, the insurer shall remain liable on the risk for losses incurred by the client company that would have been covered by the workers' compensation policy prior to the attempted cancellation.

(d) A license shall not be issued to any professional employer organization unless (i) the organization first files with the Commissioner evidence of workers' compensation coverage for all assigned employees in this State, including those leased from or coemployed with another person, and (ii) the organization certifies to the Commissioner that it has provided its workers' compensation carrier with proper and necessary documentation to allow the carrier to determine and charge a premium that is commensurate with exposure and anticipated claim experience for all employees covered under policies issued by the carrier in the name of the licensee.

(e) Each licensee shall maintain and make available to its workers' compensation carrier on an annual basis the following information:

(1) The correct name and federal identification number of each client company.

(2) A listing of all covered employees provided to each client company, by classification code.

(3) The total eligible wages, by classification code, and the premiums due to the carrier for the employees provided to each client company.

(4) Sufficient information to permit the calculation of an experience modification factor for each client company upon termination of the professional employer relationship. Information accruing during the term of the leasing arrangement that is used to calculate an experience modification factor for a client company upon termination of the leasing relationship shall continue to be used in the future experience ratings of the licensee.

(f) Every Form 19 "Employer's Report of Employee's Injury or Occupational Disease to the Industrial Commission" filed with the Industrial Commission shall identify by name and address both the licensee and the client company employing the employee who is the subject of the Form 19.

(g) A licensee shall, within 30 days of initiation or termination of the licensee's relationship with any client company, notify its workers' compensation carrier, the Commissioner, and the North Carolina Industrial Commission of both the initiation and termination of the relationship. If the client company terminates the relationship between the licensee and the client company, the notice required by this subsection shall be given within 10 days of the licensee's actual knowledge of the termination.

(h) If the professional employer services arrangement with a client company is terminated, the client company shall be assigned an experience modification factor that reflects its experience during the experience period specified by the approved experience rating plan, including, if applicable, experience incurred for assigned employees under the PEO agreement.

(i) A client company shall not enter into a PEO agreement or be eligible for workers' compensation coverage in the voluntary market if the client-workers' company owes its current or prior carrier any premium for workers' compensation insurance, or if the client company owes its current or prior professional employer organization amounts due under the PEO agreement, except for premiums or amounts due that are subject to dispute. For the purposes of this section and compliance with other laws and rules, a licensee may rely on a statement by the client company that the client company has met any and all prior premium or fee obligations, unless the licensee has actual knowledge to the contrary.

(j)   This section shall not prevent a client company of a licensee from providing workers' compensation insurance coverage for assigned employees coemployed by the client company and the licensee through a policy of insurance issued by a licensed insurance carrier in the name of the client company as the insured.

(k)   Irrespective of whether the licensee or client company maintains the policy of workers' compensation insurance for the covered employees pursuant to the PEO agreement, the licensee and the client company shall be entitled to the exclusivity of the remedy under both the workers' compensation and the employer liability provision of the workers' compensation policy or plan that either party has secured and shall both be afforded the protections provided under Chapter 97 of the General Statutes. The licensee shall be entitled, along with the client company, to the exclusivity of the remedy under both the workers' compensation and employers' liability provision of the workers' compensation policy or plan that either party has secured.

(l)   All assigned risk policies for client companies of the same licensee shall be assigned to one workers' compensation carrier in the State and in other states to the extent possible. (2004-162, s. 1; 2005-124, s. 4.)

§ 58-89A-112. Liabilities.

Subject to any contrary provisions thereof, the PEO agreement shall be interpreted for purposes of insurance, bonding, and employer's liability as follows:

(1)   A licensee is not liable for the acts, errors, or omissions of a client company or of any assigned employee or for the quality, adequacy, or safety of the goods or services produced or sold in the client company's business. A client company is not liable for the acts, errors, or omissions of a licensee or of any employee of a licensee. Nothing in this section limits any contractual liability between a licensee and the client company or limits any liability or responsibility under this Article.

(2) Employees assigned to a client company by a licensee are the employees of the client company for the purposes of general liability insurance, automobile insurance, fidelity bonds, surety bonds, and liquor liability insurance carried by the client company unless the employees are included by specific reference in the applicable PEO agreement, insurance contract, or bond. (2004-162, s. 1.)

§ 58-89A-115. Benefit plan notice.

(a) With respect to any insurance or benefit plan provided by a licensee for the benefit of its assigned employees, a licensee shall disclose all of the following information to the Commissioner and each client company:

(1) The type of coverage.

(2) The identity of each insurer for each type of coverage.

(3) The amount of benefits provided for each type of coverage and to whom or on whose behalf benefits are to be paid.

(4) The policy limits on each insurance policy.

(5) Whether the coverage is fully insured, partially insured, or fully self-funded.

(b) With respect to any insurance or benefit plan provided by a licensee for the benefit of its assigned employees, a licensee shall provide to the insurer the name and address of the insurance agent or broker responsible for securing the policy of insurance on behalf of the licensee.

(c) Whenever any insurance policy or benefit plan is cancelled, the insurance company writing the policy shall provide a notice of cancellation as required by this Chapter.

(d) The licensee shall notify the client company and the Commissioner in writing about a discontinuance and replacement, if any, of any health plan or workers' compensation insurance coverage no later than 10 business days after the discontinuance.

(e) The Commissioner, by rule, may require a licensee to file other reports that are reasonably necessary for the administration and enforcement of this Article. (2004-162, s. 1.)

§ 58-89A-120. Unemployment taxes; payroll.

A licensee is the employer of an assigned employee for purposes of Chapters 95, 96 and 105 of the General Statutes. Nothing in this section shall otherwise affect the levy and collection of unemployment insurance contributions or the assignment of discrete employer numbers under the Employment Security Law. The Department of Commerce, Division of Employment Security (DES), shall cooperate with the Commissioner in the investigation of applicants and licensees and shall provide the Commissioner with access to all relevant records and data in the custody of the DES. (2004-162, s. 1; 2011-401, s. 3.4; 2013-2, s. 9(a); 2013-224, s. 19.)

§ 58-89A-125. Posting requirements.

(a) Each licensee shall post the license issued under this Article in a conspicuous place in the licensee's principal place of business in this State.

(b) Each licensee shall display, in a place that is in clear and unobstructed public view, a notice stating that the business operated at the location is licensed and regulated by the Commissioner and that any questions or complaints may be directed to the Commissioner. (2004-162, s. 1.)

§ 58-89A-130. Contractual duties.

Each licensee is responsible for the licensee's contractual duties and responsibilities to manage, maintain, collect, and make timely payments for all of the following:

(1) Insurance premiums.

(2) Benefit and welfare plans.

(3) Other employee withholding.

(4) Any other expressed responsibility that is within the scope of the PEO agreement and that fulfills the duties imposed under this Article. (2004-162, s. 1.)

§ 58-89A-135. Compliance with other laws.

Each licensee shall comply with all appropriate State and federal laws relating to reporting, sponsoring, filing, and maintaining benefit and welfare plans. (2004-162, s. 1.)

§ 58-89A-140. Required information.

Each licensee shall:

(1) Maintain adequate books and records regarding the licensee's duties and responsibilities, including accounting and employment records relating to all PEO agreement activities, for a minimum of three years.

(2) Maintain and make available at all times to the Commissioner the following information, which shall be treated as proprietary and confidential and which is exempt from disclosure to persons other than other governmental agencies that have a reasonable, legitimate purpose for obtaining the information:

a. The correct name, address, and telephone number of each client company.

b. Each client company contract or PEO agreement.

c. A listing of each client company by classification code as described in the "Standard Industrial Classification Manual" published by the United States Office of Management and Budget. (2004-162, s. 1.)

§ 58-89A-145. Examinations.

(a) The Commissioner may conduct an examination of a licensee as often as the Commissioner considers appropriate.

(b) An examination under this Article shall be conducted in accordance with the Examination Law of this Chapter, G.S. 58-2-131 through G.S. 58-2-134.

(c) In lieu of an examination of any foreign or alien person licensed under this Article, the Commissioner may, in the Commissioner's discretion, accept an examination report on the licensee prepared by the appropriate regulator for the licensee's state of domicile.

(d) When making an examination under this Article, the Commissioner may retain attorneys, appraisers, independent actuaries, independent certified public accountants, or other professionals and specialists as examiners, the reasonable cost of which may only be recovered pursuant to G.S. 58-89A-65(d). (2004-162, s. 1; 2013-413, s. 11.1(g).)

§ 58-89A-150. Agent for service of process.

Each resident licensee shall maintain a registered agent for the service of process in this State. The Commissioner shall be each nonresident licensee's agent for service of process as provided in Article 16 of this Chapter. (2004-162, s. 1.)

Part 4. Penalties and Sanctions.

§ 58-89A-155. Grounds for disciplinary action.

(a) The Commissioner may take disciplinary action against a licensee or any person subject to licensure requirements under this Article on any of the following grounds:

(1) Being convicted or having an officer or controlling person of the licensee convicted of:

a. Bribery, fraud, or intentional or material misrepresentation in obtaining or attempting to obtain a license;

b. A crime that relates to the operation of a professional employer organization or the ability of the licensee or any officer or controlling person of the licensee to operate a professional employer organization;

c. A crime that relates to the classification, misclassification, or underreporting of employees required by State law;

d. A crime that relates to the establishment or maintenance of a self-insurance program, whether health insurance, workers' compensation insurance, or other insurance;

e. A crime that relates to fraud, deceit, or misconduct in the operation of a professional employer service; or

f. A crime that involves dishonesty or breach of trust.

(2) Engaging in professional employer services or offering to engage in the provision of professional employer services without a license.

(3) Failure to provide notice in writing of the discontinuance and replacement, if any, of any insurance coverage, to the Commissioner and client company within 10 business days of the discontinuance of any insurance coverage pursuant to G.S. 58-89A-115.

(4) Repealed by Session Laws 2013-413, s. 11.1(h), effective October 1, 2013.

(5) Failure to satisfy any of the requirements for licensure in this Article.

(b) For purposes of this section, a conviction includes an adjudication of guilt, a plea of guilty, and a plea of nolo contendere. (2004-162, s. 1; 2013-413, s. 11.1(h).)

§ 58-89A-160. Sanctions.

(a)   On a finding that a ground for disciplinary action exists under G.S. 58-89A-155, the Commissioner may suspend or terminate a license, impose a civil penalty, and seek an order of restitution under G.S. 58-2-70.

(b)   On termination of a license, the licensee shall immediately return the terminated license to the Commissioner.

(c)   Any disciplinary action taken, any temporary or permanent termination of a license, or any determination that an officer or controlling person is unqualified shall be made by the Commissioner subject to Article 3A of Chapter 150B of the General Statutes. (2004-162, s. 1.)

§ 58-89A-165. Injunctions; civil remedies; cease and desist orders.

(a)   In addition to the penalties and other enforcement provisions of this Article, if any person violates this Article or any rule implementing this Article, the Commissioner may seek an injunction in a court of competent jurisdiction and may apply for temporary and permanent orders that the Commissioner determines are necessary to restrain the person from committing the violation.

(b)   The Commissioner may issue, in accordance with G.S. 58-63-32, a cease and desist order upon a person that violates any provision of this Article, any rule or order adopted by the Commissioner, or any written agreement entered into with the Commissioner. The cease and desist order may be subject to judicial review under G.S. 58-63-35.

(c)   When the Commissioner finds that an activity in violation of this Article presents an immediate danger to the public that requires an immediate final order, the Commissioner may issue an emergency cease and desist order reciting with particularity the facts underlying the findings. The emergency cease and desist order is effective immediately upon service of a copy of the order on the respondent and remains effective for 90 days. If the Commissioner begins nonemergency cease and desist proceedings, the emergency cease and desist order remains effective, absent an order by a court of competent jurisdiction in accordance with G.S. 58-63-35.

(d) In addition to the penalties and other enforcement provisions of this Article, any person who violates this Article is subject to G.S. 58-2-70.

(e) The Commissioner is not required to post a bond for injunctive relief under this section. (2004-162, s. 1.)

§ 58-89A-170. Prohibited acts.

No person shall do any of the following:

(1) Engage in or offer professional employer services without holding a license under this Article as a professional employer organization.

(2) Use the name or title "staff leasing company", "employee leasing company", "licensed staff leasing company", "staff leasing services company", "professional employer organization", or "administrative employer" or otherwise represent that the person is licensed under this Article unless the person holds a license issued under this Article.

(3) Represent as the person's own the license of another person or represent that a person is licensed if the person does not hold a license.

(4) Give materially false or forged evidence to the Commissioner in connection with obtaining or maintaining a license or in connection with disciplinary proceedings under this Article.

(5) Use or attempt to use a license that has been suspended or terminated. (2002-168, s. 8; 2004-162, s. 1.)

§ 58-89A-175. Criminal penalty.

A person who violates G.S. 58-89A-170 commits a Class H felony. Any officer or controlling person who willfully violates any provision of this Article may be subject to any and all criminal penalties available under State law. (2002-168, s. 8; 2004-162, s. 1.)

§ 58-89A-180. Application to unlicensed professional employer organizations.

Notwithstanding any other provision of law, each provision in this Article applies to persons subject to licensure under this Article, whether licensed under this Article or not. (2004-162, s. 1.)

Article 90.

Health Insurance Innovations Commission.

§ 58-90-1: Repealed by Session Laws 2011-266, s. 1.32, effective July 1, 2011.

§ 58-90-5: Repealed by Session Laws 2011-266, s. 1.32, effective July 1, 2011.

§ 58-90-10: Repealed by Session Laws 2011-266, s. 1.32, effective July 1, 2011.

§ 58-90-15: Repealed by Session Laws 2011-266, s. 1.32, effective July 1, 2011.

§ 58-90-20: Repealed by Session Laws 2011-266, s. 1.32, effective July 1, 2011.

§ 58-90-25: Repealed by Session Laws 2011-266, s. 1.32, effective July 1, 2011.

Article 91.

Interstate Insurance Product Regulation Compact Act.

§ 58-91-1. Preamble.

The Interstate Insurance Product Regulation Compact Act is intended to help states join together to establish an interstate compact to regulate designated insurance products.

Pursuant to terms and conditions of this Article, this State seeks to join with other states and establish the Interstate Insurance Product Regulation Compact and thus become a member of the Interstate Insurance Product Regulation Commission. The Commissioner of Insurance, or the Commissioner's designee, is hereby designated to serve as the representative of this State to the Commission. (2005-183, s. 1; 2009-382, s. 35.)

§ 58-91-5. Purposes.

The purposes of this Compact are, through means of joint and cooperative action among the compacting states:

(1) To promote and protect the interest of consumers of individual and group annuity, life insurance, disability income, and long-term care insurance products.

(2) To develop uniform standards for insurance products covered under the Compact.

(3) To establish a central clearinghouse to receive and provide prompt review of insurance products covered under the Compact and, in certain cases, advertisements related thereto, submitted by insurers authorized to do business in one or more compacting states.

(4) To give appropriate regulatory approval to those product filings and advertisements satisfying the applicable uniform standard.

(5) To improve coordination of regulatory resources and expertise between state insurance departments regarding the setting of uniform standards and review of insurance products covered under the Compact.

(6) To create the Interstate Insurance Product Regulation Commission.

(7) To perform these and any other related function as may be consistent with the state regulation of the business of insurance. (2005-183, s. 1; 2009-382, s. 35.)

§ 58-91-10. Definitions.

For purposes of this Article and the Compact:

(1) "Advertisement" means any material designed to create public interest in a product, or induce the public to purchase, increase, modify, reinstate, borrow on, surrender, replace, or retain a policy, as more specifically defined in the Rules and Operating Procedures of the Commission.

(2) "Bylaws" means those bylaws established by the Commission for its governance, or for directing or controlling the Commission's actions or conduct.

(3) "Compacting state" means any state which has enacted this Compact legislation and which has not withdrawn or been terminated pursuant to G.S. 58-91-70.

(4) "Commission" means the "Interstate Insurance Product Regulation Commission" established by this Compact.

(5) "Commissioner" means the chief insurance regulatory official of a state, including a commissioner, superintendent, director, or administrator.

(6) "Domiciliary state" means the state in which an insurer is incorporated or organized; or, in the case of an foreign insurer, its state of entry.

(7) "Insurer" means any entity licensed by a state to issue contracts of insurance for any of the lines of insurance covered by this Article.

(8) "Member" means the person chosen by a compacting state as its representative to the Commission, or that person's designee.

(9) "Noncompacting state" means any state which is not at the time a compacting state.

(10) "Operating procedures" means procedures promulgated by the Commission implementing a rule, uniform standard, or a provision of this Compact.

(11) "Product" means the form of a policy or contract, including any application, endorsement, or related form which is attached to and made a part of the policy or contract, and any evidence of coverage or certificate, for an individual or group annuity, life insurance, disability income, or long-term care insurance product that an Insurer is authorized to issue.

(12) "Rule" means a statement of general or particular applicability and future effect promulgated by the Commission, including a uniform standard developed pursuant to G.S. 58-91-35, designed to implement, interpret, or prescribe law or policy or describing the organization, procedure, or practice requirements of the Commission, which shall have the force and effect of law in the compacting states.

(13) "State" means any state, district, or territory of the United States of America.

(14) "Third-party filer" means an entity that submits a product filing to the Commission on behalf of an insurer.

(15) "Uniform standard" means a standard adopted by the Commission for a product line, pursuant to G.S. 58-91-35, and shall include all of the product requirements in aggregate. Each uniform standard shall be construed, whether express or implied, to prohibit the use of any inconsistent, misleading, or ambiguous provisions in a product, and the form of the product made available to the public shall not be unfair, inequitable or against public policy as determined by the Commission. (2005-183, s. 1; 2009-382, s. 35.)

§ 58-91-15. Establishment of the Commission and venue.

(a)   The compacting states hereby create and establish a joint public agency known as the "Interstate Insurance Product Regulation Commission." Pursuant to G.S. 58-91-20, the Commission shall have the power to develop uniform standards for product lines, receive, and provide prompt review of products filed with the Commission, and give approval to those product filings satisfying applicable uniform standards. It is not intended for the Commission to be the exclusive entity for receipt and review of insurance product filings. Nothing herein shall prohibit any insurer from filing its product in any state wherein the insurer is licensed to conduct the business of insurance; and that filing shall be subject to the laws of the state where filed.

(b)   The Commission is a body corporate and politic and an instrumentality of the compacting states.

(c)   The Commission is solely responsible for its liabilities except as otherwise specifically provided in this Compact.

(d)   Venue is proper and judicial proceedings by or against the Commission shall be brought solely and exclusively in a court of competent jurisdiction where the principal office of the Commission is located. (2005-183, s. 1; 2009-382, s. 35.)

§ 58-91-20. Powers of the Commission.

The Commission shall have the following powers:

(1)   To promulgate rules, pursuant to G.S. 58-91-35, which shall have the force and effect of law and shall be binding in the compacting states to the extent and in the manner provided in this Compact.

(2)   To exercise its rule-making authority and establish reasonable uniform standards for products covered under the Compact, and advertisement related thereto, which shall have the force and effect of law and shall be binding in the compacting states, but only for those products filed with the Commission. Notwithstanding this subdivision, a compacting state shall have the right to opt out of a uniform standard pursuant to G.S. 58-91-35, to the extent and in the

manner provided in this Compact, and any uniform standard established by the Commission for long-term care insurance products may provide the same or greater protections for consumers as, but shall not provide less than, those protections set forth in the National Association of Insurance Commissioners' Long-Term Care Insurance Model Act and Long-Term Care Insurance Model Regulation, respectively, adopted as of 2001. The Commission shall consider whether any subsequent amendments to the NAIC Long-Term Care Insurance Model Act or Long-Term Care Insurance Model Regulation adopted by the NAIC require amending of the uniform standards established by the Commission for long-term care insurance products.

(3) To receive and review in an expeditious manner products filed with the Commission, and rate filings for disability income and long-term care insurance products, and give approval of those products and rate filings that satisfy the applicable uniform standard, where the approval shall have the force and effect of law and be binding on the compacting states to the extent and in the manner provided in the Compact.

(4) To receive and review in an expeditious manner advertisement relating to long-term care insurance products for which uniform standards have been adopted by the Commission and give approval to all advertisement that satisfies the applicable uniform standard. For any product covered under this Compact, other than long-term care insurance products, the Commission shall have the authority to require an insurer to submit all or any part of its advertisement with respect to that product for review or approval prior to use, if the Commission determines that the nature of the product is such that an advertisement of the product could have the capacity or tendency to mislead the public. The actions of the Commission as provided in this section shall have the force and effect of law and shall be binding in the compacting states to the extent and in the manner provided in the Compact.

(5) To exercise its rule-making authority and designate products and advertisement that may be subject to a self-certification process without the need for prior approval by the Commission.

(6) To promulgate operating procedures pursuant to G.S. 58-91-35 which shall be binding in the compacting states to the extent and in the manner provided in this Compact.

(7) To bring and prosecute legal proceedings or actions in its name as the Commission except that the standing of any state insurance department to sue or be sued under applicable law shall not be affected.

(8) To issue subpoenas requiring the attendance and testimony of witnesses and the production of evidence.

(9) To establish and maintain offices.

(10) To purchase and maintain insurance and bonds.

(11) To borrow, accept, and contract for services of personnel, including employees of a compacting state.

(12) To hire employees, professionals, or specialists, and elect or appoint officers, and to fix their compensation, define their duties, and give them appropriate authority to carry out the purposes of the Compact, and determine their qualifications; and to establish the Commission's personnel policies and programs relating to, among other things, conflicts of interest, rates of compensation, and qualifications of personnel.

(13) To accept any and all appropriate donations and grants of money, equipment, supplies, materials, and services, and to receive, utilize, and dispose of the same. At all times the Commission shall strive to avoid any appearance of impropriety.

(14) To lease, purchase, accept appropriate gifts or donations of, or otherwise to own, hold, improve, or use, any property, real, personal, or mixed. At all times the Commission shall strive to avoid any appearance of impropriety.

(15) To sell, convey, mortgage, pledge, lease, exchange, abandon, or otherwise dispose of any property, real, personal, or mixed.

(16) To remit filing fees to compacting states as may be set forth in the bylaws, rules, or operating procedures.

(17) To enforce compliance by compacting states with rules, uniform standards, operating procedures, and bylaws.

(18) To provide for dispute resolution among compacting states.

(19) To advise compacting states on issues relating to insurers domiciled or doing business in noncompacting jurisdictions, consistent with the purposes of this Compact.

(20) To provide advice and training to those personnel in state insurance departments responsible for product review, and to be a resource for state insurance departments.

(21) To establish a budget and make expenditures.

(22) To borrow money.

(23) To appoint committees, including advisory committees comprising members, state insurance regulators, state legislators or their representatives, insurance industry and consumer representatives, and such other interested persons as may be designated in the bylaws.

(24) To provide and receive information from, and to cooperate with, law enforcement agencies.

(25) To adopt and use a corporate seal.

(26) To perform any other functions that may be necessary or appropriate to achieve the purposes of this Compact consistent with the state regulation of the business of insurance. (2005-183, s. 1; 2009-382, s. 35.)

§ 58-91-25. Organization of the Commission.

(a) Membership, Voting, and Bylaws. - Each compacting state shall have and be limited to one member. Each member shall be qualified to serve in that capacity pursuant to applicable law of the compacting state. Any member may be removed or suspended from office as provided by the law of the state from which the member shall be appointed. Any vacancy occurring in the Commission shall be filled in accordance with the laws of the compacting state wherein the vacancy exists. Nothing herein shall be construed to affect the manner in which a compacting state determines the election or appointment and qualification of its own Commissioner.

Each member shall be entitled to one vote and shall have an opportunity to participate in the governance of the Commission in accordance with the bylaws. Notwithstanding any provision herein to the contrary, no action of the Commission with respect to the promulgation of a uniform standard shall be effective unless two-thirds of the members vote in favor of the uniform standard.

The Commission shall, by a majority of the members, prescribe bylaws to govern its conduct as may be necessary or appropriate to carry out the purposes, and exercise the powers, of the Compact, including:

(1)   Establishing the fiscal year of the Commission.

(2)   Providing reasonable procedures for appointing and electing members, as well as holding meetings, of the Management Committee.

(3)   Providing reasonable standards and procedures: (i) for the establishment and meetings of other committees, and (ii) governing any general or specific delegation of any authority or function of the Commission.

(4)   Providing reasonable procedures for calling and conducting meetings of the Commission that consist of a majority of Commission members, ensuring reasonable advance notice of each meeting and providing for the right of citizens to attend each meeting with enumerated exceptions designed to protect the public's interest, the privacy of individuals, and insurers' proprietary information, including trade secrets. The Commission may meet in camera only after a majority of the entire membership votes to close a meeting in toto or in part. As soon as practicable, the Commission must make public (i) a copy of the vote to close the meeting revealing the vote of each member with no proxy votes allowed, and (ii) votes taken during the meeting.

(5)   Establishing the titles, duties, and authority and reasonable procedures for the election of the officers of the Commission.

(6)   Providing reasonable standards and procedures for the establishment of the personnel policies and programs of the Commission. Notwithstanding any civil service or other similar laws of any compacting state, the bylaws shall exclusively govern the personnel policies and programs of the Commission.

(7)   Promulgating a code of ethics to address permissible and prohibited activities of commission members and employees.

(8) Providing a mechanism for winding up the operations of the Commission and the equitable disposition of any surplus funds that may exist after the termination of the Compact after the payment or reserving of all of its debts and obligations.

The Commission shall publish its bylaws in a convenient form and file a copy of the bylaws and a copy of any amendment to the bylaws with the appropriate agency or officer in each of the compacting states.

(b) Management Committee, Officers and Personnel. - A Management Committee comprising no more than 14 members shall be established as follows:

(1) One member from each of the six compacting states with the largest premium volume for individual and group annuities, life, disability income, and long-term care insurance products, determined from the records of the NAIC for the prior year.

(2) Four members from those compacting states with at least two percent (2%) of the market based on the premium volume described above, other than the six compacting states with the largest premium volume, selected on a rotating basis as provided in the bylaws.

(3) Four members from those compacting states with less than two percent (2%) of the market, based on the premium volume described above, with one selected from each of the four zone regions of the NAIC as provided in the bylaws.

(b1) The Management Committee shall have such authority and duties as may be set forth in the bylaws, including but not limited to:

(1) Managing the affairs of the Commission in a manner consistent with the bylaws and purposes of the Commission.

(2) Establishing and overseeing an organizational structure within, and appropriate procedures for, the Commission to provide for the creation of uniform standards and other rules, receipt and review of product filings, administrative and technical support functions, review of decisions regarding the disapproval of a product filing, and the review of elections made by a compacting state to opt out of a uniform standard, except that that a uniform

standard shall not be submitted to the compacting states for adoption unless approved by two-thirds of the members of the Management Committee.

(3) Overseeing the offices of the Commission.

(4) Planning, implementing, and coordinating communications and activities with other state, federal, and local government organizations in order to advance the goals of the Commission.

The Commission shall elect annually officers from the Management Committee, with each having the authority and duties specified in the bylaws.

The Management Committee may, subject to the approval of the Commission, appoint or retain an executive director for a period of time, upon the terms and conditions, and for the compensation deemed appropriate by the Commission. The executive director shall serve as secretary to the Commission, but shall not be a member of the Commission. The executive director shall hire and supervise any other staff authorized by the Commission.

(c) Legislative and Advisory Committees. - A legislative committee comprising state legislators or their designees shall be established to monitor the operations of, and make recommendations to, the Commission, including the Management Committee. The manner of selection and term of any legislative committee member shall be as set forth in the bylaws. Prior to the adoption by the Commission of any uniform standard, revision to the bylaws, annual budget, or other significant matter as may be provided in the bylaws, the Management Committee shall consult with and report to the legislative committee.

The Commission shall establish two advisory committees, one of which shall comprise consumer representatives independent of the insurance industry, and the other comprising insurance industry representatives.

The Commission may establish additional advisory committees as its bylaws may provide for the carrying out of its functions.

(d) Corporate Records of the Commission. - The Commission shall maintain its corporate books and records in accordance with the bylaws.

(e) Qualified Immunity, Defense, and Indemnification. - The members, officers, executive director, employees, and representatives of the Commission shall be immune from suit and liability, either personally or in their official capacity, for any claim for damage to or loss of property or personal injury or other civil liability caused by or arising out of any actual or alleged act, error, or omission that occurred, or that the person against whom the claim is made had a reasonable basis for believing occurred within the scope of Commission employment, duties, or responsibilities except that nothing in this subsection shall be construed to protect any such person from suit or liability for any damage, loss, injury, or liability caused by the intentional or willful and wanton misconduct of that person.

The Commission shall defend any member, officer, executive director, employee, or representative of the Commission in any civil action seeking to impose liability arising out of any actual or alleged act, error, or omission that occurred within the scope of Commission employment, duties, or responsibilities, or that the person against whom the claim is made had a reasonable basis for believing occurred within the scope of Commission employment, duties, or responsibilities as long as the actual or alleged act, error, or omission did not result from that person's intentional or willful and wanton misconduct. Nothing in this subsection shall be construed to prohibit that person from retaining his or her own counsel.

The Commission shall indemnify and hold harmless any member, officer, executive director, employee, or representative of the Commission for the amount of any settlement or judgment obtained against that person arising out of any actual or alleged act, error, or omission that occurred within the scope of Commission employment, duties, or responsibilities, or that the person had a reasonable basis for believing occurred within the scope of Commission employment, duties, or responsibilities as long as the actual or alleged act, error, or omission did not result from the intentional or willful and wanton misconduct of that person. (2005-183, s. 1; 2009-382, s. 35.)

§ 58-91-30. Meetings; acts of the Commission.

(a)   The Commission shall meet and take such actions as are consistent with the provisions of this Compact and the bylaws.

(b)   Each member of the Commission shall have the right and power to cast a vote to which that compacting state is entitled and to participate in the business and affairs of the Commission. A member shall vote in person or by any means provided in the bylaws. The bylaws may provide for members' participation in meetings by telephone or other means of communication.

(c) The Commission shall meet at least once during each calendar year. Additional meetings shall be held as set forth in the bylaws. (2005-183, s. 1; 2009-382, s. 35.)

§ 58-91-35. Rules and operating procedures: rule-making functions of the Commission and opting out of uniform standards.

(a) Rule-Making Authority. - The Commission shall promulgate reasonable rules, including uniform standards, and operating procedures in order to effectively and efficiently achieve the purposes of this Compact. Notwithstanding the foregoing, in the event the Commission exercises its rule-making authority in a manner that is beyond the scope of the purposes of this Article, or the powers granted in this Article, then that action by the Commission shall be invalid and have no force and effect.

(b) Rule-Making Procedure. - Rules and operating procedures shall be made pursuant to a rule-making process that conforms to the Model State Administrative Procedure Act of 1981 as amended, as may be appropriate to the operations of the Commission. Before the Commission adopts a uniform standard, the Commission shall give written notice to the relevant state legislative committee in each compacting state responsible for insurance issues of its intention to adopt the uniform standard. The Commission in adopting a uniform standard shall consider fully all submitted materials and issue a concise explanation of its decision.

(c) Effective Date and Opt Out of a Uniform Standard. - A uniform standard shall become effective 90 days after its promulgation by the Commission or such later date as the Commission may determine except that a compacting state may opt out of a uniform standard as provided in this Article. "Opt out" shall be defined as any action by a compacting state to decline to adopt or participate in a promulgated uniform standard. All other rules and operating procedures, and amendments to the rules and operating procedures, shall become effective as of the date specified in each rule, operating procedure, or amendment.

(d) Opt Out Procedure. - A compacting state may opt out of a uniform standard, either by legislation or regulation duly promulgated by the insurance department under the compacting state's administrative procedure act. If a compacting state elects to opt out of a uniform standard by regulation, it must (i) give written notice to the Commission no later than 10 business days after the uniform standard is promulgated, or at the time the state becomes a compacting state and (ii) find that the uniform standard does not provide reasonable protections to the citizens of the state, given the conditions in the state. The Commissioner shall make specific findings of fact and conclusions of law, based on a preponderance of the evidence, detailing the conditions in the state that warrant a departure from the uniform standard and determining that the uniform standard would not reasonably protect the citizens of the state. The Commissioner must consider and balance the following factors and find that the conditions in the state and needs of the citizens of the state outweigh:

(1) The intent of the legislature to participate in, and the benefits of, an interstate agreement to establish national uniform consumer protections for the products subject to this Article; and

(2) The presumption that a uniform standard adopted by the Commission provides reasonable protections to consumers of the relevant product.

Notwithstanding the foregoing, a compacting state may, at the time of its enactment of this Compact, prospectively opt out of all uniform standards involving long-term care insurance products by expressly providing for the opt out in the enacted Compact, and the opt out shall not be treated as a material variance in the offer or acceptance of any state to participate in this Compact. The opt out shall be effective at the time of enactment of this Compact by the compacting state and shall apply to all existing uniform standards involving long-term care insurance products and those subsequently promulgated.

(e) Effect of Opt Out. - If a compacting state elects to opt out of a uniform standard, the uniform standard shall remain applicable in the compacting state electing to opt out until such time the opt out legislation is enacted into law or the regulation opting out becomes effective. Once the opt out of a uniform standard by a compacting state becomes effective as provided under the laws of that state, the uniform standard shall have no further force and effect in that state unless and until the legislation or regulation implementing the opt out is repealed or otherwise becomes ineffective under the laws of the state. If a compacting state opts out of a uniform standard after the uniform standard has been made effective in that state, the opt out shall have the same prospective effect as provided under G.S. 58-91-70 for withdrawals.

(f) Stay of Uniform Standard. - If a compacting state has formally initiated the process of opting out of a uniform standard by regulation, and while the regulatory opt out is pending, the compacting state may petition the Commission, at least 15 days before the effective date of the uniform standard, to stay the effectiveness of the uniform standard in that state. The Commission may grant a stay if it determines the regulatory opt out is being pursued in a reasonable manner and there is a likelihood of success. If a stay is granted or extended by the Commission, the stay or extension thereof may postpone the effective date by up to 90 days, unless affirmatively extended by the Commission. A stay shall not be permitted to remain in effect for more than one year unless the compacting state can show extraordinary circumstances that warrant a continuance of the stay, including the existence of a legal challenge that prevents the compacting state from opting out. A stay may be terminated by the Commission upon notice that the rule-making process has been terminated.

(g) Not later than 30 days after a rule or operating procedure is promulgated, any person may file a petition for judicial review of the rule or operating procedure. The filing of a petition pursuant to this subsection shall not stay or otherwise prevent the rule or operating procedure from becoming effective unless the court finds that the petitioner has a substantial likelihood of success. The court shall give deference to the actions of the Commission consistent with applicable law and shall not find the rule or operating procedure to be unlawful if the rule or operating procedure represents a reasonable exercise of the Commission's authority. (2005-183, s. 1; 2009-382, s. 35.)

§ 58-91-40. Commission records and enforcement.

(a) The Commission shall promulgate rules establishing conditions and procedures for public inspection and copying of its information and official records, except information and records involving the privacy of individuals and insurers' trade secrets. The Commission may promulgate additional rules under which it may make available to federal and state agencies, including law enforcement agencies, records and information otherwise exempt from disclosure, and may enter into agreements with agencies to receive or exchange information or records subject to nondisclosure and confidentiality provisions.

(b) Except as to privileged records, data, and information, the laws of any compacting state pertaining to confidentiality or nondisclosure shall not relieve any compacting state commissioner of the duty to disclose any relevant records, data, or information to the Commission. Disclosure to the Commission shall not be deemed to waive or otherwise affect any confidentiality requirement. Except as otherwise expressly provided in this Article, the Commission shall not be subject to the compacting state's laws pertaining to confidentiality and nondisclosure with respect to records, data, and information in its possession. Confidential information of the Commission shall remain confidential after the information is provided to any commissioner.

(c) The Commission shall monitor compacting states for compliance with duly adopted bylaws, rules, including uniform standards, and operating procedures. The Commission shall notify any noncomplying compacting state in writing of its noncompliance with Commission bylaws, rules, or operating procedures. If a noncomplying compacting state fails to remedy its noncompliance within the time specified in the notice of noncompliance, the compacting state shall be deemed to be in default as set forth in G.S. 58-91-70.

(d) The commissioner of any state in which an insurer is authorized to do business, or is conducting the business of insurance, shall continue to exercise that person's authority to oversee the market regulation of the activities of the insurer in accordance with the provisions of the state's law. The commissioner's enforcement of compliance with the Compact is governed by the following provisions:

(1) With respect to the commissioner's market regulation of a product or advertisement that is approved or certified to the Commission, the content of the product or advertisement shall not constitute a violation of the provisions, standards, or requirements of the Compact except upon a final order of the Commission, issued at the request of a commissioner after prior notice to the insurer and an opportunity for hearing before the Commission.

(2) Before a commissioner may bring an action for violation of any provision, standard, or requirement of the Compact relating to the content of an advertisement not approved or certified to the Commission, the Commission, or an authorized Commission officer or employee, must authorize the action. However, authorization pursuant to this subdivision does not require notice to the insurer, opportunity for hearing, or disclosure of requests for authorization or

records of the Commission's action on the requests. (2005-183, s. 1; 2009-382, s. 35.)

§ 58-91-45. Dispute resolution.

The Commission shall attempt, upon the request of a member, to resolve any disputes or other issues that are subject to this Compact and which may arise between two or more compacting states, or between compacting states and noncompacting states, and the Commission shall promulgate an operating procedure providing for resolution of those disputes. (2005-183, s. 1; 2009-382, s. 35.)

§ 58-91-50. Product filing and approval.

(a) Insurers and third-party filers seeking to have a product approved by the Commission shall file the product with, and pay applicable filing fees to, the Commission. Nothing in this Article shall be construed to restrict or otherwise prevent an insurer from filing its product with the insurance department in any state wherein the insurer is licensed to conduct the business of insurance, and the filing shall be subject to the laws of the states where filed.

(b) The Commission shall establish appropriate filing and review processes and procedures pursuant to Commission rules and operating procedures. Notwithstanding any provision in this Article to the contrary, the Commission shall promulgate rules to establish conditions and procedures under which the Commission will provide public access to product filing information. In establishing rules, the Commission shall consider the interests of the public in having access to the information, as well as protection of personal medical and financial information and trade secrets, that may be contained in a product filing or supporting information.

(c) Any product approved by the Commission may be sold or otherwise issued in those compacting states for which the insurer is legally authorized to do business. (2005-183, s. 1; 2009-382, s. 35.)

§ 58-91-55. Review of Commission decisions regarding filings.

(a) Not later than 30 days after the Commission has given notice of a disapproved product or advertisement filed with the Commission, the insurer or third-party filer whose filing was disapproved may appeal the determination to a review panel appointed by the Commission. The Commission shall promulgate rules to establish procedures for appointing review panels and provide for notice and hearing. An allegation that the Commission, in disapproving a product or advertisement filed with the Commission, acted arbitrarily, capriciously, or in a manner that is an abuse of discretion or otherwise not in accordance with the law, is subject to judicial review in accordance with G.S. 58-91-15(d).

(b) The Commission shall have authority to monitor, review, and reconsider products and advertisement subsequent to their filing or approval upon a finding that the product does not meet the relevant uniform standard. Where appropriate, the Commission may withdraw or modify its approval after proper notice and hearing, subject to the appeal process in subsection (a) of this section. (2005-183, s. 1; 2009-382, s. 35.)

§ 58-91-60. Finance.

(a) The Commission shall pay or provide for the payment of the reasonable expenses of its establishment and organization. To fund the cost of its initial operations, the Commission may accept contributions and other forms of funding from the National Association of Insurance Commissioners, compacting states, and other sources. Contributions and other forms of funding from other sources shall be of such a nature that the independence of the Commission concerning the performance of its duties shall not be compromised.

(b) The Commission shall collect a filing fee from each insurer and third-party filer filing a product with the Commission to cover the cost of the operations and activities of the Commission and its staff in a total amount sufficient to cover the Commission's annual budget.

(c) The Commission's budget for a fiscal year shall not be approved until it has been subject to notice and comment as set forth in G.S. 58-91-35.

(d) The Commission shall be exempt from all taxation in and by the compacting states.

(e) The Commission shall not pledge the credit of any compacting state, except by and with the appropriate legal authority of that compacting state.

(f) The Commission shall keep complete and accurate accounts of all its internal receipts, including grants and donations, and disbursements of all funds under its control. The internal financial accounts of the Commission shall be subject to the accounting procedures established under its bylaws. The financial accounts and reports, including the system of internal controls and procedures of the Commission, shall be audited annually by an independent certified public accountant. Upon the determination of the Commission, but no less frequently than every three years, the review of the independent auditor shall include a management and performance audit of the Commission. The Commission shall make an annual report to the Governor and legislature of the compacting states, which shall include a report of the independent audit. The Commission's internal accounts shall not be confidential, and those materials may be shared with the commissioner of any compacting state upon request except that any work papers related to any internal or independent audit and any information regarding the privacy of individuals and insurers' proprietary information, including trade secrets, shall remain confidential.

(g) No compacting state shall have any claim to or ownership of any property held by or vested in the Commission or to any Commission funds held pursuant to the provisions of this Compact. (2005-183, s. 1; 2009-382, s. 35.)

§ 58-91-65. Compacting states; effective date; amendment.

(a) Any State is eligible to become a compacting state.

(b) The Compact shall become effective and binding upon legislative enactment of the Compact into law by two compacting states except that the Commission shall become effective for purposes of adopting uniform standards for, reviewing, and giving approval or disapproval of, products filed with the Commission that satisfy applicable uniform standards only after 26 states are compacting states or, alternatively, by states representing greater than forty percent (40%) of the premium volume for life insurance, annuity, disability income, and long-term care insurance products, based on records of the NAIC for the prior year. Thereafter, it shall become effective and binding as to any other compacting state upon enactment of the Compact into law by that state.

(c) Amendments to the Compact may be proposed by the Commission for enactment by the compacting states. No amendment shall become effective and binding upon the Commission and the compacting states unless and until all compacting states enact the amendment into law. (2005-183, s. 1; 2009-382, s. 35.)

§ 58-91-70. Withdrawal; default; termination.

(a) Withdrawal. - Once effective, the Compact shall continue in force and remain binding upon each and every compacting state though a compacting state may withdraw from the Compact ("withdrawing state") by enacting a statute specifically repealing the statute which enacted the Compact into law.

The effective date of withdrawal is the effective date of the repealing statute. However, the withdrawal shall not apply to any product filings approved or self-certified, or any advertisement of such products, on the date the repealing statute becomes effective, except by mutual agreement of the Commission and the withdrawing state unless the approval is rescinded by the withdrawing state as provided in this subsection.

The commissioner of the withdrawing state shall immediately notify the Management Committee in writing upon the introduction of legislation repealing this Compact in the withdrawing state.

The Commission shall notify the other compacting states of the introduction of such legislation within 10 days after its receipt of the notice.

The withdrawing state is responsible for all obligations, duties, and liabilities incurred through the effective date of withdrawal, including any obligations, the performance of which extend beyond the effective date of withdrawal, except to the extent those obligations may have been released or relinquished by mutual agreement of the Commission and the withdrawing state. The Commission's approval of products and advertisement prior to the effective date of withdrawal shall continue to be effective and be given full force and effect in the withdrawing state, unless formally rescinded by the withdrawing state in the same manner as provided by the laws of the withdrawing state for the prospective disapproval of products or advertisement previously approved under state law.

Reinstatement following withdrawal of any compacting state shall occur upon the effective date of the withdrawing state reenacting the Compact.

(b) Default. - If the Commission determines that any compacting state has at any time defaulted ("defaulting state") in the performance of any of its obligations or responsibilities under this Compact, the bylaws or duly promulgated rules or operating procedures, then, after notice and hearing as set forth in the bylaws, all rights, privileges, and benefits conferred by this Compact on the defaulting state shall be suspended from the effective date of default as fixed by the Commission. The grounds for default include failure of a compacting state to perform its obligations or responsibilities, and any other grounds designated in Commission rules. The Commission shall immediately notify the defaulting state in writing of the defaulting state's suspension pending a cure of the default. The Commission shall stipulate the conditions and the time period within which the defaulting state must cure its default. If the defaulting state fails to cure the default within the time period specified by the Commission, the defaulting state shall be terminated from the Compact and all rights, privileges, and benefits conferred by this Compact shall be terminated from the effective date of termination.

Product approvals by the Commission or product self-certifications, or any advertisement in connection with such product, that are in force on the effective date of termination shall remain in force in the defaulting state in the same manner as if the defaulting state had withdrawn voluntarily pursuant to subsection (a) of this section.

Reinstatement following termination of any compacting state requires a reenactment of the Compact.

(c) Dissolution of Compact. - The Compact dissolves effective upon the date of the withdrawal or default of the compacting state which reduces membership in the Compact to one compacting state.

Upon the dissolution of this Compact, the Compact becomes null and void and shall be of no further force or effect, and the business and affairs of the Commission shall be wound up and any surplus funds shall be distributed in accordance with the bylaws. (2005-183, s. 1; 2009-382, s. 35.)

§ 58-91-75. Severability; construction.

(a)   The provisions of this Compact shall be severable; and if any phrase, clause, sentence, or provision is deemed unenforceable, the remaining provisions of the Compact shall be enforceable.

(b)   The provisions of this Compact shall be liberally construed to effectuate its purposes. (2005-183, s. 1; 2009-382, s. 35.)

§ 58-91-80. Binding effect of Compact; other laws.

(a)   Other Laws. - Nothing herein prevents the enforcement of any other law of a compacting state, except as provided in subsection (b) of this section.

For any product approved or certified to the Commission, the rules, uniform standards, and any other requirements of the Commission shall constitute the exclusive provisions applicable to the content, approval, and certification of such products. For advertisement that is subject to the Commission's authority, any rule, uniform standard, or other requirement of the Commission that governs the content of the advertisement shall constitute the exclusive provision that a Commissioner may apply to the content of the advertisement. Notwithstanding the foregoing, no action taken by the Commission shall abrogate or restrict: (i) the access of any person to state courts; (ii) remedies available under state law related to breach of contract, tort, or other laws not specifically directed to the content of the product; (iii) state law relating to the construction of insurance contracts; or (iv) the authority of the attorney general of the state, including, but not limited to, maintaining any actions or proceedings, as authorized by law.

All insurance products filed with individual states shall be subject to the laws of those states.

(b)   Binding Effect of This Compact. - All lawful actions of the Commission, including all rules and operating procedures promulgated by the Commission, are binding upon the compacting states.

All agreements between the Commission and the compacting states are binding in accordance with their terms.

Upon the request of a party to a conflict over the meaning or interpretation of Commission actions, and upon a majority vote of the compacting states, the Commission may issue advisory opinions regarding the meaning or interpretation in dispute.

In the event any provision of this Compact exceeds the constitutional limits imposed on the legislature of any compacting state, the obligations, duties, powers, or jurisdiction sought to be conferred by that provision upon the Commission shall be ineffective as to that compacting state, and those obligations, duties, powers, or jurisdiction shall remain in the compacting state and shall be exercised by the agency thereof to which those obligations, duties, powers, or jurisdiction are delegated by law in effect at the time this Compact becomes effective. (2005-183, s. 1; 2009-382, s. 35.)

Article 92.

Fire-Safety Standard and Firefighter Protection Act.

(See note for effective date of this Article.)

§ 58-92-1. Title.

This Article shall be known and may be cited as the "Fire-Safety Standard and Firefighter Protection Act." (2007-451, s. 1.)

§ 58-92-5. Findings.

The General Assembly finds:

(1) Cigarettes are the leading cause of fire deaths in this State and the nation.

(2) Each year in the United States, 700-900 persons are killed due to cigarette fires, and 3,000 are injured in fires ignited by cigarettes, while in this State, there were 2,916 cigarette-related fires in North Carolina during the period 2001-2006.

(3) A high proportion of the victims of cigarette fires are nonsmokers, including senior citizens and young children.

(4) Cigarette-caused fires result in billions of dollars of property losses and damages in the United States and millions of dollars in this State.

(5) Cigarette fires unnecessarily jeopardize firefighters and result in avoidable emergency response costs for municipalities.

(6) In 2004, New York State implemented a cigarette fire-safety regulation requiring cigarettes sold in that state to meet a fire-safety performance standard; in 2005, Vermont and California enacted cigarette fire-safety laws directly incorporating New York's regulation into statute; and, in 2006, Illinois, New Hampshire, and Massachusetts joined these states in enacting such laws.

(7) In 2005, Canada implemented the New York State fire-safety standard contained in the other state laws, becoming the first nation to have a cigarette fire-safety standard.

(8) New York State's cigarette fire-safety standard is based upon decades of research by the National Institute of Standards and Technology, congressional research groups, and private industry.

(9) This cigarette fire-safety standard minimizes costs to the State and minimally burdens cigarette manufacturers, distributors, and retail sellers, and, therefore, should become law in this State.

(10) It is therefore fitting and proper for this State to adopt the cigarette fire-safety standard that is in effect in New York State to reduce the likelihood that cigarettes will cause fires and result in deaths, injuries, and property damages. (2007-451, s. 1.)

§ 58-92-10. Definitions.

For the purposes of this Article:

(1) "Agent" means any person authorized by the Department of Revenue to pay the excise tax on packages of cigarettes.

(1a) "Brand style" means a variety of cigarettes distinguished by the tobacco used, tar and nicotine content, flavoring used, size of the cigarette, filtration on the cigarette, or packaging.

(2) "Cigarette" means any roll for smoking, whether made wholly or in part of tobacco or any other substance, irrespective of size or shape, and whether or not such tobacco or substance is flavored, adulterated, or mixed with any other ingredient, the wrapper or cover of which is made of paper or any other substance or material, other than leaf tobacco.

(3) "Commissioner" means the Commissioner of Insurance.

(4) "Consumer testing" means an assessment of cigarettes that is conducted by a manufacturer (or under the control and direction of a manufacturer), for the purpose of evaluating consumer acceptance of such cigarettes.

(5) "Distributor" means any person other than a manufacturer who sells cigarettes or tobacco products to retail dealers or other persons for purposes of resale, any person who owns, operates, or maintains one or more cigarette or tobacco product vending machines in, at, or upon premises owned or occupied by any other person, or a distributor as defined in G.S. 105-113.4(3)a.

(6) "Manufacturer" means:

a. Any entity that manufactures or otherwise produces cigarettes or causes cigarettes to be manufactured or produced anywhere that the manufacturer intends to be sold in this State, including cigarettes intended to be sold in the United States through an importer;

b. The first purchaser anywhere that intends to resell in the United States cigarettes manufactured anywhere that the original manufacturer or maker does not intend to be sold in the United States; or

c. Any entity that becomes a successor of an entity described in sub-subdivision a. or b. of this subdivision.

(7) "Quality control and quality assurance program" means the laboratory procedures implemented to ensure that operator bias, systematic and nonsystematic methodological errors, and equipment-related problems do not affect the results of the testing. Such a program ensures that the testing repeatability remains within the required repeatability values stated in G.S. 58-92-15(g) for all test trials used to certify cigarettes in accordance with this Article.

(8) "Repeatability" means the range of values within which the repeat results of cigarette test trials from a single laboratory will fall ninety-five percent (95%) of the time.

(9) "Retail dealer" means any person, other than a manufacturer or distributor, engaged in selling cigarettes or tobacco products.

(10) "Sale" means any transfer of title or possession or both, exchange or barter, conditional or otherwise, in any manner or by any means whatever or any agreement therefor. In addition to cash and credit sales, the giving of cigarettes as samples, prizes, or gifts, and the exchanging of cigarettes for any consideration other than money, are considered sales.

(11) "Sell" means to sell, or to offer or agree to do the same. (2007-451, s. 1; 2010-101, s. 1.)

§ 58-92-15. Test method and performance standard.

(a) Except as provided in subsection (o) of this section, no cigarettes may be sold or offered for sale in this State or offered for sale or sold to persons located in this State unless the cigarettes have been tested in accordance with the test method and meet the performance standard specified in this section, a written certification has been filed by the manufacturer with the Commissioner in accordance with G.S. 58-92-20, and the cigarettes have been marked in accordance with G.S. 58-92-25.

(b) Testing of cigarettes shall be conducted in accordance with the American Society of Testing and Materials (ASTM) standard E2187-04, "Standard Test Method for Measuring the Ignition Strength of Cigarettes."

(c) Testing shall be conducted on 10 layers of filter paper.

(d) No more than twenty-five percent (25%) of the cigarettes tested in a test trial in accordance with this section shall exhibit full-length burns. Forty replicate tests shall comprise a complete test trial for each cigarette tested.

(e) The performance standard required by this section shall only be applied to a complete test trial.

(f) Written certifications shall be based upon testing conducted by a laboratory that has been accredited pursuant to standard ISO/IEC 17025 of the International Organization for Standardization (IOS) or other comparable accreditation standard required by the Commissioner.

(g) Laboratories conducting testing in accordance with this section shall implement a quality control and quality assurance program that includes a procedure that will determine the repeatability of the testing results. The repeatability value shall be no greater than 0.19.

(h) This section does not require additional testing if cigarettes are tested consistent with this Article for any other purpose.

(i) Testing performed or sponsored by the Commissioner to determine a cigarette's compliance with the performance standard required shall be conducted in accordance with this section.

(j) Each cigarette listed in a certification submitted pursuant to G.S. 58-92-20 that uses lowered permeability bands in the cigarette paper to achieve compliance with the performance standard set forth in this section shall have at least two nominally identical bands on the paper surrounding the tobacco column. At least one complete band shall be located at least 15 millimeters from the lighting end of the cigarette. For cigarettes on which the bands are positioned by design, there shall be at least two bands fully located at least 15 millimeters from the lighting end and 10 millimeters from the filter end of the tobacco column, or 10 millimeters from the labeled end of the tobacco column for nonfiltered cigarettes.

(k) A manufacturer of a cigarette that the Commissioner determines cannot be tested in accordance with the test method prescribed in subsection (b) of this section shall propose a test method and performance standard for the cigarette to the Commissioner. Upon approval of the proposed test method and a determination by the Commissioner that the performance standard proposed by the manufacturer is equivalent to the performance standard prescribed in subsection (d) of this section, the manufacturer may employ such test method and performance standard to certify such cigarette pursuant to G.S. 58-92-20. If the Commissioner determines that another state has enacted reduced cigarette ignition propensity standards that include a test method and performance standard that are the same as those contained in this Article, and the Commissioner finds that the officials responsible for implementing those requirements have approved the proposed alternative test method and performance standard for a particular cigarette proposed by a manufacturer as meeting the fire-safety standards of that state's law or regulation under a legal provision comparable to this section, then the Commissioner shall authorize that manufacturer to employ the alternative test method and performance standard to certify that cigarette for sale in this State, unless the Commissioner demonstrates a reasonable basis why the alternative test should not be accepted under this Article. All other applicable requirements of this section shall apply to the manufacturer.

(l)   Each manufacturer shall maintain copies of the reports of all tests conducted on all cigarettes offered for sale for a period of three years and shall make copies of these reports available to the Commissioner and the Attorney General upon written request. Any manufacturer who fails to make copies of these reports available within 60 days of receiving a written request shall be subject to a civil penalty not to exceed ten thousand dollars ($10,000) for each day after the sixtieth day that the manufacturer does not make such copies available.

(m)   The Commissioner may adopt a subsequent ASTM Standard Test Method for Measuring the Ignition Strength of Cigarettes upon a finding that such subsequent method does not result in a change in the percentage of full-length burns exhibited by any tested cigarette when compared to the percentage of full-length burns the same cigarette would exhibit when tested in accordance with ASTM Standard E2187-04 and the performance standard in subsection (d) of this section.

(n)   The Commissioner shall review the effectiveness of this section and report every three years to the General Assembly the Commissioner's findings, and if appropriate, recommendations for legislation to improve the effectiveness of this Article. The report and legislative recommendations shall be submitted no later than June 30 following the conclusion of each three-year period.

(o) The requirements of subsections (a) through (i) of this section shall not prohibit:

(1) Distributors or retail dealers from selling their existing inventory of cigarettes on or after January 1, 2010, if the distributor or retail dealer can establish that all taxes owed on the cigarettes pursuant to Article 2A of Chapter 105 of the General Statutes have been paid prior to January 1, 2010, and the distributor or retail dealer can establish that the inventory was purchased prior to January 1, 2010, in comparable quantity to the inventory purchased during the same period of the prior year.

(2) The sale of cigarettes solely for the purpose of consumer testing.

(p) The Commissioner shall implement this Article in accordance with the implementation and substance of the New York Fire Safety Standards for Cigarettes, as it read on August 24, 2007.

(q) No local government may pass any ordinance changing the performance standard set forth in this section. (2007-451, s. 1; 2009-490, s. 1.)

§ 58-92-20. Certification and product change.

(a) Each manufacturer shall submit to the Commissioner a written certification attesting both of the following:

(1) Each cigarette listed in the certification has been tested in accordance with G.S. 58-92-15.

(2) Each cigarette listed in the certification meets the performance standard set forth in G.S. 58-92-15.

(b) Each cigarette listed in the certification shall be described with the following information:

(1) Brand or trade name on the package.

(2) Brand style, as defined in G.S. 58-92-10(1a).

(3) Length in millimeters.

(4)   Circumference in millimeters.

(5)   Flavor, such as menthol or chocolate, if applicable.

(6)   Filter or nonfilter.

(7)   Package description, such as soft pack or box.

(8)   Marking pursuant to G.S. 58-92-25.

(9)   The name, address, and telephone number of the laboratory, if different than the manufacturer that conducted the test.

(10)   The date that the testing occurred.

(c)   Certifications shall be made available to the Attorney General for purposes consistent with this Article and the Commissioner for the purposes of ensuring compliance with this section.

(d)   Each cigarette certified under this section shall be recertified every three years.

(e)   For each brand style listed in a certification, a manufacturer shall pay to the Commissioner a fee of two hundred fifty dollars ($250.00). The Commissioner may annually adjust this fee to ensure it defrays the actual costs of the processing, testing, enforcement, and oversight activities required by this Article.

(f)   There is established in the State treasury a separate, nonreverting fund to be known as the "Fire Safety Standard and Firefighter Protection Act Enforcement Fund." The fund shall consist of all certification fees submitted by manufacturers and shall, in addition to any other monies made available for such purpose, be available to the Commissioner solely to support processing, testing, enforcement, and oversight activities under this Article.

(g)   If a manufacturer has certified a cigarette pursuant to this section, and thereafter makes any change to such cigarette that is likely to alter its compliance with the reduced cigarette ignition propensity standards required by this Article, that cigarette shall not be sold or offered for sale in this State until the manufacturer retests the cigarette in accordance with the testing standards set forth in G.S. 58-92-15 and maintains records of that retesting as required by G.S. 58-92-15. Any altered cigarette that does not meet the performance standard set forth in G.S. 58-92-15 shall not be sold in this State. (2007-451, s. 1; 2010-101, s. 2.)

§ 58-92-25. Marking of cigarette packaging.

(a) Cigarettes that are certified by a manufacturer in accordance with G.S. 58-92-20 shall be marked to indicate compliance with the requirements of G.S. 58-92-15. The marking shall be in eight-point type or larger and consist of one of the following:

(1) Modification of the product UPC Code to include a visible mark printed at or around the area of the UPC Code. The mark may consist of alphanumeric or symbolic characters permanently stamped, engraved, embossed, or printed in conjunction with the UPC.

(2) Any visible combination of alphanumeric or symbolic characters permanently stamped, engraved, or embossed upon the cigarette package or cellophane wrap.

(3) Printed, stamped, engraved, or embossed text that indicates that the cigarettes meet the standards of this Article.

(b) A manufacturer shall use only one marking and shall apply this marking uniformly for all packages, including, but not limited to, packs, cartons, and cases and brands marketed by that manufacturer.

(c) The Commissioner shall be notified as to the marking that is selected.

(d) Prior to the certification of any cigarette, a manufacturer shall present its proposed marking to the Commissioner for approval. Upon receipt of the request, the Commissioner shall approve or disapprove the marking offered, except that the Commissioner shall approve:

(1) Any marking in use and approved for sale in New York pursuant to the New York Fire Safety Standards for Cigarettes, or

(2) The letters "FSC," which signifies Fire Standards Compliant, appearing in eight-point type or larger and permanently printed, stamped, engraved, or embossed on the package at or near the UPC Code.

(e) Proposed markings shall be deemed approved if the Commissioner fails to act within 10 business days of receiving a request for approval.

(f) No manufacturer shall modify its approved marking unless the modification has been approved by the Commissioner in accordance with this section.

(g) Manufacturers certifying cigarettes in accordance with G.S. 58-92-20 shall provide a copy of the certifications to all distributors and agents to which they sell cigarettes and shall also provide sufficient copies of an illustration of the package marking utilized by the manufacturer pursuant to this section for each retail dealer to which the distributors or agents sell cigarettes. Distributors and agents shall provide a copy of these package markings received from manufacturers to all retail dealers to which they sell cigarettes. Distributors, agents, and retail dealers shall permit the Commissioner, the Secretary of Revenue, the Attorney General, and their employees to inspect markings of cigarette packaging marked in accordance with this section. (2007-451, s. 1.)

§ 58-92-30. Penalties.

(a) A manufacturer, distributor, agent, or any other person or entity who knowingly sells or offers to sell cigarettes, other than through retail sale, in violation of G.S. 58-92-15, shall be subject to a civil penalty not to exceed one hundred dollars ($100.00) for each pack of such cigarettes sold or offered for sale provided that in no case shall the penalty against any such person or entity exceed one hundred thousand dollars ($100,000) during any 30-day period.

(b) A retail dealer who knowingly sells or offers to sell cigarettes in violation of G.S. 58-92-15 shall be subject to a civil penalty not to exceed one hundred dollars ($100.00) for each pack of such cigarettes sold or offered for sale, provided that in no case shall the penalty against any retail dealer exceed twenty-five thousand dollars ($25,000) for sales or offers to sell during any 30-day period.

(c)   In addition to any penalty prescribed by law, any corporation, partnership, sole proprietor, limited partnership, or association engaged in the manufacture of cigarettes that knowingly makes a false certification pursuant to G.S. 58-92-20 shall be subject to a civil penalty of at least seventy-five thousand dollars ($75,000) but not to exceed two hundred fifty thousand dollars ($250,000) for each such false certification.

(d)   Any person violating any other provision in this Article shall be subject to a civil penalty for a first offense not to exceed one thousand dollars ($1,000), and for a subsequent offense subject to a civil penalty not to exceed five thousand dollars ($5,000) for each such violation.

(e)   Any cigarettes that have been sold or offered for sale that do not comply with the performance standard required by G.S. 58-92-15 shall be subject to forfeiture as contraband under the same procedures as G.S. 75D-5 or G.S. 113-412. Cigarettes forfeited pursuant to this section shall be destroyed; provided, however, that prior to the destruction of any cigarette forfeited pursuant to these provisions, the true holder of the trademark rights in the cigarette brand shall be permitted to inspect the cigarette.

(f)   In addition to any other remedy provided by law, the Commissioner or Attorney General may file an action in the superior court for a violation of this Article, including petitioning for injunctive relief or to recover any costs or damages suffered by the State because of a violation of this Article, including enforcement costs relating to the specific violation and attorneys' fees. Each violation of this Article or of rules or regulations adopted under this Article constitutes a separate civil violation for which the Commissioner or Attorney General may obtain relief.

(g)   Whenever any law enforcement personnel or duly authorized representative of the Commissioner shall discover any cigarettes that have not been marked in the manner required by this Article, such personnel is hereby authorized and empowered to seize and take possession of such cigarettes. Such cigarettes shall be turned over to the Department of Revenue and shall be forfeited to the State. Cigarettes seized pursuant to this section shall be destroyed; provided, however, that prior to the destruction of any cigarette seized pursuant to these provisions, the true holder of the trademark rights in the cigarette brand shall be permitted to inspect the cigarette.

(h)   Any penalty imposed under this Article shall be payable to the Commissioner.

(i) A violation of this Article constitutes a civil offense only and is not a crime. (2007-451, s. 1; 2009-490, s. 2.)

§ 58-92-35. Implementation.

(a) The Commissioner may adopt rules, pursuant to Chapter 150B of the General Statutes, necessary to effectuate the purposes of this Article.

(b) The Department of Revenue in the regular course of conducting inspections of distributors, agents, and retail dealers, as authorized under the Tobacco Products Tax Act, Article 2A of Chapter 105 of the General Statutes, may inspect such cigarettes to determine if the cigarettes are marked as required by G.S. 58-92-25. If the cigarettes are not marked as required, the Department of Revenue shall notify the Commissioner. (2007-451, s. 1.)

§ 58-92-40. Inspection.

To enforce the provisions of this Article, the Attorney General, the Department of Revenue, and the Commissioner, their duly authorized representatives, and other law enforcement personnel may examine the books, papers, invoices, and other records of any person in possession, control, or occupancy of any premises where cigarettes are placed, stored, sold, or offered for sale, as well as the stock of cigarettes on the premises. Every person in the possession, control, or occupancy of any premises where cigarettes are placed, sold, or offered for sale is hereby directed and required to give the Attorney General, the Department of Revenue, and the Commissioner, their duly authorized representatives, and other law enforcement personnel the means, facilities, and opportunity for the examinations authorized by this section. (2007-451, s. 1.)

§ 58-92-45. Disposition of penalties.

The clear proceeds of civil penalties and forfeitures provided for in this Article shall be remitted to the Civil Penalty and Forfeiture Fund in accordance with G.S. 115C-457.2. (2007-451, s. 1.)

§ 58-92-50. Sale outside the State.

Nothing in this Article shall be construed to prohibit any person or entity from manufacturing or selling cigarettes that do not meet the requirements of G.S. 58-92-15 if the cigarettes are or will be stamped for sale in another state or are packaged for sale outside the United States and that person or entity has taken reasonable steps to ensure that such cigarettes will not be sold or offered for sale to persons located in this State. (2007-451, s. 1.)

§ 58-92-55. Preemption.

This Article does not apply if a federal reduced cigarette ignition propensity standard that preempts this Article is enacted and becomes effective, but such inapplicability does not affect any liability for forfeiture or penalties accrued prior to the effective date of the federal law. (2007-451, s. 1.)

Chapter 58A.

North Carolina Health Insurance Trust Commission.

§§ 58A-1 through 58A-5: Recodified as Article 68 of Chapter 58.

Vision Books Order Form

Fax Orders:	1-980-299-5965
Phone Orders:	1-704-898-0770
E-mail Orders:	www.visionbooks.org
Mail Orders:	Vision Books, LLC P.O. Box 42406 Charlotte, NC 28215

Shipp To:
Name_____
Address_____
City_____State_____Zip_____
Phone_____Fax_____
Email_____@_____

Bill To: We can bill a third party on your behalf.
Name_____
Address_____
City_____State_____Zip_____
Phone____(_____)_____Fax_____
Email_____@_____

Pamphlet Number ($15.00 Each)	Qty	Total Cost
_____	_____	_____
_____	_____	_____
_____	_____	_____
_____	_____	_____
_____	_____	_____
_____	_____	_____
_____	_____	_____
_____	_____	_____
Full Volume Set 1-92	**92 Pamphlets**	**1,380.00**

Free Shipping Shipping & Handling on Full Volume Orders
Add $1.00 Shipping & Handling per pamphlet $_____

Total Cost $_____

Thank you for your order. Management!

DID YOU ENJOY THIS BOOK?

Vision Books, LLC would like to hear from you! If you or someone you know has been fasely imprisoned, we would like to hear your story. If the 'North Carolina Criminal Law and Procedure' has had an effect in your life or if you have suggestions, we would like to hear from you. Send your letters to:

Vision Books, LLC
Attn: Staff Writers
P.O. Box 42406
Charlotte, NC 28215
Email: staff@visionbooks.org

Order Additional Copies:

Fax Orders:	1-980-299-5965
Phone Orders:	1-704-898-0770
E-mail Orders:	www.visionbooks.org
Mail Orders:	Vision Books, LLC P.O. Box 42406 Charlotte, NC 28215

www.ingramcontent.com/pod-product-compliance
Lightning Source LLC
Chambersburg PA
CBHW051638170526
45167CB00001B/245